THE COINCIDENTAL ART OF
Charles Brockden Brown

THE COINCIDENTAL ART OF
Charles Brockden Brown

NORMAN S. GRABO

THE UNIVERSITY OF NORTH CAROLINA PRESS

CHAPEL HILL

© 1981 The University of North Carolina Press

Manufactured in the United States of America

Library of Congress Cataloging in Publication Data

Grabo, Norman S

The coincidental art of Charles Brockden Brown.

Includes bibliographical references and index.

1. Brown, Charles Brockden, 1771–1810—Criticism and
interpretation. I. Title.

PS1137.G7 1981   813'.2   80-39797

ISBN 0-8078-1474-1

For
JENNY FRANCHOT

Contents

Preface

Among the very first things readers note about Charles Brockden Brown's fictions is their curious and sometimes painful dependence upon coincidence. When Edgar Huntly needs a weapon, his hand just happens to fall upon a tomahawk in the darkness. Threatened women vigorously defend life and honor with penknives that pop out of nowhere just when most needed. Surely these are the classic signals of a naive, clumsy, even childish, storyteller. Because Brown neglects to prepare us adequately for the details—the tomahawks and penknives—they seem to have been manufactured on the spot to solve some particular narrative predicament. Perhaps even more unlikely are the coincidences of resemblance among his characters. It is a fortunate coincidence that Arthur Mervyn looks like young Lodi. We accept that. But he also looks like Clavering, and that second resemblance seems stretched and gratuitous. Trying to frighten Arthur away, Welbeck assumes another's voice, which just happens to be the voice of someone else known to Arthur. Wildly improbable! In *Edgar Huntly* so many characters look like others they should be numbered. Yet they manage to get through the story with a minimum of confusion. Constantia Dudley in *Ormond* bears an uncanny resemblance to her friend Sophia, and both look a lot like Ursula Monrose, otherwise known as Martinette, who of course resembles her brother Ormond.

Coincidence operates at a broader and more significant level as well.

Young Wieland starts hearing divine commands at the very time a mischievous ventriloquist saunters into the neighborhood. That's a coincidence with such catastrophic consequences that readers are still trying to puzzle it out. In *Edgar Huntly* Sarsefield by miraculous chance is mentor and surrogate father to both Clithero and Edgar, the two sleepwalkers. Why? Wouldn't relationship to one of these unfortunates have sufficed? Sarsefield teaches both young men to contrive little boxes that can only be opened by secret springs. Did it have to be Sarsefield who did the teaching? I suspect it did, because in this book, at any rate, what Brown elsewhere calls "that tissue of nice contingencies" generates far-reaching parallels of action, not merely enabling Brown to solve narrative predicaments, but actually dictating the structure and form of his story.

Coincidence, then, may sometimes strike us as a trivial annoyance, but it may also function as the foundation of the stories themselves. When we see that happening, we have to reconsider whether Brown's penchant for coincidences may not be purposeful rather than desperate. The overwhelming fact about the coincidences in Brown's fiction is that there are simply too many for them to be coincidental. Or, to put it another way, Brown's coincidence is necessary. Once coincidence becomes part of a pattern of significance, it ceases to be coincidence or accident or chance. What I want to show in the following pages is that there is more pattern and more purpose in Brown's fiction than has generally been granted, that when we let the patterns emerge from the texts, they reflect both a complex mind and a sophisticated art. Whether that art was entirely conscious or largely instinctive is probably not fully answered in these pages; Brown may not always make his visions work, but neither he nor they were naive.

This is easier to assert than it is to prove, but it is important to prove it if we are to get past the timid and hesitant state of Brown criticism and open new questions to ponder. A single instance of Brown's cleverness or skill is always dismissable as a happy accident. Likewise, the first coincidental connection one discovers in a story will not convince us of its purpose or constitute a pattern. Nor will the second or the third. But finally, many coincidences are so coherently connected that only the most perverse critic should be able to resist Brown's sense of design.

That is why I attempt to probe the structure of these stories, as Northrop Frye has urged, without the methodology—and certainly without the language—of any school of structuralist or poststructuralist criticism. I prefer to risk a good deal of New Critical close reading of the sort that some readers will find strained and fanciful. Although I very much admire the treatment of Brown in Leslie Fiedler's *Love and Death in the American Novel* and, like him, follow a psychological interpretation in large part, I do not do so from any commitment to a particular psychoanalytic school, and I avoid as much as possible the terms of psychoanalytic criticism. Nonetheless, Brown was himself thoroughly fascinated during his major creative years by the internalization of experience; there is no avoiding his psychological interests. I also minimize in this book the historical and biographical contexts, out of the conviction that a full and just appreciation of Brown's art should proceed first from a hard reading of the fictions themselves. Although I make at least a tentative assumption that these fictions have a recoverable intention, I am inclined like some neo-Aristotelians to consider this the intention of the text rather than that of the author.

Each of Brown's major texts has some apparent flaw, digression, or irrelevancy in it—the last chapter of *Wieland*, for example, Martynne's appearance with Constantia's cousin in *Ormond*, the Queen Mab episode in *Edgar Huntly*, and some would say the entire second part of *Arthur Mervyn*. Critics have traditionally overlooked, dismissed, or apologized for these faults, considering them, like the coincidences, signs of sloppy craftsmanship. My reading also treats them like the coincidences—often indeed as a special kind of coincidence—and equally purposeful and necessary. I make a strong effort to do justice to these cruxes in the stories without pretending to exhaust the possibilities for meaning in them.

What emerges from this approach is a sense of the closeness with which Brown was in touch with the American penchant for paradox, as Michael Kammen has called it, and for the doubleness that paradox implies. Patterns of doubled characters, doubled actions, and doubled meanings become central to Brown's fictive art, whether considered philosophically or formally; this conclusion is clearly pointed out in Arthur

Kimball's *Rational Fictions: A Study of Charles Brockden Brown.* How intricate and powerful such a literary fascination with doubling can be is well illustrated by John T. Irwin's *Doubling and Incest/Repetition and Revenge: A Speculative Reading of Faulkner,* as well as by the works cited in the final chapter. I do not want to suggest that each of Brown's books fits a single scheme or pattern, despite the pervasiveness of coincidental doubling. *Ormond* and *Arthur Mervyn* and *Edgar Huntly* and *Wieland* are not mere variations on one protofiction; indeed, the dynamism of Brown's experiments seems to me one of his major accomplishments.

So I mean no foreclosure of discussion of Brown, but an opening on a new plane. Some will maintain, and rightly, that the plane I offer is not that new. Brown emerges from my reading the same man he was before. He is still a moral painter, still a novelist of ideas, but the meanings of those characterizations radically alter in my readings, and I think that Brown does wear the look of a more conscious craftsman than he has been credited with wearing before. It is also true that recent work in subjects conventionally associated with Brown—feminist awareness, for example, or the traditional dynamics of Gothic fiction—has been greatly intensified and sharpened. I purposely resist the temptation to develop these aspects of Brown. Nor do I intend to claim a preeminence for Brown that he does not deserve; I intend rather to isolate in his fictions alone a number of techniques only accidentally noted before and to suggest the extent to which they justify a much more serious appraisal of his artistic value than is generally allowed. This is not a book about Brown as Gothic novelist or even about Brown as an eighteenth-century popular novelist. Everywhere I try to stick to Brown's works in their own terms, as I see them. I am constantly surprised that so modest a procedure leads so often to extensive alterations in the interpretation of the fictions. I must beg a degree of patience from readers at the outset, where each chapter begins with an objective synopsis of these very incident-intensive stories and then circles back upon that synopsis interpretively before drawing general conclusions. How better to get from the coincidences to the patterns I do not know. Even good readers of Brown should be pleased to be reminded of the order of events; the conclusions do, I believe, justify these detailed rehearsals.

Acknowledgments

My sharpest debt is to the colleagues and students who have tried for years to teach me to read: Julia Bader, Frederick Crews, Patti Hudgens, Charles Keshian, Leslie Lass, David Leverenz, Nancy Limprecht, Mark Seltzer, Jana Wainwright, and Beverly Voloshin. The blame is theirs. Dennis Berthold, William Bedford Clark, folklorist Sylvia Grider, and Jerome Loving all took time to read this study and encourage the project. Leon Howard and Annette Kolodny also read the manuscript and tried to root out its worst faults. I gratefully thank them all.

Special thanks are also due to Sydney J. Krause, general editor of the bicentennial edition of *The Novels and Related Works of Charles Brockden Brown*, who first directed my attention to Brown and whose tenacious criticism of the present study saved it from its silliest excesses. By keeping my teaching duties at a reasonable level, Texas A & M University greatly assisted with the writing of this book in the spring of 1979.

THE COINCIDENTAL ART OF
Charles Brockden Brown

Theodore and Clara

Although *Wieland; Or, The Transformation. An American Tale,* is Brown's best known and most studied romance, a description of the story will not be amiss.[1] The story is told by Clara Wieland in two stages, the first long stage apparently shortly after the event, a second stage three years later from Montpellier, France. Someone, a "revered friend" (otherwise unidentified), has requested the details of her American experience, and these she undertakes with some hesitancy, in part because the incidents are so repulsive, in part because she has suffered a kind of emotional or nervous breakdown as a result of them, in part because she is not confident others can believe what she has experienced. The recipient and his (or her) companions are not identified. Clara begins with the history of her family and the most notable event in her early memory, the bizarre death of her father Theodore. Theodore, a mercantile apprentice in London, was early converted to a strict form of protestant Christianity and came to America to convert the savages. His failure to persist in his calling bred deep guilt and anxiety in him and a feeling that he had disappointed his God. When Clara was six, her father died, apparently by spontaneous combustion, in the place of his worship, an event that remains continuously on the minds of his children—Clara and her older brother Theodore.

Financially comfortable with their inheritance, the young Wielands imbibe a liberal Rousseauistic education on their neighboring estates on the Schuylkill River. Theodore pursues classical studies and religious history, and eventually marries Catherine Pleyel, whose brother Henry joins their happy circle. Music, books, sewing, intellectual discussions, and dramatic presentations employ much of their time, as do Theodore and Catherine's four children. The scene is idyllic as these innocent companions gather one May afternoon to discuss the beauties of sublime nature. Theodore leaves them for a short time to retrieve a letter left at his father's temple, and when he returns, his disturbed attitude is quickly communicated to the others. He explains that at the foot of the hill leading to the temple he was warned away by his wife's voice, coming from the stairs of the temple itself. But Catherine had not been absent from the others, and the young people fruitlessly puzzle this strange experience. Theodore is sure of what he heard. Pleyel, who is highly rationalistic and skeptical by temperament, suggests that Theodore suffered a delusion of his senses.

Some time later, however, Pleyel's confidence in his judgment is shaken when he too—and in Theodore's company—hears Catherine's voice at the temple. Without much further knowledge, Clara concludes that she has evidence, "proofs of a sensible and intelligent existence, which could not be denied" (p. 45). In time the information transmitted by this supernatural voice is confirmed by natural means, and Pleyel learns that his German fiancée has died. The small company are much occupied with these strange occurrences, when into their life comes another young man, distantly known by Pleyel, named Carwin. Totally captivated by his face and his voice, Clara experiences a series of perturbing premonitions of death and disaster and troubled dreams. In that state, she too hears voices—this time of two men apparently planning her murder—in the small room immediately next to hers. In panic she runs to her brother's house and faints at the door, where she is found when a voice again speaks to Theodore urging him to help her. Clara's conclusion is: "This was the third instance of a voice, exerted for the benefit of this little community" (p. 59).

Quite disturbed, Clara has a dream in which her brother entices her towards a destructive pit. Agitated, she retreats to the palisade where the temple is located and is warned away again by a mysterious voice. At the same time Pleyel receives information not to the credit of Carwin, but when suspicions are allayed, Carwin is taken into the group's confidence about the voices. He suggests that the agency is probably human and some form of mimicry, but there is no widespread acceptance of this explanation.

Clara now discovers that her affection for Pleyel has turned to love, and she looks forward eagerly to telling him so. But Pleyel does not appear for a planned play performance, and Clara returns home disappointed and frustrated. Seeking her father's memoirs, she approaches her closet, only to be met by a voice telling her again to "Hold, Hold!" from opening it. Believing that Theodore is within, she insists on opening the door, only to find Carwin there. Carwin implies that his intention had been to ravish Clara, but that she had been saved again by the mysterious warning voice. He leaves Clara to contemplate the mystery, and she concludes that she is indeed under the protection of some benevolent providence.

She sinks into a stupor in which she fears and then imagines that Pleyel has met with an accident, even death, from which she is startled by footsteps and the sounds of doors opening. Pleyel himself accosts her, but with accusations of profligate behavior which he claims to have both seen and heard. Waiting for no explanation, he bolts from the house, and Clara hurries to her brother to ask his advice. Theodore treats her "wickedness" very sternly, and she feels she must go to Pleyel to explain more coherently what had happened. With sinking confidence, she presents herself to Pleyel, but he is extraordinarily cold toward her, indicating that he has himself witnessed her wicked sexual liaison with Carwin, whom he has also found to be wanted for murder. Pleyel leaves her to her misery.

As she returns home, she finds a letter from Carwin desiring an interview with her at her home, and she resolves to meet him. When she returns home late at night, however, she discovers a series of strange lights and voices, a fleeting glimpse of Carwin's face, and a practically incoherent letter from him. Then she discovers the murdered body of Catherine lying in her own bed. Utterly shocked, she sits amid the carnage when

Theodore enters, apparently deranged and responding to voices whose commands only he can hear. He seems to threaten Clara, but a clamor from outside the house frightens him into flight.

Thrown into fever and delirium, it is some time before Clara recovers and can be told not only that the children and their governess Louisa had also been destroyed, but that the murderer had been caught, tried, and sentenced—and that he was her own brother! Only when she reads the transcription of his testimony, that he was acting on the commands of an angel of God and therefore carrying out the divine will, can she accept that he in fact did the deed. The realization again brings her to the point of death. When she recovers, she reveals that her suspicions now fall on Carwin as the agent behind Theodore's madness, but at the same time her trust in her own senses and reason are sadly shaken, and she wonders if she too, having heard voices, may not be as insane as her brother.

She resolves to move to Europe to regain her health and to that end visits her own house one last time to retrieve her father's memoirs and her own journal. In the gloomy dusk and morbid associations of the house, Carwin once more appears. He confesses to his mimicry of others' voices and to the unhappy consequences they produced but denies being the cause of Theodore's butchery. But he also admits that he has learned, by curiously prying into Clara's diary, some private matters that permitted his successful biloquism. Clara is unpersuaded, sure that Carwin's malignancy is the cause of her catastrophes. Into their interview suddenly appears Theodore himself. Clara accuses Carwin, but Theodore orders him to begone. A long interview ensues, which culminates in Theodore's intention to finish his supposed duty by killing Clara. At the crucial moment a disembodied voice orders him to "Hold!" and tells him that he has been insane to believe in his voices. The effect is crushing to Theodore, who stabs himself to death.

Carwin disappears, Clara (again accosted by violent dreams) moves to France and marries Pleyel. She returns to a condition that permits her to relive and retell her ghastly story and to moralize upon the changes that she has undergone and all around her have suffered.

The more one looks at and thinks about that story, the less satisfactory this or any other summary seems to be—including Clara's. When she sums up her experience at the end of the book, we give momentary acquiescence, but almost immediately fall into doubt or uneasiness. Theodore, she tells us, was transformed to a man of sorrows because his notions of moral duty were not just, nor were his conceptions of divine attributes, whereas she herself lacked "ordinary equanimity." The "double-tongued deceiver"—presumably Carwin, although he is not specified—remains in the very last sentence of Clara's account the cause of all the misfortune. That is too pat, too glib. And it simply does not agree with the story she has just told us. Indeed, each of the three errors is open to immediate question.

Let's begin, where Clara does, with the story of her father's odd death. Her father was a man of extreme spiritual scruples. He believed he had a command from God. He also believed he had failed that command, had disobeyed God, and awaited a terrible fate that must destroy him, no matter how far off that time might be. He is, in short, a puritan who knows he stands on God's left-hand side. This does not free him but entraps him. His worship not only persists, but is so intense that no available religious discipline can contain it. Thus he can serve the interests of sects such as the Moravians but cannot join them. His private worship takes on all the characteristics of idiosyncratic superstition. He erects a temple where he worships alone. His devotions call him at regular hours and at inconvenient ones, like those of a Jesuit retreat. And it is during his devotions that he dies, in a loud bang and flash of light with no visible cause. His brother-in-law, a man of science generally and also a physician, attests to the peculiarities of his death. And his diary, along with family tradition (apparently), attests to his premonitions of fiery destruction. On the night of his death he suffered from several fits of alternating revery and frenzy, from which he "complained, in a tremulous and terrified tone, that his brain was scorched to cinders" (p. 14).

This burning image is Clara's, which we are inclined to overlook at first reading because, after all, the narrative too is hers. But reflecting upon it, we realize that her father's death is part of her explanation of the subsequent events. She apparently intends to explain her brother's madness by including this extraordinary event (certainly Clara need not relate it for the stated purpose of her narrative). If it is important to an understanding of Theodore, we cannot forget that it is at least equally important to Clara. What it represents is the extraordinariness of experience, clearly beyond the reach of scientific or rational explanation, that bespeaks the reality of supernatural agency. "Such was the end of my father," she explains. "None surely was ever more mysterious" (p. 19), and she continues to emphasize the impression that this event made upon her as a six-year-old.

I emphasize this reflexive aspect of the narrative because the final American experience for Clara is another conflagration as her dream and her house simultaneously dissolve in flame and smoke (p. 236). Her apocalyptic view is no unimportant aspect of her story, and it is well to realize that early. Brown's own Quaker upbringing may be included here in a parody of the explosive consequences of an inner light—he had reason to reject his family faith—but I see no strong evidence for that. Clara's general view, however, that Theodore's madness relates to their father's peculiar death, deserves attention.

Theodore is a young man of moral seriousness who thinks about his responsibilities as a man of means and freedom. Like Jefferson, he has concluded that the agricultural life is best, and he respects the duties of wealth without falling prey to its blandishments. So he is to some degree a social idealist. But he is also a classicist, a rationalist deeply interested in religious questions, and something of a purist (we must not overlook that his chief avocation is the editing of Cicero). Moreover, he is "grave, considerate, and thoughtful" (p. 22), conspicuously sober and ruminative, and especially interested in testing the validity of religious opinions. He is a considerable pedant, yea, even unto textual criticism: "He was diligent in settling and restoring the purity of the text. For this end, he collected all the editions and commentaries that could be procured, and employed months of severe study in exploring and comparing them. He never betrayed more satisfaction than when he made a discovery of this kind" (p. 24).

But Theodore's temperament is a strange blend of intellectual rigor and speculation. "Moral necessity, and calvinistic inspiration, were the props on which my brother thought proper to repose" (p. 25), says Clara, implying a peculiar mixture of rational with irrational thought. Thus his logical activities in no way preclude his belief in active supernatural agencies, and Clara clinches the connection when she comments, "His father's death was always regarded by him as flowing from a direct and supernatural decree. It visited his meditations oftener than it did mine. The traces which it left were more gloomy and permanent" (p. 35). Pleyel's light skepticism is no effective constraint to such notions, and indeed, Pleyel's failure to explain the voices he and Theodore hear together tends to remove Pleyel's position as a serious counterexplanation to Theodore's. The functional weakness of Pleyel's position is illustrated when he discovers the apparent confirmation of the news of his fiancée's death. At that point, Theodore, busy writing an essay on Socrates' daemon, finds his readiness to accept some supernatural agency for the voices increased (p. 48).

Yet at his trial, the notion that he acted because of possession by some daemon is the first one Theodore rejects (p. 176). Indeed, his entire defense or justification rings with moral necessity and New-Light inspiration. Theodore argues that all human views and judgments are but "bounded views and halting reason" and no way "the measure of truth" (p. 176). True virtue resides in obedience to God's will, and wrong, criminal, or insane as such obedience must be viewed by the more limited dictates of convention, moral sense, conscience, or sentiment, such obedience is the inescapable duty of the truly moral man. Theodore's logic is impeccable.[2] He knows what God wills and he carries out that will despite his contrary sympathies. Moreover, he has not gone beyond earlier American theologians by acting contrary to scripture. The lessons of Job and especially of Abraham and Isaac are deeply within him, and I think we must conclude that Theodore's actions are a logical and reasonable and necessary consequence of his views of God's omniscience and omnipotence. Could he form juster notions of divine attributes? Surely not. However one comes to know God's will, Theodore has come to know it, and no moral creature could behave otherwise. Are God's demands unreasonable, inhumane, inhuman?—consider Job, consider Abraham, and be still. So Clara is wrong in her final appraisal of her brother.

She seems even more perverse in her judgment of Carwin, the "double-tongued deceiver." In the final scenes of the book, Carwin reveals himself as the agent of stupid mischief rather than the engineer of evil. He is desperate, scared, appalled at what his machinations have wrought, eager for understanding and relief, if not forgiveness. He is a second-rate seducer and trickster, content with Judith if he can't have Clara, rightly aware that he has set into motion a series of actions over which he has no control and, in a sense, no responsibility. His tricks have been prompted partly by his pride in his uncommon ventriloquistic abilities, partly by his delight in intrigue, and mainly by his curiosity and need to protect himself. He is a most shabby villain, indeed. But he has a strange sense of honesty about it all, and one cannot help wondering at Clara's insistence that it is he who wrought all the evil.

From the outset it seems that, if Carwin is peculiar, Clara's response to him is even odder. She begins her introduction to Carwin with a claim of revulsion and terror: "If thus, on the very threshold of the scene, my knees faulter and I sink, how shall I support myself, when I rush into the midst of horrors such as no heart has hitherto conceived, nor tongue related?" (p. 49). Yet the description that follows is not one of horror, but of fascination. Carwin's appearance, especially his face, fixes Clara's imagination inexplicably. She cannot shake him; his mellifluence literally triggers a burst of tears. "The tones were indeed such as I never heard before; but that they should, in an instant, as it were, dissolve me in tears, will not easily be believed by others, and can scarcely be comprehended by myself" (p. 52). Though their encounter is momentary, Clara's fancy is utterly preoccupied with Carwin—she sketches him and spends half a night contemplating the sketch, the first link in a necessary series leading to wretchedness (p. 54).

This meeting with Carwin occurs after Catherine's voice has been mysteriously heard twice: once by Wieland alone, the second time by Wieland and Pleyel in company. The first time the voice is heard Pleyel rejects Theodore's description. Possibly Theodore heard a voice, but he only imagined it was Catherine's. One way or another, Theodore's senses were deceived, and any mystery about the event is finally only a natural mystery. Clara's response is quite different, based not upon thought but upon feeling. She immediately senses a "shadowy resemblance" between this event and her father's rather spectacular death. What strikes her most directly is the similarity of "sensations" produced by both events. Talking the matter over with her melancholy brother, Clara has him declare what she herself believes, that their father's death flowed "from a direct and supernatural decree" (p. 35) and that such a decree could be manifest to the understanding by other than visual means. In short, the supposition is laid that the voice might be a divine or at least supernatural manifestation. But it deserves noting that Theodore only confirms what Clara herself feels.

After the second audition, the range of explanations is narrowed. Since Pleyel hears Catherine's voice too, he concludes that no deception from the fancy has occurred. Clara, however, entertains no question now that the voice is supernatural: "Here were proofs of a sensible and intelligent existence, which could not be denied. Here was information obtained and imparted by means unquestionably super-human" (p. 45). In her troubled thoughts that night she surmises that the superhuman agent must also be virtuous: "the idea of superior virtue had always been associated in my mind with that of superior power" (p. 46). Thus the voice rescued Theodore from some unknown danger and now rescued Pleyel from his uncertainty regarding his fiancée's faithfulness and well-being. This is a curious interpretation of the second voice and very specious reasoning. For the voice has informed Pleyel that his promised is dead, hardly a happy rescue. Why does Clara's mind leap to such an explanation? One obvious reason is the context into which the voice appeared. Pleyel is trying to persuade Theodore to go to Germany and claim an inheritance that will permit him to carry his social idealism into practice. And he, too, is eager to discover the fate of his long-silent baroness. Clara experiences no compassion at the news of the death of the baroness: "for though this object of his love be snatched away, is there not another who is able and willing to console him for her loss?" (p. 46). Rather cold-blooded musing, indeed, but we see that Clara's notion that the voice is virtuous proceeds from her relief that she will not now lose two dear men, her brother and Pleyel.

Clara is not only able and willing; she's ready! And it's into that readiness that Carwin strolls. Not only does Brown want us to make this inference, Clara does too, pausing in her account of the fascination with Carwin to tell her readers: "Perhaps you will suspect that such were the first inroads of a passion incident to every female heart, and which frequently gains a footing by means even more slight, and more improbable than these. I shall not controvert the reasonableness of the suspicion, but leave you at liberty to draw, from my narrative, what conclusions you please" (p. 54). The day following the first meeting with Carwin is stormy and tumultuous, and Clara is visited by gloomy premonitions of anguish and death. "Something whispered that the happiness we at present enjoyed was set on mutable foundations" (p. 54). That whisper will soon be made palpable. She tries to drive off her dejection by singing, but the song proves to be a ballad filled with images of "violence and carnage." And then her father's clock strikes midnight—a clock of his own making that Clara has inherited—striking the time when he himself went off to his fatal devotions years earlier.

Immediately after this sequence of troubling sounds, Clara hears a whisper at her ear. No one is visible. The whisper occurs yet again, but Clara does not tell us what it says, and not even a satanic toad shows itself. But now her attention is directed toward the small closet that adjoins her bedroom, the room whose main function is to house Clara's "books and papers" (p. 57). She hears two voices apparently arguing over whether to murder somebody, perhaps her. Terrified, she bolts from the house, runs to her brother's, and there falls into a faint. Her brother learns of her need only when another disembodied voice alerts him: "'Awake! arise!' it exclaimed: 'hasten to succour one that is dying at your door.'" (p. 59). No wonder that Clara is convinced that this is a "third instance of a voice, exerted for the benefit of this little community" (p. 59), for Pleyel moves into her house to protect her, even though he and Theodore suspect the whole episode has been a dream. When she claims that "this arrangement gave general satisfaction," we are not surprised.

The uncertainty of what is dream and what is reality is reinforced by the ensuing episode. Clara falls asleep in a summerhouse overlooking the river. She dreams that Theodore beckons her into a pit, but a hand stops her and a voice saves her from destruction by crying out, " 'Hold! hold!' " The sound breaks her sleep, awakens her in the dead of night, and leaves her effectually unable to move. Now to her awakened mind comes another voice through the latticework, warning her away from the summerhouse by reminding her of her father's death. When the light from Pleyel's lantern penetrates her darkness, she is horrified, remembering the inexplicable lights that accompanied her father's destruction. She is utterly confused and cannot tell whether the pit and the voice were not both part of the same dream. But now she concludes that her protective agent is not superhuman: "A human being was at hand, who was conscious of my presence, and warned me hereafter to avoid this retreat. His voice was not absolutely new, but had I never heard it but once before?" (p. 66).

The narrative problem here is this. Clara knows at the time of writing that Carwin has confessed to being all these voices, yet she presents her own state of mind as if she did not know his explanation. If she now believes that the guardian virtue that protects her is at least to some extent human, she will not relinquish her sense of its virtue. But it is at this point that Carwin is formally introduced into the community by Pleyel (a nice irony). The oddness of his dress and demeanor and the peculiarities of his rumored past are overlooked as the entire question of the voices is proffered to his judgment. Carwin plays all sides of the question. He allows that history offers manifold evidence that "human beings are, sometimes, admitted to a sensible intercourse with the author of nature" (p. 74) but insists that the appearance of such intercourse is often deceptive, the result of tricks done with mirrors or speaking tubes to project the voice. Thus he agrees both with Theodore, who maintains "the probability of celestial interference" (p. 75), and with Pleyel, who will only warrant what his senses tell him. Carwin argues that none of the experiences escapes the possibility that all the voices are the product of mimicry, an explanation that none of his companions will accept. In short, Carwin tells the truth, knowing that the predispositions of his companions will make the truth forceless. We have, then, Clara the narrator explaining a true view of the matter that she herself cannot accept at the time it is first offered and that she persists in rejecting long after the events of her narrative have been played out.

The month that follows intensifies Clara's emotional confusions and excites her imagination. She overlooks the shock of Pleyel's loss and comes to believe that his dispirited manner is owing to his love for her. The notion grows into a certainty but seems completely groundless. Nonetheless, it culminates in a day of intense frustration when Clara eagerly anticipates his arrival and his supposed profession of love. When he fails to arrive, Clara's disappointment is very keen. What were formerly images of unreal happiness now become images of discouragement, but the important thing is Clara's awareness that she has become subject to the creations of her own mind. "Thus fallen into ruins was the gay fabric which I had reared! Thus had my golden vision melted into air!" she laments. "How fondly did I *dream* that Pleyel was a lover!" (my emphasis). And she concludes that her opinions have been built from "the most palpable illusions" (p. 81).

Conscious that this is the case, she nonetheless pursues her illusory way after suppressing an impulse to write a letter to Pleyel that will declare her love. Emotionally out of control, she then imagines Pleyel's death by drowning, conscious all the while that "thus was I tormented by phantoms of my own creation" (p. 83). This habitual fantasizing she explicitly links with her sexual awakening, though her language is so circumlocutious here as practically to hide that admission:

> I can not ascertain the date when my mind became the victim of
> this imbecility; perhaps it was coeval with the inroad of a fatal
> passion; a passion that will never rank me in the number of its
> eulogists; it was alone sufficient to the extermination of my peace;

it was itself a plenteous source of calamity, and needed not the concurrence of other evils to take away the attractions of existence, and dig for me an untimely grave. [p. 83]

And it is just then that she determines to reread her father's memoirs, which are kept in her private closet with her other books and papers.

Sexually charged, hyperimaginative, deeply frustrated, and yearning for her father's comfort, she approaches her closet door. Memories of the murderous voices flood back upon her, and she records that "a sort of belief darted into my mind, that some being was concealed within, whose purposes were evil" (p. 84). Presumably she means within the closet, but there is a nice ambiguity in the sentence that makes it possible the evil being is within her own mind. Terrified, she nonetheless approaches the door when again a voice cries out, "Hold! hold!"—the same voice that warned her at the summerhouse from falling into the pit of her dream. The thought raises again the image of her brother beckoning her to destruction, and while she consciously resists the thought that her brother is her foe, "the frantic conception that my brother was within, that the resistance made to my design was exerted by him, had rooted itself in my mind" (p. 88). Not understanding herself why she wants to bring him out and persisting in attempts to open the closet door despite what she believes to be a "divine" warning against doing so, she finally succeeds in revealing the hidden presence—not her brother but Carwin!—the first major transformation of the subtitle.

What follows would be high comedy, had Brown been conscious of it. Quite caught, Carwin puts on an amazing spur-of-the-moment act of bravado. He confesses his impulse to divest Clara of her honor but mysteriously vows to refrain from his purpose, and, as if to buttress his otherwise foolish position, he claims to be the antagonist of Clara's guardian spirit, that voice "beyond the compass of human organs" (p. 90). Then he backs out with all the awkward aplomb of Stan Laurel or Harold Lloyd. The great irony of the scene is that he does not satisfy Clara's barely suppressed sexual desires. Not only does he not rape her, he is not even her brother! In a very confused state, she tries to slow down her careening emotions. Carwin, of course, in braving out his discovery, has unintentionally confirmed her reliance upon supernatural power:

> How thankful should I be to the power that has interposed to save me!
>
> That power is invisible. It is subject to the cognizance of one of my senses. . . . Perhaps he is a human agent. Yet, on that supposition his atchievements are incredible. Why should I be selected as the object of his care; or, if a mere mortal, should I not recognize some one, whom, benefits imparted and received had prompted to love me?" [pp. 94–95]

Such musings are interrupted by the sound of footsteps outside her door. Again Clara prepares to be assaulted, but is not. The steps retreat, and Clara's mind reverts to images of Pleyel's death. This time not only has he drowned, but it is she who finds his body. "I dwelt, with an obstinacy for which I could not account, on the idea of his death. I painted to myself his struggles with the billows, and his last appearance. I imagined myself a midnight wanderer on the shore, and to have stumbled on his corpse, which the tide had cast up. These dreary images affected me even to tears. I endeavoured not to restrain them. They imparted a relief which I had not anticipated" (p. 101). Better a dead body than nobody at all!

By the following morning, it appears that Clara's hostile imagery has been premature. Not only is Pleyel alive, he is hopping mad, shocked, outraged at Clara's flagitious behavior, and he tells her so quite plainly. Clara speculates that Pleyel has misconstrued her late meeting with Carwin and wonders that he should be so quick to condemn her when an equally plausible construction would be that she had been involuntarily and criminally assaulted by Carwin. She resolves to seek her brother's advice. From Theodore she learns that Pleyel believes he has actually seen and heard her and Carwin during their sexual interlude. Clara protests that that could only be so if someone had been taught to mimic her, and so she comes, almost unwittingly, to the same explanation for extraordinary sensations that Carwin had given earlier—mimicry. Theodore is not notably affected by this theory, and Clara goes off to the city to make her vindication to Pleyel directly.

But Pleyel is by then fortified by considerable thought, new information, and convinced sensory experience. He explains to Clara that she has long been a model of virtue for him, indeed, that he judged his fiancée according to her approximation of Clara's standards. Because Clara had already handled one sexual threat responsibly—from "that specious seducer Dashwood"—he was not at first worried by her fascination with Carwin. But when he once stole into her chamber, as she was writing at her diary, he saw just enough of what she was writing to suspect something suspicious about the summerhouse and a meeting there. What is more, he has learned that Carwin is an escaped murderer "in league with some infernal spirit" (p. 130). "Bloodshed is the trade, and horror is the element of this man" (p. 131), reasons Pleyel, and, on his way back with the news, he is arrested near the summerhouse by a sound of laughter, Clara's laughter, and made privy to a very incriminating conversation between Clara and her paramour. Offended in his perceptions—all through his *hearing*—and betrayed in his trust, sensing that he had but foolishly supposed Clara needed a protector, he leaves.

Sick and desolate, Clara nonetheless returns home to an interview with Carwin, an interview she fears and detests yet seeks out compulsively. She returns late at night to find a light burning in her room and, despite her fright, again persists in approaching her bedroom and closet: "If my angel were not weary of fruitless exertions to save, might not a new warning be expected? Who could say whether his silence were ascribable to the absence of danger, or to his own absence?" (p. 147). But the warning does again ring out—"*hold! hold!*"—this time accompanied by a confused image of a face shrieking and distorted but strangely blended with the image of Carwin. "This visage was, perhaps, pourtrayed by my fancy. If so, it will excite no surprize that some of his lineaments were now discovered. Yet affinities were few and unconspicuous, and were lost amidst the blaze of opposite qualities" (p. 148). Then, with thoughts of her father's death in "a meteorous refulgence," she discovers Catherine murdered in her bed, murdered in her place.

It is many pages later that Clara reverts to the question of the nature of the voices, which her uncle attributes to delusions of the imagination, just as Pleyel first ventured to explain Theodore's initial encounter with the mysterious voices. But Clara is no more disposed to accept that explanation than when she was at first exposed to it, though now her confidence that the voices are supernatural is decidedly shaken—"I believe the agency to be external and real, but not supernatural," she tells her uncle (p. 178). Yet the news that her maternal grandfather committed suicide in response to such voices (pp. 178–79) and so offers her an inheritance of madness from both her parents, shakes up the assured tone in which she denied the supernatural agency. Thrust into concern for her own sanity here, transformed "from rational and human into a creature of nameless and fearful attributes" (pp. 179–80), withdrawn and suicidal, Clara's notions of divine agency return.

> Some times I conceived the apparition to be more than human. I had no grounds on which to build a disbelief. I could not deny faith to the evidence of my religion; the testimony of men was loud and unanimous: both these concurred to persuade me that evil spirits existed, and that their energy was frequently exerted in the system of the world.
>
> These ideas connected themselves with the image of Carwin. Where is the proof, said I, that daemons may not be subjected to the controul of men? [p. 180]

Clara's concern here becomes not whether there are supernatural agents, but whether her guardian voices have been agents of good or evil, whether they conspire with or oppose Carwin, whether Carwin controls them or they him. As her health returns, so does her prior assurance of the supernatural nature of the voices, but now in a new perplexity, because she begins to be more and more accepting of her brother's self defense (p.

181). In brief, she is coming to agree with Theodore's view of reality, which the world judges to be mad.

As her sympathies for Theodore return, her passion for Pleyel dissipates. And as it does, back into life springs his previous fiancée, Theresa de Stolberg, clearing the way again for a conflict between the two main threats in her consciousness, Theodore and Carwin. This seems to be why Clara returns so imprudently to her house, to her chamber, to her innermost closet, where the two had struggled in her imagination once before. By now, however, she has been told that Theodore is totally deranged, that his divine calling will not have ended until he destroys both Clara and Pleyel, and that he has several times escaped from confinement to kill her. Earlier, before her closet door, she was shocked by the thought that her brother had become her foe; now indeed he has. Her consciousness that what began as a premonition in a dream has now become reality is quite clear:

> I recollected the omens of this destiny; I remembered the gulf to
> which my brother's invitation had conducted me; I remembered
> that, when on the brink of danger, the author of my peril was
> depicted by my fears in his form: Thus realized, were the creatures
> of prophetic sleep, and of wakeful terror! [pp. 189–90]

Clara is telling us quite forthrightly that her dreams, the illusions, the delusions of which she earlier complained, have all become real. This is a matter to which we shall have to return. But for the present, consider the other emphasis of this passage, the recurrence of recollection and remembrance. It is to seek "memorials" that she returns to her house. Most particularly, it is to retrieve and destroy her shorthand journal, a manuscript "which contained the most secret transactions of my life" (p. 191). Clara is here restaging an important psychodrama. In the same room where she had earlier sought consolation in her father's memoirs, she has now come to witness some kind of reenactment:

> Here it was that the incomprehensible behaviour of Carwin was
> witnessed: this the stage on which that enemy of man shewed

himself for a moment unmasked. Here the menaces of murder were wafted to my ear; and here these menaces were executed. [p. 193]

The nice feature of this passage is its conflation of the two major scenes that occurred here earlier—Clara's near rape and murder, and Catherine's vicious destruction. The recollection revives Clara's suicidal morbidity; stage and mood set, enter the characters. First, Carwin.

What Clara expected in this interview is not quite clear; what is clear is that Carwin exculpates himself entirely from all involvement in Theodore's mad mission. Yet he confesses all. He has spied. He has mimicked voices (confirming the theory that he had declared so openly earlier). He has ruined Clara's reputation though he could not steal her honor. He has turned to the servant Judith instead. He has been caught unawares in the most compromised circumstances. He has even discovered Catherine's body, and it was indeed he whose face and voice Clara perceived just prior to finding Catherine's corpse. He even claims a kind of responsibility for what has happened, although it is indirect and rather self-aggrandizing: "yet had I not rashly set in motion a machine, over whose progress I had no controul, and which experience had shewn me was infinite in power?" (pp. 215–16). Because she has never heard of biloquism or ventriloquism, Clara rejects the entire story: "He attempts to give an human explanation of these phantasms; but it is enough that he owns himself to be the agent; his tale is a lie, and his nature devilish. As he deceived me, he likewise deceived my brother, and now do I behold the author of all our calamities!" (p. 216). Into such reasonings, such conclusions, enter Theodore.

Totally fallen from the noble and judicious man we earlier saw, and practically unconscious that Carwin is there, Theodore announces that Clara is fated to die. Though death as a solution to living has several times occupied Clara's thoughts, this form of it she is unprepared for: "I who had sought death," she reflects, "was now thrilled with horror because it was near. Death in this form, death from the hand of a brother, was thought upon with undescribable repugnance" (p. 218). Suddenly what seemed so improbable—Carwin's mimicry—occurs as a form of salvation to Clara. She tells her brother all the mischief has been Carwin's, and slowly, with difficulty, but with a sense of its importance, Theodore recognizes Carwin's presence and asks him solemnly and ominously if it had indeed been he who spoke the night of Catherine's death. Carwin, quite according to form, answers so ambiguously, so pitifully, that Theodore dismisses him, and once again Carwin exits, "his knees beating one against another," from the fatal chamber.

In the strained silence that follows, the transformation we saw earlier repeats itself, this time reversed. Originally, we remember, it was Carwin who emerged threateningly from the closet when Clara expected Theodore. Here the threat shifts back:

> What shall I say! I was menaced, as I thought, with death, and, to elude this evil, my hand was ready to inflict death upon the menacer. In visiting my house, I had made provision against the machinations of Carwin. In a fold of my dress an open penknife was concealed. This I now seized and drew forth. It lurked out of view; but I now see that my state of mind would have rendered the deed inevitable if my brother had lifted his hand. This instrument of my preservation would have been plunged into his heart. [p. 223]

Clara's intentions are revealed when she throws down the weapon in a fit of self-abhorrence. The sound generates in Wieland a series of rather rapid alterations of mood. Or perhaps the alterations are Clara's. The uncertainty seems more than accidental. Indeed, the scene culminates in a joining of their views regarding Carwin. Theodore announces:

> "I was indeed deceived. The form thou hast seen was the incarnation of a daemon. The visage and voice which urged me to the sacrifice of my family, were his. Now he personates a human form: then he was invironed with the lustre of heaven."

But he adds, "This minister is evil, but he from whom his commission was received is God" (pp. 225–26).

The point here is that Theodore's view of Carwin and Clara's most recently urged view now have coalesced, have become identical. Carwin again appears but, instead of exercising his marvelous ventriloquial powers to save Clara, stands dumbly for a time and then leaves. Theodore, in an apparently lucid moment, had returned the knife to Clara; it is now her turn to return it to him. But not until she, too, hears a "voice, louder than human organs could produce, shriller than language can depict, burst from the ceiling, and commanded him—to *hold!*" (p. 229). What supremely delicious irony. Now for the first time Clara hears the same voice Theodore hears, and mutually they acknowledge it to be superhuman. And yet its opening words are the very words Carwin has uttered numerous times before in his malicious trickery. Joined fully now in Theodore's frenzy, she practically puts back into his hand the knife with which he kills himself. Her observation that "my hands were sprinkled with his blood as he fell" (p. 232) is indeed more than physical description.

Through all this, Clara never relinquishes the thought that Carwin is to blame. Yet, if his former appearance ill fit the agency of Satan, Carwin's appearance after Theodore's self-destruction hardly sits with that of Clara's savior:

> Carwin, as I said, had left the room, but he still lingered in the house. My voice summoned him to my aid; but I scarcely noticed his re-entrance, and now faintly recollect his terrified looks, his broken exclamations, his vehement avowals of innocence, the effusions of his pity for me, and his offers of assistance.
>
> I did not listen. [p. 232]

Indeed she did not. Clara's narrative, in short, betrays Carwin's behavior and appearance in such a manner that she contradicts and undercuts her own stubborn insistence on his villainy. This, even though she is addressing a reader (the unknown recipient of her narrative) who may have already heard Carwin's side of the story: "He has told thee his tale, and thou exculpatest him from all direct concern in the fate of Wieland" (p. 233). Is she addressing the recipient of her story here or her revered uncle? Either way, this is the first point at which Clara's frantic defensiveness becomes obvious, and as it does so, she becomes increasingly agitated.

Suddenly she professes not to care how the events are explained, or what Carwin's motives or purposes might have been, just so she can focus upon him all responsibility: "I care not from what source these disasters have flowed," she blurts out, now joining herself to her brother in one plural pronoun, "it suffices that they have swallowed up our hopes and our existence." Whether Carwin has told her "revered friend" the truth, she does not care, so as her turmoil and confusion and longing for death mounts, she ends her narrative in a hallucinatory state, judging Carwin by condemning him to his own self-judgment, banishing him by words, then falling to silence.

"My work is done!" exclaims Clara at the very end of that narrative, but we know the story is not. Indeed, the narrator has only fallen into yet another of her many swoons, this one to last three years. When she emerges, she does so to tell another story, the Stuart-Conway-Maxwell story, which everyone agrees is a disastrous digression. We may see, however, that the digression is purposeful. Up to the end of chapter 26 we have witnessed Clara's progressive involvement in her brother's and her family's madness and her deepening and unshakable conviction of Carwin's responsibility, until she cracks under the stress. We have also witnessed her reliving of that experience by narrating, by seeking through language to account for her complicity in madness, in order to persuade us that whatever horrors have occurred are the fault of another, Carwin, until her narrative voice also cracks and ceases under the impossible pressure. Consciousness, time, and narrative voice all cease at the same instant of realized impossibility. Shall we say the story has combusted spontaneously, very like the elder Wieland? Let's.

Certainly when Clara takes up her tale again in the final chapter, the tone and the story have changed. Time has returned to obliterate the most intense of emotions, making turbulence subside, converting fluctuations to calm (p. 234). But it is not just time that works the change. Nor is it the sensible intervention of her uncle-physician Mr. Cambridge. Clara confesses to a positive gratification in nursing her mad sickness:

> In relating the history of these disasters I derived a . . . species of gratification. . . . Having finished my tale, it seemed as if the scene

were closing. A fever lurked in my veins, and my strength was gone. Any exertion, however slight, was attended with difficulty, and, at length, I refused to rise from my bed. [p. 235]

Amid talk of her recovery there is thus this experience of complete torpidity, at least outwardly. For inwardly the experience of telling the story has cast her into the most harrowing and energetic of dreams, dreams of "phantastical incongruities" in which her "uncle, Wieland, Pleyel and Carwin were successively and momently discerned amidst the storm." Cast into a chaotic inferno—darkness shot through with light, she on the verge of a dark abyss or gazing from the ridge of volcanic power terrified with immensity—Clara creates or recreates her condition. But now she feels as if a real difference has occurred. The dream world may be confusing, but she is not confused about its being a dream. "However strange it may seem, I was conscious, even during my dream, of my real situation" (p. 236). But once more Clara is wrong, for her inferno is external as well as internal. She is literally engulfed in the fire of her own house (the scene of her horrors) burning down around her. At least we can say that this is her last error of that sort, for in a way Clara expires in that fire—the same way the young boy drowns into poetry in "Out of the Cradle."

What is gone is the theater of Clara's musings, the chamber of her memories, the closet of her inmost secrets, the bed of her passionate death. She began this episode with the remark, "It is true that I am now changed" (p. 235), and she concludes it with, "My habitation was levelled with the ground, and I was obliged to seek a new one. A new train of images, disconnected with the fate of my family, forced itself on my attention, and a belief insensibly sprung up, that tranquillity, if not happiness, was still within my reach" (p. 237). Both the image of the new habitation and of locomotion matter here. Throughout the earlier narrative we have seen characters, particularly Carwin and Clara, confined by chains of necessity, compelled to follow trains of images to horrid destinations. Clara has solved the problem by switching trains.

This readjustment of her mind propels her to happiness in two pages— a return to Europe, return of her love for Pleyel and even, after the death of Theresa, marriage with him and their settling in Montpellier. Fair enough, but Carwin has apparently not been able to keep from telling his view of the story, possibly to the recipient of this narrative and certainly to Clara's uncle, in whom he found "a more impartial and indulgent auditor" (p. 239) than Clara had been. Mr. Cambridge believes that Carwin may have influenced Wieland indirectly but cannot be held responsible for Wieland's "maniacal illusion." How incredible that Clara seems suddenly so content with that explanation and can picture him as the American farmer with a future life of innocence and usefulness. And yet it is not so incredible when we consider how her tabula has been razed. She is now in the act of making a new house, a new habitation, a new comprehension, and therefore a new story.

That story is the Maxwell-Stuart-Conway story, a totally vapid tale of conventional relationships, a sentimental tragedy of seduction, betrayal, infidelity, wounded and redeemed honor, and the susceptibility of good but weak men (and women) to the deceits of unscrupulous villains. Clara now offers this as an explicit analogue to her own earlier narrative. In short, Clara has turned her own tortured experience into formula fiction, life into soap, so that she can moralize upon it and somehow make it livable. Larzer Ziff and other modern critics have strongly urged the function of Clara as an antisentimental heroine.[3] I would grant that urging and yet maintain that Clara is an antisentimental creation whose only mode of survival or understanding of existence is to be a sentimental heroine. So I see the process as reversed: Clara begins under stress in a very real and very distasteful situation. She addresses a sympathetic, or at least friendly, auditor and until her final collapse she senses that every defensive maneuver is simultaneously self-betraying. All that is left to her then, she slowly comes to see, is the conventionalizing of experience. Amid all the ambiguities, the uncertainties, the mysteries, *that* is perhaps the only way. Surely the story she now tells is lame, the parallels she draws at the end between herself and Louisa's mother and especially between Carwin and Maxwell, totally inadequate. Surely we are meant to recognize Clara's saving falsifications, to turn away, as I stated at the outset of this chapter, from Clara's conclusions.

What we seem to have then is two stories, one of which disgusts all readers by its patent inadequacies, the other of which nearly destroys its teller. Let me suggest that the chief difference between these two stories is their relative externality. The formulaic nature of the concluding story resides chiefly in its abstractness (partly a result of its brevity), in the fact that all the characters are stock and the motivations so obvious they are barely stated. The story is all event and so leads to simple, facile, and totally unsatisfactory generalizations about experience. If that is correct, then one would expect certain features to mark the first story—namely, that it would be much longer, that its length would be a product of its exploration of the motives behind and within events, that it would be interiorized so intensely that we might understand its unbearable effects upon its teller, and that finally it might prove incapable of satisfactory generalization. But such an expectation is complicated by the imagined psychological state of the narrator, whose purpose is to attain the pat satisfaction of the externalized story. Let me try again. Clara is looking for the comfort, health, and sanity that language can provide so that she can live with and live beyond her devastating experience. Her first lengthy attempt fails, but the second attempt succeeds. In short, her defensive posture in the first telling leads her to attribute to external events what are really internal problems. Let me illustrate.

Clara begins her first narrative with the story of her family, especially her father's religious calling, his sense of failure and guilt, his surrogate worship, and his mysterious death. At one level Clara is telling us that her brother killed his wife and children *because* he inherited from his father a destructive morbidity, an irrational religious predilection. The elder Wieland is thus like Carwin an indirect cause but a necessary condition for the younger Theodore's commitment to irrational commands. Clara externalizes Theodore's inheritance of guilt, faith, and obedience to a sense of divinity. She thus tends at first to hide that she also shares that inheritance by making it so obvious an aspect of her story. Indeed, it is Clara who pores on the death of her father all through her childhood, and she, not her brother, who ponders whether it is divine punishment or the bitter coincidence of merely natural forces. What Clara reveals, perhaps betrays, to us is her own more vital inheritance, her fascination with the mystery of her father's death. To put it another way, what she imputes to and exteriorizes in her brother is first of all true of herself.

Clara's chief mechanism for the central transformation of this narrative is the dream itself. We have seen several times how powerful her dream projections are. The most obvious is the early dream of her brother beckoning her to join him in such a way that she must plunge into a horrid abyss. We have seen how her narrative is the movement toward a kind of identity with Theodore attainable only over the bodies of Theodore's wife and children. When she declares that the dream has become reality—"Thus realized, were the creatures of prophetic sleep, and of wakeful terror" (p. 190)—she is telling truth in more than one way. Theodore has become her foe; of that she is conscious. But we know additionally that the dream is being fulfilled in other ways as well. She is approaching a kind of union with her brother, and through him, with her father. That is to say, she is coming to enlightenment about the initial perplexity, knowledge of the mystery of death. Her desire for that union has obvious erotic overtones that she reveals even as she tries to damp them by imagining alternatives to that knowledge. Carwin is her own self-generated sexuality—raw, irrational, irresponsible, violent, even criminal. His is the repulsive attraction of the disembodied voice, the idea with neither personal nor social connection, abandonment completely without duty. He is therefore a kind of personification of an impulse in Clara that is essentially antinomian. He is the replica also of that aspect of her father that refused or failed to carry out his obedience to the source of creation, whereas Theodore is his obverse twin, the replica of his father's duty, obedience, and guilt. In one sense, Theodore and Carwin are opposites, and so we might expect Clara to be choosing between them; in another, since they both share features of her father, Clara wants both, and her narrative, at key points as we have seen, nearly confuses them —when she expects her brother she discovers Carwin, and when she prepares to destroy Carwin, it is Theodore she kills.

The choice of either is impossible, and the impossibility is put in essentially sexual terms. She cannot be entirely united to Theodore because of the obvious incestuous connections, yet she can very much desire to supplant his wife and children. That Catherine is bludgeoned beyond recognition in Clara's own bed may be the fitting, if rather extreme, recognition of Catherine's persistent lack of identity throughout Clara's story. But if she cannot hope to be wholly possessed by and of Theodore, neither can she surrender to Carwin's utter lawlessness, no matter how strong her fascination.

The only possible alternative to Theodore's mad devotions and Carwin's licentiousness is Pleyel. He is both honorable and passionate. He is available and proximate. That he is promised to another (out of obligation, not love, we are assured at the end) is no problem: Clara merely kills his fiancée, wills her death, we might say, and equally wills her back to life when it is convenient. But she also wills Pleyel's death, and I think we must ask why. One answer is obvious: she is pleased to think of him dead because that nurses her melancholy and permits her to show how much she valued him. The dream is disturbing but also pleasing. Clara must resist Pleyel because he is neither her fatherly madness nor her private sexuality. Too much has been made, perhaps, of Pleyel's rationality and skepticism, since the principles he most clearly represents are sensible social duty, reasonableness and sanity. Clearly he is susceptible to deceit and mistake, but he is Clara's life principle and therefore quite in opposition to both Theodore and Carwin, although he is in amity with both. He refuses to subject himself to Clara's dreams of him (and therefore to both Theodore's desire to kill him and Carwin's more successful conying). His response to Clara's supposed liaison with Carwin is totally consistent with Clara's final story of conventional seduction, which is to say that it is susceptible to correction and change.

To put my argument most baldly, as Clara's initial narrative proceeds, it increasingly implicates her in madness and murder. Full recognition that her simple account has become a very deep confession indeed is what makes her story crack. Clara cannot accept her lust for her father/brother or the death that full knowledge of them represents. Neither can she give full rein to the sexual desires represented in Carwin, and one is tempted to see her pig-headed blaming of Carwin for every misfortune as, finally, an inability to live with herself. But when she finally banishes Carwin in her ultimate hallucination, she has nothing left.

Well, not quite. What she needs is some mediating principle that joins deadly knowledge and acceptable sexuality. And this she finds in her uncle-physician Mr. Cambridge. This avuncular figure, her mother's brother, fits the role exactly. He is, first, very knowing, and he is roughly her father's age. Indeed, when they return to Europe, it is essentially as father and daughter. Moreover, he can tell Clara—again the telling—of others whose experiences correspond to hers, can tell her that her mother too had a father whose pursuit of private voices led to his destruction. At the same time, he shares Pleyel's rationalism. This means that he is content with the explanation that natural causes can account for moral peculiarities. As I remarked above, he seconds, and therefore shares, Pleyel's view of the delusive origins of Wieland's actions. In doing so, of course, he speaks for the delusions that also control Clara's distress. Being in this essentially asexual position, he can not only mediate between Clara and Pleyel and so join her to her social role as wife and mother, he can even reconcile her to Carwin's maladroit mischief.

Like a modern psychoanalyst, Mr. Cambridge has brought Clara into a state of social adjustment. A compassionate healer has made it possible for one human being to persist in living. But Charles Brockden Brown is obviously suspicious about the satisfactoriness of that solution. That so feeble a fabric or fabrication as Clara's Stuart-Maxwell-Conway concoction could possibly sustain sane, human, and humane relationships remains to be seen. It may wrap up a plot, but it cannot end the story.

Constantia

Charles Brockden Brown's first novel of transformations, with its spectacular and bizarre episodes of death by spontaneous combustion, biloquism, and dream projections, might understandably generate certain expectations for the second novel. Those expectations are met, at least to some extent, by *Ormond: or the Secret Witness.*[1] Again we have the predicament of a young lady's education into reality by threats to her virtue, her life, and her integrity. For a ventriloquist, we have a master of disguises who can make himself a witness to the most secret desires and affairs of others. And in place of the Wielands' spectacular enlightenments, we have the very vividly portrayed miseries of urban disease in a period of intense political revolution. But such similarities are at first deflected by a number of very marked contrasts between *Ormond* and *Wieland*. The most obvious of these is the narrative stance. Although this is again a story told by a young woman, the narrator is not the central figure in the story. That figure, Constantia Dudley, is therefore unable, except at second hand, to reflect any of the psychological complexity that marks Clara's story. There is also an apparent difference in the ostensible purpose of the story, which is in the form of a communication to an I. E. Rosenberg, a German interested in American society and manners and for unexplained reasons "anxious" to learn about Constantia. The narrator disclaims any artistic design; indeed, at the outset, we are so buffeted with details and events that there is no reason to suspect that disclaimer.

But that, too, is a difference. The early biography of the elder Wieland is similarly crammed with details, but they subside by the second chapter as we get into the adventures of our central characters. Here the profusion of details persists, and we learn very quickly that the story being told is another sentimental tale of a young lady in sexual and social danger, a variant of the Conway-Maxwell-Stuart story of *Wieland*. The substitute story from one book thus becomes the primary story of another.

No surprise, then, that this story initially appears to minimize internal psychological states and focuses on the details of the exterior world. Absent are the powerful forces of madness and unreason, superstition and religion. There is no supernatural in *Ormond*; in its place there is only the arena formed by sex and marriage, where social principles such as politics and economics meet. To the degree that this substitution is conscious on Brown's part, I think we can say that *Ormond* became for Brown a test of the assumptions that finally ruled Clara's solution in *Wieland*. As *Ormond* proceeds, however, the sentimental romance form becomes itself transformed into something quite different from what it appeared to be in *Wieland*.

Let us begin with a moderately objective recapitulation of the story S. C. tells. Brown's profusion here makes every summary statement at least mildly interpretative through the necessity of selection, but you, Gentle Reader, will no doubt make your own corrections. *Ormond* begins with a story of a man's fall from a state of power to one of submission. Stephen Dudley, Constantia's father, is an artist whom necessity drives to business and finally to ruin through an elaborate embezzlement scheme concocted by a young man named Thomas Craig. Craig secures Dudley's confidence and then his dependence, so that when he finally absconds with the proceeds of Dudley's pharmacy, Craig leaves Dudley bereft of all normal resources. Bankrupt and ashamed, but determined to support his small household, Dudley moves from New York to a poor suburb of Philadelphia. He tries to work as a technical writer, a legal copyist, but the work destroys his spirit, and a series of catastrophes—drink, the death of his wife, and his blindness—move the small family into what we now call the inner city.

Everything comes to depend upon his sixteen-year-old daughter Constantia, who proves very able despite her naiveté, youth, and rather powerful imagination and intellectual curiosity. They are now in the heart —or perhaps the craw—of society, which slowly breaks down their seclusive habits. Indeed, it is because of their straitened means that they first become aware of the yellow fever epidemic that progressively involves the entire city in a dance of death. Food prices go up, shortages of service are encountered at every turn, Constantia's work as a seamstress disappears, and so we learn that the first effects of social disease are economic. The Dudleys are relatively ignorant of the course of the disease itself but feel its pocketbook pinch severely.

When the yellow fever does come home to them, it comes hard. The death of their landlord gives them some respite from financial woes, but that hope is pulled away almost at once when a new and harder landlord, M'Crea, comes to collect. Constantia tends a sick neighbor and is finally left to streek her out and arrange for her body to be carted off. The Dudleys themselves suffer the disease at least mildly and attribute their survival to the meager fare of hasty pudding on which they have had to rely for diet. One of Constantia's few acquaintances, Sarah Baxter, tells her of the miseries experienced by a French couple, the Monrose father and daughter, during the height of the pestilence, when the father dies and the weakened daughter buries him crudely by lantern light in their garden and then disappears without a trace into the darkness of the city. Into the abandoned Monrose house Constantia moves her own family, but not even that tactic saves them from desperation, and they soon have to surrender their most prized possessions, her father's comforting lute and her own gold-mounted miniature portrait of her dear friend Sophia.

Not only do such measures gain nothing, but more positive signs of hope and help cannot be accepted, thus increasing her woe. Accosted by ruffians on the streets, Constantia is saved by a middle-aged man named Balfour, who moves from defender to suitor rather quickly. But Constantia rejects him on the grounds of his too limited mind and sensibility. Balfour's sister, angered by what she supposes to be Constantia's mistreatment of her brother, sees to it that what little work as seamstress is still left to Constantia dries up. Utterly reduced, Constantia seeks the help of an acquaintance of happier times, Mr. Melbourne. But on her way she encounters none other than Thomas Craig, the author of many of these calamities.

She pursues him to the house of one Ormond, where Craig sends her fifty dollars with which she happily goes off to pay her debts. But before she can determine how next to act, she and her father are arrested on the complaint of M'Crea that they have passed him a forged banknote. Hailed before a magistrate with images of prison looming before them, they discover a very sympathetic justice indeed in the person of Mr. Melbourne, who alleviates much of their pressure and worry and assures Constantia of new business through his wife. Meanwhile Ormond, who merely passed Constantia when she was coming from her interview with Craig and who has heard of her misfortunes from Craig (who blamed them on the malice of his brother), resolves to help the Dudleys.

With the advent of Ormond roughly one-third of the way through the story, the character of the narrative alters conspicuously. Chapter 12 is an extended character sketch of Ormond through the maxims by which he lives. Believing that service to one's self is the only attainable good, Ormond is comfortably independent of society. His chief social end, therefore, is to know the intentions, plans, and motivations of others so that he can control them for his own sake. He bends to that end an extraordinary talent for theatrical imitation, a talent so powerful that it goes far beyond normal acting and even controls the reality within which he and others operate, although he himself remains impenetrable. This character is complicated by its isolation, for he has not yet met his equal in a woman. Ormond has indeed converted Helena Cleves, a gorgeously soft, musically talented, and mentally pliant young lady, from a possible wife to simple mistress. Although he is opposed to marriage, some element in him seems to be leaning in that direction. To discover the worth of the Dudleys, he has entered their house disguised as a Negro chimney sweep and, pleased with what he finds, he provides the Dudleys with sufficient means to keep them going. He also introduces Constantia to Helena, a relationship that deepens into confidentiality and friendship, despite Constantia's realization that Helena is not married.

With mixed feelings, Constantia agrees to speak to Ormond on Helena's behalf regarding marriage. But the effort is not only fruitless, it clarifies how foolish such a marriage of unequals would be; it leads progressively to Ormond's discontent with his mistress, to Helena's progressive melancholy, and to his stirred appreciation of Constantia's sharp mind. Sufficiently quickened, that appreciation turns to desire; Ormond tells Helena he can be her lover no more, though he will continue to maintain her. He then proposes marriage to a somewhat surprised Constantia, who not only rejects him, but sends him away filled with genuine remorse at the pain he has caused Helena. The rejection has been too strong for Helena, who commits suicide, resigning Ormond to Constantia. In several ways Constantia assumes Helena's place—she inherits Helena's house (originally owned by Stephen Dudley, who lost it to Ormond, who had given it to Helena) and leaves behind all financial difficulties. She is a perfect student of Ormond's peculiar brand of knowledge and her education explodes under his tutelage. Her father even regains his sight, and the fortune of the Dudleys is clearly on the rise. What she does not know is that Ormond's earlier revulsion toward marriage is again in full force and that he now wants Constantia as mistress, not as wife.

After some months, Ormond leaves but writes to the Dudleys vividly and regularly. During his absence, Constantia again encounters the lady who purchased her father's lute, Lady Martinette de Beauvais. Martinette, Constantia's most formidable encounter, is international, cosmopolitan, adventuresome, and quite intimidating. Constantia feels much in common with Martinette in temperament and education, though not in experience, and she is puzzled and somewhat repulsed by Martinette's savage commitment to liberty. As she relates her story, we discover that she is Miss Monrose of chapter 7, whose house the Dudleys had moved to after she disappeared into the sick night.

Meanwhile, Stephen Dudley, who is not entirely pleased with Ormond's attitude towards his daughter, determines that he will travel to Italy and that his daughter should accompany him. Constantia is pleased to do so, especially because the trip may permit her to find her friend

Sophia. But just as the trip seems certain, she discovers her father dead "in some terrific and mysterious manner." Doubly bereft and shocked, she tries to locate the miniature portrait of Sophia she had given to M'Crea as a pledge when she was at her lowest ebb. In pursuing the miniature, she comes upon its subject herself, Sophia, who has returned to find her. In chapter 23 Sophia comes into the story as a participant; it takes her three chapters to recount her adventures with a profligate and crazed mother, many travels, marriage, her return to America, familiarity with the yellow fever epidemic, and her search for Constantia's papers after coming to believe that Constantia had died during the plague. But now they are totally and rapturously reunited, and the stage is set for the last phase of the story.

Ormond suddenly reappears to Constantia, professing to know all that has occurred since Dudley's death and the reunion with Sophia. He warns Constantia about some impending danger and destiny and, after some ominous and rather mysterious predictions, he withdraws. The young ladies determine to leave for Europe, but Constantia insists on one last visit to the house she received from Helena. While in the upstairs closet-study, she sees Ormond, who has not been around for two months, riding to the house. Frightened but resolute, she opens her door to leave the closet, when she discovers a body whom she only half identifies. She is then confronted by Ormond. After confessing that the body is Craig's and that Craig killed Dudley at his command, Ormond admits that he then killed Craig to win Constantia's gratitude and acquiescence. Now his main purpose is to violate her honor as well as her body, be she dead or alive. Locked in the house with this threat, Constantia resolves to die herself because she cannot kill another. Meanwhile Sophia, concerned for Constantia's safety, has hurried to be with her but arrives just in time to peek through a keyhole at a disheveled and distraught Constantia. With help, she releases Constantia and comes upon a "scene of . . . complicated havoc" in which Constantia has stabbed Ormond at the last possible moment. Sophia then ties up her narrative with a few details and bids farewell to I. E. Rosenberg.

Telling it this way, one inevitably suppresses a number of crucial concerns in the narrative. In fact, only when one reflects upon the story do elements in it emerge that not so much supplant the plot but reinforce it in perhaps unexpected ways. For example, consider the opening episode, the reduction of the Dudley family through the schemes of Thomas Craig. Stephen Dudley, the artist who goes blind through adversity, suffers from defective moral vision from the beginning. He sees himself as painter, the sensitive appreciator of man's memorials to his noblest visions. We see him so preoccupied with his vision of Italian dignity and beauty that he can neither see, appreciate, nor control the everyday reality before him. What makes him susceptible to Craig's scheme is, first of all, a series of deceptions practised upon him, but behind those deceptions lies his own temperamental and cultivated blindness. Constantia is not entirely free from that affliction herself.

Craig succeeds in bilking Dudley by appealing to his impaired vision; that is, he shows Dudley letters and written witnesses to his character and to his own testimony about his background and family. Over time Dudley comes to accept these as proofs of Craig's sincerity and worthiness, because the letters come from Craig's mother and also from Dudley's business associates in England, providing a kind of independent corroboration of Craig's stories. Dudley eventually realizes, much too late, that not only are the letters false, but they also falsify by a kind of impersonation, by the successful mimicry of other personalities and characters as well as their handwriting. Only an accidental display of inconsistent evidence, also a letter, pricks Craig into desperate and unsuccessful pretences until he decides the game is up and he had better leave. Simple forgery is, of course, Craig's occupation, as we learn from the fifty-dollar banknote he sends to Constantia later. But Brown is showing us more than that; Craig's talent is for imitation, and it is a quill-keen talent, though exercised in the rather limited genre of double-entry bookkeeping. It is keen enough to persuade Ormond later that Constantia has had an affair with Craig, persuasion wrought by letters purported to be by Constantia and only contestable by her: "'Those letters never were received from me, and are forgeries. His skill in imitation extended no farther in the present case than my handwriting. My modes of thinking and expression were beyond the reach of his mimicry'" (p. 124). Ormond's response is interesting. He talks of Craig as a very adept entertainer and can even concede his own losses to Craig as worth the exhibition.

Ormond's appreciation for that kind of show is not limited to Craig as actor. Indeed, it was Helena's talent for mimicry that drew and held him to her—"Ormond was an accurate judge of the proficiency of Helena, and of the felicity with which these accomplishments were suited to her character. When his pupil personated the victims of anger and grief, and poured forth the fiery indignation of Calista, or the maternal despair of Constance, or the self-contentions of Ipsipile, he could not deny the homage which her talents might claim" (p. 107). Yet Ormond is aware that her talent for mimicry and acting needs external direction, for she cannot originate, generate, or create: "She was no poet. She listened to the rehearsal without emotion, or was moved, not by the substance of the passage, by the dazzling image or the magic sympathy, but by something adscititious; yet usher her upon the stage, and no poet would wish for a more powerful organ of his conceptions. In assuming this office, she appeared to have drunk in the very soul of the dramatist. What was wanting in judgment was supplied by memory, in the tenaciousness of which she has seldom been rivalled" (p. 106).

That talent is, along with her music and painting, one of the reasons for Ormond's keeping her. But Brown presumably dwells on it to enhance Ormond's own superiority in this area. Craig is limited not only by his acting range and his medium, but also by his stupidity and the trivial reach he exercises. Helena's mimicry is broader but purposeless, whereas Ormond himself is a supreme master of imitation and disguise, which he sees as a means to power. "It enabled him to gain access, as if by supernatural means, to the privacy of others, and baffle their profoundest contrivances to hide themselves from his view. It flattered him with the possession of something like omniscience. It was, besides, an art in which, as in others, every accession of skill was a source of new gratification. Compared with this, the performance of the actor is the sport of children. . . . He blended in his own person the functions of poet and actor, and his

dramas were not fictitious but real" (p. 96). We will return to the effects
of this talent on the story; I must first underscore that final quotation,
where Ormond is described as the poet of reality, a quotation that forces
us back to Dudley's blind separation of reality from art and his refusal to
tend to the first.

At issue in the first chapters of the story is the relationship between
state of mind and state of fact. Most broadly and simply, the narrative
shows us the effects of misfortune on Dudley's mind as he falls out of
contact with society. As he loses his art, his business, then his friends,
even the wife he married in his beloved Italy, and finally his sight, Dudley
becomes locked into his own mind. He finds solace in the music he makes
on his lute, but there is another compensation as well, though it enters
the story rather inconspicuously. All Dudley can do is talk about what he
sees in his mind, what he remembers of the world. Such talk marks the
beginning of Constantia's education and whets her curiosity, at once
teasing and informing her desire to know. As the yellow fever forces its
insidious way into their neighborhood, there is as much concern about
the panic it generates as about its initial effects. Neighbor Whiston, for
instance, comes daily with unwelcome news of the disease. Whiston is
the bearer of a "tainted atmosphere" that not only destroys others after
his death, but also infects them much earlier with images of terror. This
motif treads softly in the story at first.

Its implications deepen, however, by chapter 7, which is introduced by
Sophia in a strangely self-conscious manner:

> In spite of redundance and obscurity in the style of the narrative
> [told to Constantia by Mrs. Baxter], Constantia found in it
> powerful excitements of her sympathy. The tale, on its own ac-
> count, as well as from the connection of some of its incidents with a
> subsequent part of these memoirs, is worthy to be here inserted.
> However foreign the destiny of Monrose may at present appear to
> the story of the Dudleys, there will hereafter be discovered an
> intimate connection between them. [pp. 50–51]

The inserted tale is that of Mr. Baxter, who spies on his Monrose neighbors and witnesses the burial of M. Monrose by his daughter. What is

strange about the story is that it is no more redundant and obscure than anything else in Brown and hardly needs apology as a digression because it is connected to subsequent events. Moreover, although the point is made with Brown's usual ambiguity, it is nonetheless clear that Baxter's death may not have been from yellow fever. He is so sure that the elder Monrose died of the pestilence that he believes himself to have caught it. Baxter immediately sickens after what he sees, even though search of the Monrose house produces "no proof that Monrose had fallen a victim to the reigning disease." The chapter ends with the rather bland observation that Baxter's "case may be quoted as an example of the force of imagination. He had probably already received, through the medium of the air, or by contact of which he was not conscious, the seeds of this disease. They might perhaps have lain dormant, had not this panic occurred to endow them with activity" (p. 58). Much later in the story, Martinette, now revealed as the lady earlier known as Miss Monrose, reconfirms this oddity: "The rueful pictures of my distress and weakness which were given by Baxter existed only in his own fancy" (p. 173).

Still, with both Dudley and Baxter, we have only the commonplace observation that the imagination can enhance the effects of experience. So perhaps what follows is merely coincidental. For Constantia is stirred by Baxter's image of Miss Monrose: "She imagined that Ursula Monrose would prove worthy of her love, and felt unspeakable regret at the improbability of their ever meeting" (p. 59). Yet meet they will, though not quite consciously, in that very chapter, and Brown's preparation for that meeting is very studied and carefully prepared. First, a simple substitution occurs when the Dudleys literally occupy the place of the Monrose father and daughter, which they can only do on the condition of giving up two most prized possessions, her father's lute and her own miniature portrait of Sophia. Constantia's attachment to that miniature is peculiar, at least, in its intensity, which is practically religious: "Habit had made this picture a source of a species of idolatry. Its power over her sensations was similar to that possessed by a beautiful Madonna over the heart of a juvenile enthusiast. It was the mother of the only devotion which her education had taught her to consider as beneficial or true" (p. 61). As we saw, when Constantia goes to sell the lute and finds a fascinating lady engaged with the shopkeeper, the power of visual forms for her is not limited to the miniature. "The accuracy and vividness with which pictures of this kind presented themselves to her imagination resembled the operations of a sixth sense. It cannot be doubted," cautions the narrator, "that much was owing to the enthusiastic tenor of her own conceptions, and that her conviction of the truth of the picture principally flowed from the distinctness and strength of its hues" (p. 63). What chiefly arrests Constantia about the strange lady is her heroic and contemplative genius. "The female was absorbed, so to speak, in the rational creature, and the emotions most apt to be excited in the gazer partook less of love than of reverence" (p. 63). Apparently one religious image has been replaced with another; Sophia has been equated with this strange lady who will end up buying the lute and who will turn out to be Miss Monrose herself under another name. An additional turn is given to those substitutions of character when Sophia tells us that the strangely defeminized lady strongly resembles Constantia herself.

Again, many pages later in chapter 19, Brown intensifies the connection among these three. Reencounter with the lute brings to mind Constantia's earlier meeting with the lady who bought it. "She forgot not their similitude in age and sex, and delighted to prolong the dream of future confidence and friendship to take place between them. Her heart sighed for a companion fitted to partake in all her sympathies" (p. 155). The sighing itself generates melancholy images of her lost Sophia, who is so intensely and so forcibly revived in her reminiscence "as almost to produce a lunatic conception of its reality" (p. 155). At the very moment she is conjuring an image of Sophia's death, who should enter her room and her consciousness and her longing but Martinette de Beauvais, a woman decidedly peculiar in her conversation and deportment: "These exhibited no tendencies to confidence, or traces of sympathy. They merely denoted large experience, vigorous faculties, and masculine attainments" (p. 157). That is to say, she talked only about the attainments of men, but the ambiguity of phrasing invites us to acknowledge Martinette's own masculinity as well and this is indeed borne out in the long story of her adventurous life.

As soon as her story is told, Martinette politely disappears, Mr. Dudley suffers his sudden death, and, a week after his burial, Constantia's longing for Sophia returns (p. 180). It begins with the same kind of recollected consciousness, with the singing of their song, and, what is more, with renewed yearning for the portrait. Again we begin with the mundane and with Constantia pursue the miniature from M'Crea, to a goldsmith, to a young man named Martynne, who cannot be found. The search is tedious and discouraging. However, when she is seated in Martynne's last home, she discovers not the portrait but the portrait come to life. Sophia herself is there and, in the ecstasy of discovery, Constantia swoons, making room for Sophia to enter more palpably into her own narrative. Shall we say that Brown is showing us the possibility that Constantia, with her peculiar sixth sense about visual forms, her debilitated state because of the death of her father, her frustrated plans to go to Europe, the quiet disappearance of Martinette, and the discouraging trek for her miniature, has willed Sophia into existence and converted the image into substance, has imagined art into reality? Why not? Or, to put it more profitably, why would Brown construct that possibility?

Brown's most obvious reason would be to create a character equal to Ormond. Remember that he began with a series of images of deception, forgery, disguise, acting, and impersonation, all culminating in Ormond himself as the poet who invents his reality. Now we have seen another series of images created by characters who to varying degrees endow their imaginings with destructive and sickening force. Sophia has told us, in her first extended review of Ormond through the maxims by which he lives, that "he had not hitherto met with a female worthy of his confidence" (p. 97); in other words, he has not yet met a woman who was his match. And, as we noted, Ormond's character comes in part from the sense of power his theatrical talents provide. Ormond is conscious of his ability and uses it arrogantly for knowledge and omniscience; whereas Constantia is innocent of her own power and nonetheless uses it, humbly, for the same thing—knowledge. When their relationship becomes a contest, Constantia's poetic and creative power stands to Ormond's power as his impersonations stand to Craig's. But that is leaping to the end of

the story, if not to its purpose, so let's back away once again and look
from a greater distance.

Let's begin again, then, with the question of the title of the story and
the obvious suspicion that Ormond is the "secret witness." Most conspicuously, Ormond is the secret witness to Constantia's conversations
with Sophia as they plan to avoid Ormond and take themselves to Europe. Ormond simply listens at an unexpected canvas door or enters
through it to penetrate Constantia's innermost thoughts, plans, intentions, and secrets. Thereby he learns things irksome to himself and, feeling rebuffed and offended, brings about the catastrophe at the end of the
story. If that flimsy canvas is Constantia's moral maidenhead, then the
physical rape that is threatened at the very end is anticlimactic indeed, for
Ormond has penetrated more than her body before that final assault. But
there have been suggestions throughout the story that Ormond's secret
witnessing signifies more than a device for sexual adventuring. At the
outset (pp. 94–95) we see him as a bluntly sincere man without much
regard for social conventions and with a gift of mimicry that amounts to
an art. There are hints not only that he will put this acting talent to some
high political or moral use but also that he senses in it more immediate
uses: "He was delighted with the power it conferred. It enabled him to
gain access, as if by supernatural means, to the privacy of others, and
baffle their profoundest contrivances to hide themselves from his view. It
flattered him with the possession of something like omniscience. . . . He
blended in his own person the functions of poet and actor, and his dramas
were not fictitious but real" (p. 96).

Ormond is, in short, something of a Paul Pry (in anticipation of Haw-
thorne's Coverdale). But he is a Paul Pry who hopes to gain control over
men's opinions and bring them thereby unconsciously into line with his
own political idealism:

> Ormond aspired to nothing more ardently than to hold the reins
> of opinion—to exercise absolute power over the conduct of others,
> not by constraining their limbs or by exacting obedience to his
> authority, but in a way of which his subjects should be scarcely

conscious. He desired that his guidance should control their steps, but that his agency, when most effectual, should be least suspected. [p. 147]

But if Ormond's ambitions are grandiose, his actions are ludicrously inappropriate. All we see him actually do is pass himself off as a black chimney sweep in order to get a firsthand view of the Dudleys' character and condition (pp. 110–11), an impressive performance surely, but hardly of the significance implied. One is hard put to imagine why Brown introduces what should have been a major dimension of his title character and then abandons it to such trivial maskings.

When Ormond finally confronts Constantia in the locked closet, he stuns her with his information about her private conversations and unexpressed intentions. But we know that he has either overheard these or pried into Constantia's letters and memoirs. His claims go beyond that, however, to include the omniscience he was said to aspire to so ardently. "What do I know? Everything. Not a tittle has escaped me. Thy letter is superfluous; I know its contents before they are written" (p. 212). And but a moment before he has maintained sarcastically, "Thinkest thou I would refrain from knowing what so nearly concerns us both? Perhaps your opinion of my ignorance extends beyond this. Perhaps I know not your fruitless search for a picture. Perhaps I neither followed you nor led you to a being called Sophia Courtland. I was not present at the meeting. I am unapprised of the effects of your romantic passion for each other. I did not witness the rapturous effusions and inexorible counsels of the newcomer. I know not the contents of the letter which you are preparing to write" (p. 212). Here the claim that Ormond has not only followed but also led Constantia opens up some surprising possibilities. When we look back to chapter 22, where the search for the portrait and the meeting with the narrator occurs, there are no hints of any such guidance except perhaps in a metaphorical sense. In this chapter Constantia discovers her murdered father's body and is led to thoughts of Sophia, whose portrait she sets out to regain. Pursuit of the portrait also brings her to Sophia herself.

Is it possible that one of the characters in that chapter is Ormond in disguise? The possibilities are remote. The former landlord M'Crea, who held the portrait, has an individual existence established well before Ormond's consciousness of the Dudleys. The goldsmith D——, to whom the portrait was sold, has too public a reputation and visibility, although it is he who identifies the purchaser of the picture as Martynne and directs Constantia to the house on Front Street. Furthermore, the otherwise unidentified lady of the Front Street mansion testifies to Martynne's activities in a way that seems to preclude him—besides the fact that he is never present with Constantia. That lady herself is a possibility—anyone who can do a black chimney sweep ought to be able to play in drag—but although she is never adequately presented or characterized, Sophia's presence in her apartments seems at first to have been another of Brown's damnable coincidences. Yet we must remember that she is the only other person present when Constantia and Sophia are rejoined, and Ormond later claims to have been present at that point. Moreover, that Martynne and Sophia should occupy the same apartments by accident is almost too much to swallow.

It seems then that Ormond's claims, like his claim to have restored Mr. Dudley's sight, are claims for a remote agency of sorts. He has started the machinery of events, in truth, but comes to believe that he controls every consequence and can predict every outcome. His hubris in this regard is both surprising and unprepared for but easier to believe in some respects than his reduction at the end to a mere seducer and rapist, even if his primary target is psychological, as he implies (that is, he explains that Constantia's loss of honor will have no effect on her public esteem but will be known only to her and to him).

Constantia's destiny is certainly linked closely to Ormond's actions, especially in his relationship to the two contrasting characters of Constantia and Helena. Ormond the social idealist and atheist keeps Helena the spontaneous creator and creature of sensual beauty in his charge. He is attracted to Helena almost exclusively because of her physical beauty and sensitivity. What Helena lacks, however, is mind and intelligence, qualities that so mark Ormond himself. By contrast, Constantia appears to have her share of winning physical and sensible attractions but is distinguished primarily by her intelligence. Ormond, in short, falls for the part of himself that he sees in Constantia and that we are told is primarily a masculine trait. When Ormond bluntly chooses between these two women—the one pliant, willing, and weak; the other strong from adversity, uncertainly willing, and certainly not pliant—the weaker dies by her own hand. Before that happens, however, two curious things occur. The first is that Constantia must assume a masculine role when she becomes the father/brother seeking to rectify Helena's wronged situation. She goes to argue with Ormond that he should marry Helena. But her own intelligence informs her that she herself is more suited to Ormond than is Helena, because she has more of that sympathetic male quality of intelligence. Their shared sense Brown takes some pains to emphasize: "I have acted an uncommon and, as it may seem, an ambiguous part," confesses Constantia early on (p. 128), but the result of her awareness and her connection with Ormond seems "like a doubling of existence" (p. 131) that derives from, on Constantia's part, a "manlike energy" (p. 131). Given their increasing proximity of moral stance, it is no wonder that the upshot of this relationship is Ormond's rejection of Helena by his retreat from the role of lover to that of father and brother (pp. 134–35). This emphasis upon resemblance is one of the appeals Ormond makes in his proposal of marriage to Constantia, immediately before discovering Helena's suicide: "Is there no part of me in which you discover your own likeness?" (p. 138). We also have to remember that Helena's last testament returns Dudley to his property, makes his life comfortable again, gives him the means to resecure his eyesight, and ends the extraordinary tests to which fate has put Constantia. In a way, Constantia has become Helena's substitute, so Ormond changes his desire to marry and determines to have her on the same terms he had Helena.

At that very point (chapter 19), Sophia reintroduces Martinette de Beauvais, formerly seen only as the unfortunate Miss Monrose during the yellow fever outbreak of the early chapters. The situation in which this reintroduction occurs is important. Constantia, now bereft of her friend Helena, thinks back to her loving friend Sophia, whom she has not seen or communicated with for years. Martinette steps into that longing situation most handily, and as she does, she brings to realization even more than Constantia herself a masculinity of character that both fascinates and repels Constantia. Helena had female beauty and sensibility; Constantia added to that an intelligence not unequal to Ormond's. Martinette brings a radical freedom that erases all constraints, especially sexual constraints, in the name of freedom. Her physical actions have been that of a battlefield soldier. She has killed for her cause; she does not shrink from danger, threat, hardship, or cruelty and describes herself feeling "as if imbued with a soul that was a stranger to the sexual distinction" (p. 167).

In going beyond Constantia in her masculinity, Martinette approaches the condition of Ormond himself, a parallel that occurs to Constantia at the opening of chapter 21 (p. 170). If Ormond was the East—the wild and barbaric adventurer of Siberia, the leader of a troop of Cossacks who was ready to kill his friend Sarsefield over a captured woman and then to try to expiate his sin by waging fierce and savage war—Martinette was Constantia's West, her Occident, her introduction to the more sophisticated but no less bloody and cruel politics of liberty in Europe. That they will prove to be brother and sister is no surprise, for Martinette is merely a female Ormond. She is modified perhaps by the fact that her ideal is, mirror fashion, a completely untrammeled liberty, whereas his is a subtle and insidious but no less absolute control. Now, after Helena's death, Constantia is conscious of both these forceful personalities. Both appeal to her, but both go beyond what she instinctively senses is right. She listens to both but accepts neither, and one must wonder if Martinette is not indeed merely a mimic performance of Ormond, a sly appeal through bisexuality.

Just at this juncture Mr. Dudley is found murdered, and Constantia's thoughts and longings turn again to Sophia. Thus, precisely at the point where Constantia's longings are keenest, the narrator becomes a major actress in her own story. By her own testimony, Sophia is not intellectual:

> I have indeed much to learn. Sophia Courtland had never been
> wise. Her affections disdain the cold dictates of discretion, and

spurn at every limit that contending duties and mixed obligations prescribe. [p. 207]

For four-fifths of this story, Sophia has repressed herself as agent; but now, with Ormond and Martinette both having gone too far, she is free to introduce herself upon the stage (chapter 23, p. 185). Although confessedly lacking in masculine wisdom, she is powerfully passionate.

Once on stage, Sophia performs with the kind of ambiguity that Brown seems ineluctably drawn to. She presents herself first as Constantia's half-sister. Of Mr. Dudley she says, for example, "Life itself was the gift of her [Constantia's] father, but my virtue and felicity are her gifts" (p. 185). Is Stephen Dudley literally her father? Or has he given her life only in the sense that he supported and raised her until her seventeenth year? She never mentions another father. In a sense it seems that she is claiming to be the offspring of Dudley and Constantia. Whatever Brown's intention here, there is no question about the queer intensity of the Sophia/Constantia affection—it is friendly, it is sisterly, above all it is passionate. That Sophia's ardent longing brings her fresh from a marriage to Courtland across the ocean to seek out her "sister" is not itself unusual, perhaps. What is unusual is that nowhere does Sophia express a similar attachment to her new husband. Their courtship has been decidedly restrained:

Sufficient opportunity was afforded us, in an unrestrained and domestic intercourse of three months, which succeeded our Roman interview, to gain a knowledge of each other. There was that conformity of tastes and views between us which could scarcely fail, at an age and in a situation like ours, to give birth to tenderness. My resolution to hasten to America was peculiarly unwelcome to my friend. He had offered to be my companion, but this offer my regard to his interest obliged me to decline; but I was willing to compensate him for this denial, as well as to gratify my own heart, by an immediate marriage. . . .

A week after my mother's death, I became a wife, and embarked the next day, at Naples, in a Ragusan ship, destined for New York. [p. 191]

If there is sexual innuendo in the terms "intercourse," "knowledge," and "birth," there may have been passion in the relationship; but there is no passion in the description. How different the reunion with Constantia:

> The succeeding three days were spent in a state of dizziness and intoxication. The ordinary functions of nature were disturbed. The appetite for sleep and for food were confounded and lost amidst the impetuosities of a master passion. To look and to talk to each other afforded enchanting occupation for every moment. I would not part from her side, but eat and slept, walked and mused and read, with my arm locked in hers, and with her breath fanning my cheek. . . .
>
> And yet, O precious inebriation of the heart! O pre-eminent love! what pleasure of reason or of sense can stand in competition with those attendant upon thee? Whether thou hiest to the fanes of a benevolent deity, or layest all thy homage at the feet of one who most visibly resembles the perfections of our Maker, surely thy sanction is divine, thy boon is happiness! [p. 207]

Immediately, Sophia displaces all other contenders for Constantia's love—Mr. Dudley, Ormond, Helena, Martinette—and equally at once draws Ormond's antagonism. Constantia becomes both the prize and the field of their combat, and what begins with Ormond eavesdropping through a canvas wall ends with Sophia peeping through a keyhole. The nature and perhaps even the identity of the secret witness of the subtitle have changed.

How are we to read this peculiar relationship? The one quality that can be confirmed by the story is its secretiveness. Ormond calls it a "romantic passion for each other," filled with "rapturous effusions" as well as "inexorible counsels" (p. 212). Sophia reports Constantia's perplexity at Ormond's penetration of their private affairs:

> Her interviews and conversations with me took place at seasons of general repose, when all doors were fast and avenues shut, in the midst of silence, and in the bosom of retirement. The theme of our discourse was, commonly, too sacred for any ears but our own;

disclosures were of too intimate and delicate a nature for any but a
female audience; they were too injurious to the fame and peace of
Ormond for him to be admitted to partake of them: yet his words
implied a full acquaintance with recent events, and with purposes
and deliberations shrouded, as we imagined, in impenetrable
secrecy. [p. 212]

The point is reenforced only slightly later in the story: "All human pre-
cautions had been used to baffle the attempts of any secret witness. [Con-
stantia] recalled to mind the circumstances in which conversations with
her friend had taken place. All had been retirement, secrecy, and silence"
(p. 215). Surely Brown is here inviting us to entertain the prospect of
Constantia and Sophia as lovers, a relationship whose complex possibilities he treated in the separate short story "Jessica" that he published
in *The Monthly Magazine* in the summer of 1800.[2] One suspects the
stories belong together.

Jessica, confined at home, writes to her friend Sophia a series of letters
detailing her infatuation with a young boarder. The letters record in polite and muted tones Jessy's unmistakable attraction to Colden—at least
unmistakable to everyone but Jessica herself. As her passion grows, so
does the intensity of her communications. Colden's room is immediately
next to hers; its nearness to her bed generates the greatest perturbation:

> How shall I part with this sweet recess? When they were alive it
> was my sister's [sic] work room, but now it seems, I must enter it
> no more. A stranger will possess it and a *man*! How chilling is that
> thought my [Sophia]!
> Besides my own bed room is *so* near; a slight partition divides
> them, for the two apartments were once the same and the two
> doors are not ten inches asunder. I cannot go on; I cannot move
> about; I cannot stir a step, but. . . . [p. 131]

As much self-betrayal as there is in this passage about the Jessica-Colden
relationship, the more interesting feature of it is its intention to titillate
Sophia's sexual curiosity and to raise her ardor.

Jessica claims to resist her sexual attachment to Colden and to do so she recalls her loving desire for Sophia:

> You honoured me once you know, with your company for one night. How delighted I was, yet how ashamed to introduce you to my humble cot. Shall I ever forget that night! we talked till past three; and such unbosoming of all your feelings, all your pleasures and cares, and what you called your foibles; spots in the sunny brightness of your character. Ever since that night have I been a new creature; to be locked in your arms; to share your pillow with you, gave new force, new existence to the love which before united us. [pp. 137–38]

And she adds, "often shall we pass such nights when thou and I are safe together at Wortleyfield." What she would be safe from is her own heterosexual passion and perhaps the kind of entrapment that marriage, as much a threat as rape, seems to imply. Sisterhood and its comfortable alternative to marriage rather than lesbian behavior may well be Brown's concern here, but the homoerotic overtones of the story are unmistakably there. Also, when we realize that Brown was finishing *Ormond* and writing "Jessica" at the same time, I think we can safely assume some spillover from one story to the other.

In "Jessica," Sophia acts as a kind of passive seductress; in *Ormond*, Sophia is equally successful but much more aggressive. Just how aggressive is rather surprising. As we think back upon the story from our present vantage point, we realize that its main action is the reification, the progressive realization, of Sophia herself and of Constantia's incorporation into her. When Constantia and Sophia are finally joined, the incorporation is made fairly explicit: "Henceforth the stream of our existence was to mix; we were to act and think in common; casual witnesses and written testimony should become superfluous" (p. 208). But until that point we have a series not of joinings but of substitutions. Constantia moves into the place of her father, then into Ursula Monrose's place, then into Helena's, then partially into Martinette's, totally into Martynne's, and to some extent into Ormond's himself, before she disappears into Sophia's voice. So though it is a critical commonplace to see Constantia consciously set against the contrasting foils represented by other women in the story, especially Helena and Martinette,[3] I believe we must go beyond that to see these characters as stages in Constantia's development or as reified projections of possibilities of being, essentially possibilities of sexual character. We have already seen how Constantia equals Ormond's mimic poesy by creating realities from her own vivid fantasies, especially by conjuring up Sophia herself. But that action is itself enfolded in Sophia's narrative, so we might equally urge that Sophia has made all these characters, has generated them and therefore been them, and has indeed been the real secret witness of the title. In short, we might conclude that Sophia *is* Ormond.

Thus the story operates rather like an optical illusion. At first we see everything so clearly through Sophia that she seems utterly transparent, and she remains so despite the constant recalls to her existence as a person and not merely a voice, that is, Constantia's chronic yearnings and the miniature itself. By the story's end we seem to have only Sophia—her life, her marriage, her search for Constantia, her involvement with Martynne and Constantia's cousin—until all the other characters tend to disappear or become relatively insubstantial (including both Constantia and Ormond), operating like characters in a dream. Perceived this way, Constantia's adventures take on a new coherence that deserves tracing once again.

These adventures pose as a series of tests or temptations, all in terms of Constantia's sexual identity or perhaps more properly a progressive elimination of sexual possibilities. All of the tests involve some sense of conflict between male and female principles. Adversity leads Constantia first to take on the head of household role. She becomes her father, bearing his responsibilities for the family and also taking on his knowledge of the world through his intense memories of art and love and beauty in Italy, a world apart. But this has to be a temporary and incomplete role for Constantia, who at the earliest stages can only see for herself marriage as an appropriate station in life. But she has been jilted once and has come to realize that marriage is an economic fact as well as an affective one. That it cannot be strictly economic is demonstrated by Balfour's suit. Balfour is nothing but social station and economic comfort. He wants a wife, not a woman, and is hardly a test at all. Constantia recognizes that there is no satisfactory solution in that, but it is interesting that the Balfour episode occurs as the first indication of her character. Her own father has taught her the unsatisfactory nature of the father/daughter relationship and has given her a masculine education that cannot stay within the confines of Balfour's benevolent but much too narrow sensibility.

Yet the image of dependency is still strong with Constantia, and so she finds her sympathies touched not by Ursula Monrose herself but by Baxter's view of her—the poor, fatherless, weak woman in a world of danger. Her next real possibility, however, is not Ursula, but Ormond's Helena. Having refused marriage on Balfour's terms, might she not accept Ormond's? Should she, like Helena, be the kept mistress of a man of the world? We are told that Helena and Constantia were formerly acquainted, which I take to mean that the possibility of Helena's role had already been entertained and to some extent dismissed by Constantia. With the possibility at hand, however, Constantia significantly vacillates. She knows that the relationship is degrading, but at the same time it is an extension of the father/daughter relationship that gives full adult acknowledgment of her femininity. With that comes not only economic comfort but imaginative freedom. By inheriting Helena's estate, she also comes into Helena's sexual completeness, but that is not enough. It does have the effect of utterly changing her relationship to her own father, who can now be restored in sight so as to see quite clearly the hazard of Ormond's presence. In effect, Ormond is Dudley writ large, now with animal spirit enough to be the knowledge of the world turned to vicious power. He is a heady object for Constantia, a form of masculinity both attractive and dangerous, dangerous to Constantia's own masculine expectations and especially dangerous to Dudley.

But Constantia can only be Ormond's equal, not the subject of his control. Such a state belongs to Martinette, Constantia's reformed ambition. Constantia can no longer be the daughter, the sickling, or the mistress. But she now discovers she cannot satisfactorily be the hybrid man/woman Martinette either. Her aspirations toward equality in the name of total freedom are as bloody, brutal, and repulsive as Ormond's impulse towards total control. Martinette is simply Ormond in another guise. Each lacks the ideal blend of masculine/feminine traits that Constantia seems to be growing toward. As that notion of a satisfactory state becomes clearer in Constantia's imagination, it takes the form of that secret witness in the background, her lost Sophia. And it does so just at the moment when we are forced to note the resemblances between Constantia and Martinette and Sophia.

One more unsatisfactory state has to be projected before Sophia can fully appear. Constantia thus follows her own masculine qualities beyond those of Martinette and becomes a man, Martynne—Martinette with her *ette* off. What this figure means is difficult to see, for the plot does not require his existence at all; he need not have been named Martynne. Indeed, the entire episode involving him, Constantia's look-alike cousin Ridgley, and Sophia operates at a level of apparently trivial everyday experience. Indeed, Martynne's devotion to Sophia's miniature is essentially a parody of Constantia's much more serious attachment. That is why Sophia can believe at this point that Constantia's death is confirmed. The substitution of Martynne, the foppish male of drawing-room comedy and a kind of Billy Dimple, for Constantia is an impossibility and an imposture. Indeed, Martynne has presented himself as a forger, rather like Thomas Craig. Thus the possibility of achieving Sophia by a suppression of her femaleness is displayed as ridiculous, an awareness that is underscored by the first detailed description of the miniature itself. Sophia says that Constantia "and myself were desirous of employing the skill of a Saxon painter, by name Eckstein. Each of us were drawn by him, she with the cincture of Venus, and I with the crescent of Dian" (p. 201). As we realize by now, this is the state toward which the story has been tending from a very early point—the right adjustment between urge and restraint, between energy and balance. Martynne is the masculine urge to dalliance and vapid relationships.

In rejecting (actually in not even being tempted in the direction of)

Martynne, Constantia has exhausted a broad range of possibilities. She knows that a full and responsible sexual identity cannot be that of father/daughter, nor of submissive mistress, nor of swaggering equal, nor of coquette. She also knows that no matter how much a father, brother, or companion in knowledge she may be, she cannot give up her femininity. Only in a just compact of generative energy with chaste restraint is fulfillment possible for Constantia, and that comes only in joining Sophia's existence to her own, making the final image a reality. Everything short of that is a forgery, a disguise, a fraud, and must be put out of existence—and so it is. Dudley dies, Helena dies, Craig dies; Martinette and Martynne are removed from the scene of her action; only Ormond is left to test the constancy of Constantia's new realization. So that the final challenge to her acceptable state is appropriately a direct sexual assault. Put another way, before Constantia can rest in her chastity, she has to face her strongest sexual urges in the most forthright way possible. These take the form of her most admired, most similar, and therefore most attractive image among them all, Ormond.

On no other terms, I submit, are the actions of Ormond and the catastrophe itself sensible. Are we to suppose this worldly, unconventional, intelligent, and talented man, who is involved in schemes for the betterment of the world, who is extraordinarily assertive and yearning to control men and nature—are we to suppose him so smitten to possess Constantia sexually that he attacks her in sexual madness? Well, possibly. But I doubt it. Ormond exists only as the chief opponent to the joining of Constantia and Sophia (Venus and Dian) and so is as much an internal aspect of Constantia herself as he is a purely independent existence. His claims to omniscience, then, are not mad, but true, in the sense that he is the companion of Constantia's impulses and yearnings. The final attack comes only after Ormond exhibits himself in his rawest power. He kills the initial symbol and agent of forgery, Craig, and expects to be welcomed with gratitude for exposing himself in his true form. He knows the most intimate of Constantia's confidences to Sophia because he is Constantia's erotic principle itself, disguised as father, suitor, teacher, seducer, adventuress, and sister. He has indeed led her to Sophia and followed her at the same time, for he is the need that makes Sophia possible. He is Sophia's savage and brutal double, the contrary principle that when fully in the saddle obliterates Sophia as an active force.

For all her exertions and desperation, Sophia is finally useless in Constantia's final struggle. By the time she arrives at the house that once belonged to Helena, and before that to Dudley himself, Sophia sees through the keyhole only the distraught and disheveled figure of Constantia. She does not witness the attempted rape. She does not witness Constantia's final destruction of Ormond. In fact, there is never any considered explanation. All we know is that Constantia survives the complicated havoc. Mimicry is dead, the Ormond aspect of Venus has met his quietus with a bare penknife, and Constantia never says another word. Venus and Dian are joined as Sophia rules the end of her narrative with placid sureness.

Under the polite placidity, however, lurk chasms of ambiguity. We do not know whether Constantia finally surrendered to her sexuality before puncturing it. We also do not know if we are to take the Sophia/Courtland image as Brown's notion of a satisfactory resolution to the question of sexual identity, a socially agreeable if passionless arrangement, a sort of mutual relinquishing of both power and independence. But if *Ormond* is the book I have described, we do know that Brown has demonstrated a very complex novelistic technique for exploring human experience. We can see that Brown's narrative methods are not limited to a single problem but can respond sensitively to a range of genuine psychological insights, even when his mechanisms seem superficially trite and conventional. If *Ormond* has in general used the same kind of self-reflection to expose a genuine psychic experience as *Wieland* did, it is still quite a different book. Merely to claim that *Ormond* repeats Brown's interest in the general problem of the reliability of the senses may be true, but it is manifestly insufficient. It is as if Brown has said, well, Clara may hide her encounter with madness under a conventional sentimental tale, but when we put such a tale itself to the test, as Sophia may be said to do, it turns out to offer very little relief.

THREE

Edgar

At least with *Edgar Huntly*, everyone agrees on the story's psychological purposes, although there is no consensus on the ultimate purpose or the extent to which we should credit Brown's psychologizing.[1] Thus, for example, some readers will be content to acknowledge that the somnambulism shared by Edgar and his alter ego Clithero is too coincidental not to spring from a similar observation about human nature: that guilt will manifest itself in our fantasies or dreams and finally, if necessary, our involuntary actions. Again, as Edgar follows his mazy and circuitous path through the rugged forests, his physical confusions equate with his mental perplexities, so that there is at least a rough but definite correspondence between his state of mind, his external appearance, and the natural world in which he operates. When Edgar is in the dark, so to speak, he is literally in the dark; when problems beset him, the going indeed gets rough; when he is relieved and enlightened, he emerges from caverns to gaze upon sublime landscapes. So there is an obvious reciprocity between his mental states and external conditions. The reciprocity is such that each seems to inform and symbolize the other, and we never quite know whether nature is being internalized or his emotional and mental states are being externalized. The process seems to work both ways at once.

The different element in *Edgar Huntly* is at first the high intensity of the narrator. Clara Wieland believed herself in control of her story, re-covered from its frightful suggestions. Sophia tells *Ormond* with the studied coolness of an outsider. In Edgar we have a narrator still totally distraught by the most incredible shocks and adventures, one who tries to set incidents in order but is purposely unwilling to wait for a condition of satisfactory repose and full understanding. In his choice to tell im-petuously for fear of losing the essence of his experience, we have a narrative technique that Poe will focus on a generation later. We also cannot be too misled by the rational tone of voice in which Edgar tells his tale, for, as the story shows us, character has no distinguishing voice in a Brown fiction. Only reason speaks, madly, criminally, tenderly, virtu-ously, and in a uniform voice. Another new element is the manner in which Brown presents this fiction in his preface "To the Public." He offers himself here as a "moral painter" who will avoid customary subjects and settings and who will, on the contrary, "exhibit adventures, growing out of the condition of our country." So his tale will not, like Cooper's *The Pioneers* twenty-three years later, be descriptive of places and social manners but will somehow use "the condition of our country" to paint morally. Of course, Brown's exasperating fuzziness of meaning keeps one from being entirely sure about his intention, but the possibility is there, nonetheless, that his preface is announcing a way to read him as well as the general subject of the story. However, let us try yet again to say in synopsis what happens.

The narrative is addressed in a state of high excitement to Mary, the sister of the recently murdered Waldegrave. Passing the tree where the murder occurred, Edgar compulsively seeks it out, finding there a half-naked man wailing remorsefully and digging at the ground. Edgar returns the next night and again sees the same man, who is apparently acting in his sleep. Suspicious that this is Waldegrave's murderer, Edgar follows him on a long and apparently aimless trek through the moonlit wilder-ness, until he disappears into a cavern. For a third night Edgar follows this man, who turns out to be a neighbor's servant, an Irishman named Clithero Edny. Edgar connives to meet with Clithero in order to con-front him with his suspicions and accusations. Stunned by the encounter,

Clithero puts off responding until a week later, when he meets Edgar again to tell him his story in the heart of the wilderness.

Clithero explains that Edgar, through "a tissue of destructive errors," has nonetheless struck very close to home. Odd circumstances caused him to be raised and educated as a companion to Mrs. Lorimer's son. Clithero eventually supplants that son in Mrs. Lorimer's favor and in her house, where this benevolent lady honors him with trust and "maternal regard." But she has a twin brother, Wiatte, who is as mean and evil as she is kind and generous. Although he has undertaken a life of crime and been transported and supposedly killed, he has left behind a beautiful daughter named Clarice. Clithero experiences increasing agitation at his growing affection for Clarice, until he decides his only honorable course must be to leave Mrs. Lorimer. But she refuses to release him and offers Clarice to him instead.

At that point, Mrs. Lorimer's former lover, Sarsefield, and her twin brother Wiatte somehow materialize together. Plans to apprehend Wiatte (to keep him from somehow harming Mrs. Lorimer) fail. But as Clithero goes on an errand for Mrs. Lorimer to receive an amount of money, he is assaulted by a thief, whom he involuntarily kills. The thief turns out to be Wiatte, which plunges Clithero into despair because he knows that Mrs. Lorimer believes her own life to be vitally connected with her brother's. In killing Wiatte, he has surely killed his benefactress. Or has he? Clithero enters her chamber stealthily, discovering a form in her bed still breathing. But when she awakens, what then? The news will surely kill her. Better to dispatch her thus, unconscious. Just as he is about to stab her with a convenient dagger, a divine voice behind him interrupts the action with a shriek. It is Mrs. Lorimer herself, and now he sees that he nearly murdered Clarice. He blurts out the fact that he has killed Wiatte, watches Mrs. Lorimer crumple to the floor, and flees. Ending his story in regret that Edgar has recalled all this misery to his consciousness, he disappears into the forest.

Determining to help Clithero, Edgar tries to follow him, especially because Sarsefield is also his own mentor. He enters the cavern into which Clithero first disappeared and ultimately emerges into a scene of rugged natural grandeur. From the edge of a precipice, he sees Clithero across a deep ravine. Edgar calls out, but Clithero disappears. Edgar then sees that a tree might be felled to bridge the abyss and returns for an axe and food. Back again, he succeeds in bridging the gap and finds Clithero asleep atop a hill. Puzzled about how best to act, Edgar simply leaves the food and returns to neighbor Inglefield's to spend the night. There, in the room that the murdered Waldegrave formerly occupied, he discovers a secret box of Clithero's. The box is empty, but once opened cannot be reclosed. Edgar then digs at the base of the somber tree and finds another box, which proves to contain Mrs. Lorimer's account of her love for Wiatte and her justification for agreeing to his transportation.

The following day is very stormy, but Edgar again makes the trek to Clithero's retreat, this time with the Lorimer manuscript. There is no sign of Clithero, and Edgar just barely makes it back across his makeshift bridge when it collapses. He also has a near brush with a vicious panther, who lunges for him but falls into the chasm and dies. That night Edgar dreams of Waldegrave. Edgar guesses that he seems to be warning him not to do as he had promised sister Mary he would, that is, not to write a transcription of Waldegrave's and Edgar's correspondence, because some of its attitudes might corrupt the young lady. He goes to his own secret box to retrieve the letters but finds them unaccountably missing. The theft is extremely perturbing, and so is his uncle's arrival to ask what Edgar has been doing rummaging about the attic in the middle of the night. Edgar protests that it was not he, and a search of the house indicates nothing out of order.

At that point a stranger named Weymouth arrives to inform Edgar that Waldegrave's surprisingly ample estate (since passed on to Mary) consisted mainly of funds that Waldegrave was holding for him. Weymouth's story stuns Edgar "as if it had existed in a dream." Edgar is also shocked because, if the story is true, and he clearly believes it, Edgar and Mary must forsake their hopes for marriage.

Suddenly the story swerves. A new series of incidents occurs, utterly bewildering to the narrator but causing fear and horror. Edgar tells of becoming conscious in total darkness and dumb pain. He is suddenly reduced to fighting for survival and comprehension at once. Slowly he reasons that he may have been thrown into a pit in a cave like one he formerly encountered while following Clithero. He succeeds in climbing out of the pit but there meets a panther, which he kills and eats. The eating sickens him, but he recovers and, following the sound of water, comes eventually to the mouth of the cave and a glowing fire. Around the fire are several sleeping Indians and a bound girl. When the guard leaves the cave, Edgar follows and is forced to kill him with weapons stolen from the sleeping Indians. Refreshed by water, he returns to the cave and releases the girl. After painful wandering they discover a hut, where Edgar learns that the gun he has picked up is his own, a gun given him by Sarsefield. He can only conclude that his uncle and his sisters have now been massacred by these very Indians, which steels his resolve to kill two more once they are tracked to the cabin. Before a rescue party arrives with the girl's father, a fourth Indian has to be killed as well. Edgar tells what has happened and then slumps into unconsciousness.

When he recovers, all are gone except the dead Indians and one remaining savage, whom Edgar kills only after repeated shots and a final bayoneting. In a freakish gesture Edgar sticks the Indian's musket upright in the ground and stumbles off to find relief. At one house he finds food and learns that the hut he had occupied with the girl belonged to a strange old Indian called Queen Mab. Now refreshed and oriented, he sets off for home. But once again he gets lost and is trapped on a cliff above a river, where he nearly dies from exposure and from attack by a band of men. Desperate, Edgar fires at one of them and then leaps into the river amidst a hail of bullets. Recognizing increasingly familiar ground as he leaves the river for the road, Edgar encounters further signs of Indian ravages at the Selby house. He then moves on to another house, noting signs of desertion immediately before he enters. Wandering through the rooms, he comes upon the missing packet of Waldegrave's letters and, immediately after that, Sarsefield himself.

Sarsefield expresses his wonder at Edgar's still being alive and tells of the community's simultaneous chase of the Indians and its attempt to find Edgar, who had apparently wandered off into the woods several nights earlier in his sleep. Indeed, it turns out that Edgar, thinking them savages, had fired his last shot at Sarsefield and the other villagers, whereas they had fired at him in the river in the belief that he was a savage. Edgar mentions Clithero, thus generating an outburst of vindictiveness from Sarsefield. Before explanations can be made, however, Edgar goes up to bed, is roused by shouts and gunfire, permits an Indian to escape through his window, and then discovers that Clithero is badly injured below stairs. Sarsefield refuses to help Clithero and tries to take Edgar away with him. But Edgar cannot desert the badly wounded Irishman. He stays to hear Clithero's story of recovering his desire to live because of Edgar's kindnesses and then of being captured by savages. Clithero is put into the bed Edgar just left, and Edgar goes off to tell Clithero's story to Sarsefield, who is enough mollified at least to tell Clithero he knows what happened. Sarsefield then goes off to New York to join his pregnant wife Euphemia Lorimer and Clarice. Edgar explains that Waldegrave was killed by a savage Indian provoked by old Deb, or Queen Mab. Then Clithero, who was not as sick as he looked, recovers and disappears.

Here Edgar's letter to Mary, composed during a couple of weeks immediately after these adventures, ends, with Edgar presumably off to rejoin Sarsefield and his family in New York and now ready to take Clithero's place with Clarice. But a strange reversal occurs in three concluding letters. The first is a brief one from Edgar to Sarsefield warning him that Clithero is on his way to New York to find Mrs. Lorimer. The second one, also from Edgar to Sarsefield, describes how Clithero has taken up Queen Mab's hut as his dwelling and how Edgar, attempting to assure him that he did not truly kill Mrs. Lorimer, has revealed her whereabouts and, in the process, provoked Clithero's truly savage mania. The third letter is Sarsefield's response. It scolds Edgar's indiscretions, pointing out that the very threat, once come to Mrs. Lorimer's attention, resulted in her miscarriage and blasted Sarsefield's greatest hopes. It also describes Clithero's capture and his apparent death by drowning as he was on his way to an asylum. Sarsefield bids Edgar farewell, and we are left with no certain sense of the consequences of all these activities.

Perhaps because the action is so physical and so diverse—Brown displays prodigal invention here—this story seems to lose its way amid its own details, especially in the protracted forest chase and Indian fighting of the second part. The opening questions regarding Waldegrave's murder, dutifully explained at the end, have disappeared as vital questions; the many hints at some special significance to Clithero's involved adventures are quite disproportionate to the final function he serves; Weymouth's strange claim upon Mary and Edgar's happiness and comfort is utterly forgotten; the digression on Queen Mab strikes one as quite pointless; the sudden plunge into the wilderness is effected solely out of narrative desperation; and Sarsefield's coincidental role as mentor to both Clithero and Edgar blatantly confesses Brown's failure to resist self-parody. But we have seen that in Brown's fiction purpose often lurks in such indirections. Moreover, the story itself provides one sequence of controlled and purposeful images, which may help us to modify this sense of aimlessness.

That sequence is the series of houses Edgar visits through the second half of the book as he attempts to return home. The first of these is Deb's hut. We take no particular notice, I suspect, of the care devoted to its description, despite the fact that it contains Brown's most realistic detail: "In the bucket was a little water, full of droppings from the roof, drowned insects, and sand" (p. 175). But the shelter itself is rendered thus:

> It consisted of a few unhewn logs laid upon each other, to the
> height of eight or ten feet, including a quadrangular space of similar
> dimensions, and covered by a thatch. There was no window, light
> being sufficiently admitted into the crevices between the logs. These
> had formerly been loosely plastered with clay; but air and rain had
> crumbled and washed the greater part of this rude cement away.
> Somewhat like a chimney, built of half-burnt bricks, was perceived
> at one corner. The door was fastened by a leathern thong, tied to a
> peg. [p. 174]

The description is appropriate, if not necessary, but seems nowhere obtrusive. Its purposive function becomes clear when Edgar, having killed his last Indian, comes to the second house:

> This dwelling was far different from that I had lately left. It was as small and as low, but its walls consisted of boards. A window of four panes admitted the light, and a chimney of brick, well burnt and neatly arranged, peeped over the roof. [p. 192]

That purposive sense is then expanded by the description of the Selby house, with its neighboring barn:

> It was the model of cleanliness and comfort. It was built of wood; but the materials had undergone the plane, as well as the axe and the saw. It was painted white, and the windows not only had sashes, but these sashes were supplied, contrary to custom, with glass. In most cases the aperture where glass should be is stuffed with an old hat or a petticoat. The door had not only all its parts entire, but was embellished with moldings and a pediment. I gathered from these tokens that this was the abode not only of rural competence and innocence, but of some beings raised by education and fortune above the intellectual mediocrity of clowns. [p. 208]

Edgar cannot stop there, however, but pushes on to yet another house, apparently a public house or inn, where the meeting with Sarsefield and Clithero and the final events of the story transpire. He does not describe this building.

The pattern here is obvious: Edgar is moving from frontier wilderness to settled order. But he is also moving from ignorance to knowledge, from survival to ease, from isolation to society, and from the hunt to the farm to the village. In general this appears to be, to put it most simple-mindedly, progress from a bad state to a good one, from anxiety to rest. In fact, however, there is an increasing countermovement throughout this part of the book. If Queen Mab's hut is a scene of wild fighting, killing, and destruction, the final scene in the public house is one of equal turmoil. We have moved from poverty to simple subsistence to drunkenness, death, and familial disregard, and finally to another pursuit with gangs of men chasing other gangs of men—shooting, beating, torment, and tumult. Where formerly the whole Norwalk region was the arena for such animal behavior, the arena in the last scenes has narrowed to one house though the action remains the same. Now this is a rather jolting observation, but I would like to suspend it temporarily. My primary point here is not what the pattern means but the existence of a pattern, evidence of conscious purpose on Brown's part. We shall return to its significance.

Edgar characterizes the progressive nature in this pattern almost inadvertently but in a way useful for exploring some of the earlier parts of the story. At the second house on his return, Edgar for the first time gets his geographical bearings and recovers his sense of duty to return to "Solesbury, my natal *township*." The page on which that occurs (p. 197) is filled with animal comparisons—leopard, elk, lynx, and roe—in none of whose gifts Edgar will be outdone. Indeed, "I have ever aspired," he says, "to transcend the rest of animals in all that is common to the rational and brute, as well as in all by which they are distinguished from each other" (p. 197). With due allowance for Edgar's smugness here, we may still have a sense of the rightness (for this book) of the animal-man conjunction when we remember that this is not the first time men and animals have been brought together in this story.

Edgar's first moonlight pursuit of Clithero led to an all-night wait outside the entrance to a cave where Clithero had disappeared. Edgar assures us that his position is such that Clithero could not emerge unseen:

> My attention was at length excited by a sound that seemed to issue from the cave. I imagined that the sleeper was returning, and prepared therefore to seize him. I blamed myself for neglecting the opportunities that had already been afforded, and was determined that another should not escape. My eyes were fixed upon the entrance. The rustling increased, and presently an animal leaped forth, of what kind I was unable to discover. [p. 44]

Clithero goes in; animal comes out. In Brown's carefully drawn atmosphere of unsolved murders, moonlight, brooding trees, and mysterious men digging in their sleep, there is certainly room for a little lycanthropy.

It is some time later, having heard Clithero's story and having followed him to his mountain retreat, that Edgar encounters another animal, one that he "hoped was no more than a raccoon or opossum, but which presently appeared to be a panther. His gray coat, extended claws, fiery eyes, and a cry which he at that moment uttered, and which, by its resemblance to the human voice, is peculiarly terrific, denoted him to be the most ferocious and untamable of that detested race" (p. 126). Edgar points out that he is no hunter, "My temper never delighted in carnage and blood" (p. 127), though he makes an exception of panthers. And, being a mean hand with a tomahawk, he has collected many a panther skin as a trophy —humanlike voice and all. This time, however, he is unarmed and seriously concerned that he may make a meal for this particular varmint. He does not relish "being rent to pieces by the fangs of this savage" (p. 128). Edgar escapes the attack of this animal but stresses his determination not to travel again without a tomahawk, given the possibility that this panther's mate may still be around.

Three chapters later, Edgar will face another panther and in desperation kill and feast on it. Before that happens, however, we have been witness to Clithero's slow transformation into a filthy, emaciated, brutish form, marvelously hirsute for so short an absence but still recognizable as essentially human. When Edgar spies Clithero, "pinched with famine," he calls out in common recognition as well as to capture his attention, "*Man! Clithero!*" Now tortured by his own hunger and driven to kill to satisfy it, what is Edgar Huntly doing but joining Clithero in an utterly reduced human condition? This is joining in more senses than one, for when Edgar eats the panther he takes into himself the savageness that is Clithero—murderous, mad, and driven—the savageness that is man in his essential nature. This is man communing with his savage self. The effect is sickening but sustaining. Edgar understands that his vile feast is necessary for survival; what he cannot see, but which we must, is Brown's point that at bottom the animal in us cannot be dismissed or plastered over. Stand back far enough from it—from the top of Norwalk Ridge, for example—and nature bears a grand and sublime aspect; crawl into its innards—the darkness of the pit and the cave—and nature without form is tearing and bloody, a primal energy to eat and to make life glow. The view is not pretty. In outsavaging the panther, Edgar has become the panther, a mechanism for mayhem and a threat to society.

Edgar, of course, is quite unaware of the extent of his fall. Utterly dislocated in time and space when he regains consciousness in the pit, he works his way slowly and arduously upward and back to a human condition. As the earth delivers him again into the human condition, Edgar sees how the world has changed more than he realizes how he has. For what he emerges into is a world of savages—panther-men in a hunting world of death and injury, human existence at its most physical. Somewhere apart is the world of the first part of Edgar's story, a settled social world of order and law, of villages and farms, of courtships and friendships where human contact is sustained by letters, accounts, messages, and memoirs. The world Edgar is reborn into is a world of animal silence, hostility, and direct contest. Intentions take the form of bullets here and survival depends on keeping one's mouth shut. It is not a world of explanations. Brown's theme is not more fully conceived or better treated until Conrad.

Edgar shows himself quite adept at handling his new situation. He kills one Indian with a hatchet, cleanly shoots three more, and butchers a fifth with his bayonet out of kindness. He is very careful, this man whose temper never delighted in blood and carnage, to demonstrate the necessity of the killings to Mary, but his explanations ring more than slightly hollow. In the first place, there is a nasty streak in Edgar. He revealed it in one of his earliest interviews with Clithero. He has just reawakened Clithero's guilt and remorse by his accusations; Clithero "looked up, and fixed his eyes upon me with an expression of affright. He shuddered and recoiled as from a spectre" (p. 52). Edgar's reaction to that incident is not one of righteous self-approval; it is enjoyment at the prospect of "generous sympathy, which filled my eyes with tears, but had more in it of pleasure than of pain" (p. 53). Edgar has attacked and won, and he likes it. But there is another qualification, not entirely of temperament but mixed with early experience, a kind of psychological preparation. Edgar's parents were murdered in his childhood by Indian "assassins," and only an accidental tempest had kept Edgar himself from "captivity or death." Edgar's recall of that event should warm any Freudian's heart:

> Most men are haunted by some species of terror or antipathy, which they are, for the most part, able to trace to some incident which befell them in their early years. You will not be surprised that the fate of my parents, and the sight of the body of one of this savage band, who, in the pursuit that was made after them, was overtaken and killed, should produce lasting and terrific images in my fancy. I never looked upon or called up the image of a savage without shuddering. [p. 165]

Add to these qualifications Edgar's desperation, his physical prowess, and his strong survival instinct, and the result is a formidable engine for destruction.

Edgar, of course, does not see himself quite that way; he is merely a bewildered victim of circumstances who is forced to kill. He has indeed, as his puzzled fellow villagers recognize, become confounded with the foe. Brown effects a very nice touch in keeping us sympathetic to Edgar's actions by maintaining his point of view in the narration and by embedding Edgar's involuntary moral state in a powerful, if gory, image. When Edgar revives after his blood-glut at Deb's hut, he has been deserted and left for dead, pillowed upon the body of one of his own victims.

> My head had reposed upon the breast of him whom I had shot in this part of his body. The blood had ceased to ooze from the wound, but my dishevelled locks were matted and steeped in that gore which had overflowed and choked up the orifice. I started from this detestable pillow, and regained my feet. [p. 186]

Born again out of a kind of death, if not burial (as in the darkness of the cave), Edgar recovers more quickly this time his sense of what has happened and begins to separate himself from his own bestiality: "I formed a sort of resolution to shun the contest with a new enemy, almost at the expense of my own life. I was satiated and gorged with slaughter, and thought upon a new act of destruction with abhorrence and loathing" (p. 187).

But no sooner has he done so than the one remaining Indian comes along. "My eye was now caught by movements which appeared like those of a beast. In different circumstances, I should have instantly supposed it to be a wolf, or panther, or bear. Now my suspicions were alive on a different account, and my startled fancy figured to itself nothing but a human adversary" (p. 187). This time, however, despite his new sort of resolution, or perhaps because of it, he only wounds the Indian twice, having finally to dispose of him by the "cruel lenity" of driving his bayonet through the man's heart. As with the panther in the cave, the act of violence crashes Edgar to the ground. But his paroxysm of disgust and remorse is only momentary, and when he remembers that no such tenderness would have affected the Indian, he turns to an act of exultation that he wisely does not try to explain: "Prompted by some freak of fancy, I stuck his musket in the ground, and left it standing upright in the middle of the road" (p. 190). With this macho monument planted in phallic defiance and with his manhood proclaimed and demonstrated, Edgar undertakes his trek back to civilization.

Edgar has now died twice—once in the pit and again upon his savage pillow. Both times his encounters have ended in screaming convulsions, not his but those of his victims. In both cases we see the real difference between Edgar and his savage confederates. Edgar has speech, and they do not. He has used it earlier for pleasure, just to bounce his echo off the canyon walls, to help locate himself in the dark by seeing where sounds returned from, and to bridge the gap between himself and the almost utterly lost Clithero. For all his physical prowess, what separates him from panthers and Indians is his speech. Those Indians have not come from any Cooper novel but from some nightmare without words. Their lack of speech is their real savageness, and it is this lack that makes them so terrible and so easily destroyed. Their unintelligibility is their inhumanity, just as it is Edgar's when, having tried to explain to the captive girl's father what has happened, he sinks into a deadly swoon and is left behind as offal.

His first hope lies, therefore, in the conversation with the woman at the next rude house he visits. But speech only gives him alarm, rumor, and misdirection. This larger confusion of identity is demonstrated by Edgar's becoming the hunted again rather than the hunter. What he has come to see is that, whether caught in nature's bowels or isolated on its heights, man in a purely natural state is man imprisoned and dangerous. For the complex return to Solesbury is finally marked by encounters with men whose only communication is with yells and savage calls; these Edgar is now in no emotional state to judge correctly. He is the prey and society is his enemy, though neither sees correctly who the other is. Edgar's father is long dead. He is now sure his uncle is also dead, and he is right. His nearest parental figure is Sarsefield, but Sarsefield is a leader in the hunt after the savages—the hunt that finally aims its sights at Edgar himself. Edgar is indeed the foe, though in a sense neither Edgar nor Sarsefield is in a position to understand. Indeed, Edgar fires his last shot at Sarsefield with the very gun Sarsefield had given him, and Sarsefield and the society he represents responds with a flood of bullets that miss Edgar only by chance.

So if Brown has been a long time getting there, the maze has had a predetermined path and end from the start. It is the confrontation between Edgar and Sarsefield, the central issue in this book. Before examining that, however, let's consider where we have come. Out of a hurried and pell-mell tumble of incidents, we have seen two series of images merge. The first was the progress of architecture from the cave back to the public house; the second, a series of animal associations that turns Edgar out of conventional time and sets him back into a primitive condition of brutishness and savagery before he can come again into a civilized state. We have seen that these sequences of images join the two parts of a story that otherwise breaks in the very middle with Edgar's plunge into total darkness. What, we have to ask, accounts for that precipitous reversion? One answer, the answer Sarsefield gives and Solesbury (and apparently Edgar) accepts, is that he too has become a sleepwalker. When he first misses Waldegrave's papers and accompanies his uncle on a search of the house, we begin to suspect that much. So our question then becomes, what turns him suddenly to a half-naked, night-wandering sleepwalker? What makes Edgar Clithero? And that in turn becomes, what makes Clithero Clithero?

When we first see Clithero he is crazed with remorse, digging to no apparent purpose around the elm tree where Waldegrave was killed. He is not apparently burying or recovering anything but is himself shattered with sorrow and remorse. We know almost at once that he is a sleepwalker, because Edgar views him from a distance just as later he will view the panther and the Indians. Edgar is actually observing himself, although he does not know this himself at the time. But Clithero practically tells him (and thereby Brown tells us) about the relationship: "You, like others," Clithero says, "are blind to the most momentous consequences of your own actions" (p. 55). For this is how Clithero explains his own predicament first, upon the killing of Wiatte: "My exertions were mechanical. My will might be said to be passive, and it was only by retrospect and a contemplation of consequences that I became fully informed of the nature of the scene" (p. 85). The implication here might well be that we are all sleepwalkers, and that, when he has a chance to reflect upon Clithero's story, is the implication Edgar draws. Can Clithero be blamed, Edgar wonders, for actions in which will and intention play no part at all? (p. 101). Very near the end of the story, contemplating it all, Edgar remarks that Clithero's deed "was neither prompted by the will nor noticed by the senses of him by whom it was done. Disastrous and humiliating is the state of man! By his own hands is constructed the mass of misery and error in which his steps are forever involved." And he continues, "How little cognizance have men over the actions and motives of each other! How total is our blindness with regard to our own performances!" (p. 250).

These passages, which are so redolent of the moral logic of Jonathan Edwards's *Nature of True Virtue*, suggest that the act of reflection, the conscious telling of the story, may make us alert to events but does not guarantee our understanding of the springs that bring those events about.

As a case in point, we see that Clithero has uncovered parts of himself that he knows and parts that he does not know. By his accusations, Edgar may be said to have dug up Clithero's buried self. The diction in Clithero's preface to his own tale—*bury, entangled, disclosure, groundless, awakened*—all spin off the act in which Clithero is first seen:

> Fain would I be relieved from this task. Gladly would I bury in oblivion the transactions of my life. But no! My fate is uniform. The demon that controlled me at first is still in the fruition of power. I am entangled in his fold, and every effort that I make to escape only involves me in deeper ruin. I need not conceal, for all the consequences of disclosure are already experienced. I cannot endure a groundless imputation, though to free me from it I must create and justify imputations still more atrocious. My story may at least be brief. If the agonies of remembrance must be awakened afresh, let me do all that in me lies to shorten them. [p. 56]

Accused of one murder, he confesses to another and in the act becomes himself murdered by Edgar's accusations. So, somehow, is justice served.

I think we have to suppose, however, that Clithero's story is simultaneously one of burial and of disclosure. The disclosure is obvious; Clithero may not even be aware of the burial. But the narrative reflects the degree of control Clithero imposes on the incidents in its high degree of patterning. That patterning is especially evident in the resemblances of the characters, which amounts almost to outrage. Clithero grows up with Clarice and Euphemia Lorimer's nameless son. The two boys become mirror reversals of one another: Clithero the responsible moral fop, the true son an irresponsible profligate. Mrs. Lorimer herself has a twin brother who looks so like her that in infancy and youth they could not be distinguished. She is a paragon of taste and virtue, but he "seemed to relish no food but pure unadulterated evil." This brother, Arthur Wiatte, comes into the story fully in conjunction with a rival—Sarsefield, Euphemia's lover. It falls to Euphemia's lot to banish both the evil Arthur and the benevolent Sarsefield. The mutual connection of their fates is emphasized by the fact that both men return to Euphemia's life and come into Clithero's high fortune simultaneously. Even Clithero expresses bewilderment at their mutuality: "That Sarsefield should be so quickly followed by his arch-foe; that they started anew into existence, without any previous intimation, in a manner wholly unexpected, and at the same period—it seemed as if there lurked, under those appearances, a tremendous significance, which human sagacity could not uncover" (p. 82). Certainly Clithero's sagacity cannot uncover that significance; but equally certainly, we are invited to try. The scheme of resemblances is complicated even further by the fact that Euphemia's bastard niece, Arthur's daughter, looks so much like Euphemia that even Clithero, her promised husband, mistakes the one for the other.

Now I frankly do not understand all this. Clithero may be right that the parallels and resemblances are beyond human sagacity. It is clear, however, that the patterning is there, that it is certainly conscious, that it is a feature only of Clithero's story, and that it implies significance, namely, it contains some valuable truth about human nature and experience and must thereby be as true about Edgar as it is about Clithero. One is literarily tempted to see some point in the fact that this is an Irish story. But these characters are clearly not the Irish savages of Spenser, or Swift's Yahoos, or Brackenridge's Teague O'Regan, and the later famous Irish wanderer who leaves the citizenry like a shot off a shovel has only the most distant connection with Clithero and the others. One is also tempted to see in Clithero's destructive attachment to Mrs. Lorimer's "maternal regard" a crude Oedipal pattern, especially when the young Clarice is offered as an appropriate sex substitute for the middle-aged mother. The dream of possessing the mother sexually is fully developed by Jocasta's declarations in Sophocles' play, so we risk no anomalies in suggesting such proto-Freudian possibilities. But where would they lead us? Clithero has Mrs. Lorimer's trust, her favor, and her love. He even has her body in Clarice's form. As her agent, he has her property as well. He seems to feel no threat to his own fortune from either Wiatte or Sarsefield, although he is vaguely conscious of some threat to his future (p. 82), a vague discomfort perhaps caused by Wiatte's return and the fact that he might exert "the parental prerogatives" and block Clithero's marriage to Clarice.

It seems instead that the patterning, all the correspondences and re-semblances, are designed to indicate Clithero's uncertainty of his own identity. Is he the real son or an illegitimate heir? Indeed, he has all his good fortune from the death of Mrs. Lorimer's husband (the substitute for Sarsefield). It seems to come down to this: you do not get Mrs. Lorimer without Wiatte and Sarsefield, you do not get Clarice without Wiatte, you do not enjoy fortune without reasonless opposition, and you do not enjoy peace without grief. If the values these characters represent are so vitally linked, their denial is too; that is, you cannot destroy Wiatte without also destroying Euphemia. Put with unforgivable moralism, you cannot rid yourself of evil without destroying the good as well. Haw-thorne's much neater allegory in "The Birthmark" and Melville's com-plex symbolism in *Billy Budd* develop the same ambivalences. Wiatte's motiveless malevolence is as much a part of Mrs. Lorimer as is her benevolence. You cannot destroy one without fatal hurt to the other.

Clithero's story—obviously a twice-told tale, once to himself and once to Edgar—is a confession of such ambiguities. In fact, his fortune is the direct result of Wiatte's having forced Euphemia to marry the licentious old man Lorimer. So though Clithero's conscious regard is entirely for Mrs. Lorimer's safety and protection, a part of Clithero is elsewhere. When Clithero kills Wiatte, he blames himself primarily for ingratitude. He has not shown his gratefulness to Mrs. Lorimer sufficiently for his social and personal advancement. But he also has an unspoken debt of gratitude to Wiatte, without whose actions none of Clithero's good for-tune would have occurred, a debt of which Clithero seems refreshingly unconscious. Had this deeper debt been conscious, we might have had sufficient reason for Clithero's anxieties. As it turns out, however, they come from another and rather unexpected source.

If consciously Sarsefield is Clithero's friend and Wiatte merely an ob-noxious disturbance, their mutual reappearance is a definite threat to Clithero's well-being, and this he senses intuitively. Wiatte might forbid his marriage with Clarice. Sarsefield will certainly supplant him in Eu-phemia's affections. Clarice's postponement of their marriage stimulates his uncertainty. All three steal his rest, especially Sarsefield, who rouses

Clithero from a deep and frustrated sleep with the information that
Wiatte has returned (p. 79). Clithero registers the significance of that
event involuntarily, as he stumbles in his narrative:

> At this period of his narrative, Clithero stopped. His complexion
> varied from one degree of paleness to another. His brain appeared
> to suffer some severe constriction. . . . In a short time he was
> relieved from this paroxysm, and resumed his tale with an accent
> tremulous at first, but acquiring stability and force as he went on.
> [p. 79]

Clithero's disturbance here is primarily important as a kind of exclama-
tion point. Edgar is thus saying: this is an important episode. Is Clithero
remembering the beginning of his demonic sleepwalking? Is he trying to
bring to consciousness something he cannot quite understand but knows
matters? Is he merely recoiling from the recollection of the terrible deeds
that follow? Whatever that brief interval of struggle means, it surely
punctuates the story and gives more than common weight to the observation with which the story resumes: "On waking, as I have said, I found
my friend [Sarsefield] seated at my bedside."

Sarsefield's invasion of Clithero's sleep is very important, for all the
information about Wiatte comes from him. Clithero never sees Wiatte
until he is attacked. All he has is Sarsefield's insinuations—reminders of
Wiatte's promise of vengeance against Euphemia, a story of his rude and
threatening call upon her, and the conspiracy to ward off future attempts
by Wiatte against his sister. Knowingly or not, Sarsefield fuels Clithero's
anxieties and brings on the impossibility of sleep (pp. 82–83). Moreover,
by making Clithero so intensely conscious of Wiatte, Sarsefield is showing Clithero an aspect of himself that Clithero cannot afford to examine.
For what is Clithero but a man who has usurped the property and luxury
of another's life? Wiatte is, in a sense, Euphemia's nameless son returning
to retrieve his own, and Clithero sees himself as the same kind of dissolute thief who attacks him for Euphemia's "large sum." That in part
accounts for Clithero's persistent sense of the justice in his own punishment. It may also account for the mazy and circuitous reasoning that fol-

lows his killing of Wiatte and leads to the attempt to murder Euphemia. That reasoning begins in a stupor. "I found that I had trodden back the way which I had lately come, and had arrived within sight of the banker's door. I checked myself, and once more turned my steps homeward" (p. 87). Clithero realizes there is no going to this bank but once. In killing Wiatte, Clithero loses both Euphemia and Clarice, but in realizing that loss, he becomes Wiatte himself, determined to obliterate the richness that he cannot himself enjoy. This impulse of mean vengeance quails before Euphemia's imperious commands, and Clithero runs off laden with guilt and shame, abandoning both Euphemia and Clarice and all the wealth they represent to a victorious Sarsefield.

On first announcement, that threat of displacement seems a rather trivial cause for Clithero's woes. His material well-being jeopardized, Clithero realizes in himself murderous and vengeful impulses. Acting upon them, full of reasons and wide awake, he brings his whole world down on his own head. Now banished, only by night and in his sleep can he let his guilt and remorse be expressed in frantic digging. Is he covering up, burying the evidence of Euphemia's virtue so as to forget it? Or is he in his frenzy trying to recover the virtuous image that is her book? In a way it does not matter. What matters is that the murder of Waldegrave has regenerated all Clithero's agitation again and given him a location for digging. He says, "I can no otherwise account for my frequenting this shade than by the distant resemblance which the death of this man bore to that of which I was the perpetrator. This resemblance occurred to me at first" (p. 99). But if the death of Wiatte means what I have suggested, what can the death of Waldegrave mean? What is the nature of the resemblance?

Although occurring worlds apart, the two murders and their attending circumstances have a great deal in common. Edgar's happiness and social promise derive utterly from the death of his closest friend. Marriage with Mary depends entirely on the $8,000 she has inherited upon her brother's death. That money, through marriage, will go far to alleviate Edgar's very precarious situation. He and two younger sisters are living with their uncle and relying entirely on his kindness. If the uncle dies, his estate passes on to his son, who will drive Edgar and his sisters out. So, like Clithero, Edgar is on the lip of a fully satisfying social existence but also on the brink of ruin. Perhaps his desperate condition overcomes any squeamishness at the cost of his soon-to-be-enjoyed comfort.

Even the noble youth Waldegrave had his dark side, one that Edgar would prefer to hide or bury. Indeed, Edgar both thinks and dreams about this after hearing Clithero's story and pursuing him through the cave to the other side of Norwalk Ridge. After he returns from his arduous journey, Edgar dreams that Waldegrave appears to him in some angry and unquiet mood. The experience reminds him that he had promised to transcribe Waldegrave's letters for Mary and that he had also promised Waldegrave he never would because of their damaging and possibly corrupting ideas. In fact, thinks Edgar, these ideas are so caught up in Waldegrave's character and person that they cannot be expunged: "mixed up with abstract reasonings were numberless passages which elucidated the character and history of my friend. These were too precious to be consigned to oblivion; and to take them out of their present connection and arrangement would be to mutilate and deform them" (p. 133). So Edgar is consciously torn between exposing or concealing Waldegrave's mind, but he has already acted unconsciously in his sleep, hiding the packet of letters much as Clithero has buried Mrs. Lorimer's book.

Now the ideas that Edgar feels obliged to hide are Waldegrave's "early" commitments to a kind of materialism, which led him "to deify necessity and universalize matter; to destroy the popular distinctions between soul and body, and to dissolve the supposed connection between the moral condition of man anterior and subsequent to death" (p. 132). Waldegrave himself had renounced these youthful experiments in atheism but feared that his sister, untrained in metaphysics and without opportunity to discuss and debate the positions, might find her religious faith undermined. There was good cause to worry, because Edgar himself did not follow Waldegrave's conversion: "I did not entirely abjure the creed which had, with great copiousness and eloquence, been defended in these letters" (p. 133). So we see Edgar's situation more clearly—an ambivalent materialist about to enjoy the material fruits of another man's fortune—a situation close to Clithero's at the moment of his catastrophe.

Which brings us, finally, back to the question of Edgar's sudden thrust into utter blankness. What happens is the sudden threat to all Edgar's material hopes. When Weymouth arrives with the story of having left 7,500 dollars in Waldegrave's keeping (money that Edgar has built his future on), his bubble bursts. Weymouth cannot prove his claims, but the tissue of circumstances he presents is compelling, and even his open honesty argues in favor of his claims. He admits to Edgar, "The frailty of your virtue and the strength of your temptations I know not" (p. 149). Indeed, he does not, but neither does Edgar, who is conscious of no wrongdoing. But it is curious that Waldegrave kept no letters and made no notes to warrant Weymouth's claims. Edgar had been privy to all Waldegrave's activities and, as his executor, had looked through all his papers with Mary. Weymouth puts the question to him directly: "Are you qualified, by your knowledge of his papers, to answer me explicitly? Is it not possible for some letters to have been mislaid?" Edgar assures him that he is qualified to answer but slips the main question. We then remember that only the preceding night Edgar had lost his own packet of Waldegrave's letters. If Edgar has hidden the one uncomfortable side of Waldegrave while sleeping, may he not have done the same with even more disagreeable evidence involving the loss of Mary's fortune and his own? If he has, the visit from Weymouth puts him under incredible pressure—his open, reasonable, and daylight self in powerful opposition to his exhausted, driven, and desperate midnight self. Weymouth's shock pitches Edgar totally into Clithero's dark state.

We have already traced Edgar's violent tracks back from that darkness to civilization, but there is yet another episode in the story that needs attention, the episode of Old Deb, or Queen Mab, at whose rude hut Edgar destroys most of the Indians, returns the young girl to her father, swoons, and is left for dead. This old Indian woman is invested with a kind of mythic stature in Edgar's description (pp. 193–96), despite his bemused tone. Because of her great age, she seems to be timeless. When the Delawares moved out before the usurping English in the 1750s, "she declared her resolution to remain behind and maintain possession of the land which her countrymen should impiously abandon" (p. 193). Attended by three wolves, she becomes the one remaining testimony to the

Indian presence in the area. Her entire society is her trio of beasts; her goddesslike conversation is entirely the giving of praise, blame, and commands to them, for she refuses to speak English. Since her people left, she assumes the role of queen in the area (for which the young Edgar nicknamed her Queen Mab), demanding provisions, food, and other necessities. Deb's stubborn refusal to join her people is not, I think, from a sense of ownership, as Ikkemotubbe's is in Faulkner's legend; rather, "possession" carries here a sense of jurisdiction or place, an identity of status. The English have usurped her jurisdiction with their cultivation. Indeed, her original village site is now where the barn and orchard of Edgar's uncle stand, so we can understand that to her the "English were aliens and sojourners, who occupied the land merely by her connivance and permission, and whom she allowed to remain on no terms but those of supplying her wants" (p. 194).

Edgar's condescension is ironic. Deb truly is the presiding genius of the wild, jealous of her royal perquisites and insulted by the condescension of the English interlopers in her domains. As it turns out, it is some such sense of jurisdiction that has set her fellow Indians to revenge themselves upon the English on her account. Waldegrave was merely their first random victim, but this entire episode of hostilities is laid to Queen Mab's direction and encouragement (p. 252). Proud and arrogant, she will not be snuffed out. One is tempted to suggest that her title is the creation of Edgar, that in a vague sense he has created this destructive will himself.

Such an interpretation would indicate that Edgar is at least symbolically the force behind Waldegrave's murder and that he is an active contender for the rights of place, even before his symbolic assumption of brutal and savage activities brought on by Weymouth's appearance. Whether Edgar as somnambulant Indian—his guards, his conscious virtues, his will, his senses, and his responsibility all sunk in slumber—is the actual killer of Waldegrave, there is no sure telling. But it is highly possible, as I have tried to intimate.[2] The pattern now begins to cohere. Clithero and Edgar are, each in his own ways, like Queen Mab. Insulted by circumstances, cheated of the place they had counted on, usurped in their hopes and expectations, they unleash their silent dogs of vengeance and murder and unbury their wild unsociability, that essential self Edgar spied when he called out, "*Man! Clithero!*"

So, at the end of this story, they do it together. Edgar's necessary opposition to Sarsefield is treated so dramatically that we cannot be sure that Edgar really understands or appreciates his complicity in Clithero's final mad deeds. We remember that Edgar has just discovered Waldegrave's papers in a strange room. Into the room comes Sarsefield, and Edgar melts with joy and exhaustion and relief after his protracted ordeal. But Sarsefield barely recognizes and credits that this is his pupil, his child (p. 220). Indeed, what gives Sarsefield the most trouble is that Edgar just will not die. Sarsefield describes in detail his discovery that Edgar is missing (after going to wake him up just as he had Clithero much before) and his joining in the chase of the Indians. He dwells especially on the "startling spectacle" of "an Indian, mangled by repeated wounds of bayonet and bullet. . . . His musket was stuck in the ground, by way of beacon attracting our attention to the spot" (p. 231). Sarsefield apparently does not see or recognize the hostility in that beacon. Nor does he really see how important it is that Edgar has shot at him with the very gun he used to carry, even though the gun is Sarsefield's main means of identifying Edgar through his wild and savage appearance.

The gun itself, which Edgar retrieved from one of his victims, is first examined in Deb's hut—a double-barreled fusil:

> This piece was of extraordinary workmanship. It was the legacy of an English officer, who died in Bengal, to Sarsefield. It was constructed for the purposes not of sport but of war. The artist had made it a congeries of tubes and springs, by which every purpose of protection and offense was effectually served. A dagger's blade was attached to it, capable of being fixed at the end, and of answering the destructive purpose of a bayonet. On his departure from Solesbury, my friend left it, as a pledge of his affection, in my possession. [pp. 177–78]

This strange pledge of affection is Sarsefield's legacy of usurpation. The double-barreled construction is just too juicy. The most obvious implication is that the two barrels are the two protegés of Sarsefield, Clithero and Edgar.

But Sarsefield indicates that his own purposes are not hostile. "My motives," he tells Edgar, "in coming to America were numerous and mixed. Among these was the parental affection with which you had inspired me. I came with fortune, and a better gift than fortune, in my hand. I intended to bestow both upon you, not only to give you competence, but one who would endear to you that competence, who would enhance, by participating, every gratification" (p. 234). In short, Sarsefield comes to relieve all Edgar's anxieties—with money, love, family, the protection of his sisters, even the offer of Clarice. Edgar will truly supplant Clithero. Sarsefield has the power to make this happen (p. 236). Indeed, that seems to be the problem, he has the power.

This announcement has the immediate effect of dividing this would-be father from his would-be son. Edgar is reminded of Clithero and, in saying his name, provokes instant outrage in Sarsefield: "I will not occupy the same land, the same world, with him," he insists (p. 237). Ironically, within a very short time they will occupy the same house. Almost at once after this outburst, Edgar wearies and is put to bed. He then hears the voices below and a shot. Shortly after, an unarmed Indian enters the room, sees Edgar in bed with his gun aimed, and dives through a window. No wonder. What is wonderful, however, is that Edgar does not shoot. Edgar says, "His flight might have been easily arrested by my shot, but surprise, added to my habitual antipathy to bloodshed unless in cases of absolute necessity, made me hesitate" (p. 240). Habitual antipathy indeed! Edgar can state whatever consoling and justifying reasons he wants, but the fact is he has a clean shot at the enemy and he lets him go. After all, Edgar would only be killing part of himself, and that he cannot do.

Almost at once Sarsefield returns, profoundly disturbed, to announce that Clithero himself has returned from the dead. By not killing the Indian Edgar has in effect reinvigorated the Clithero impulse. Sarsefield, although a surgeon, refuses to restore the badly wounded Clithero or even to attend him. Edgar clearly does not understand this, but he intuits that he cannot leave his battered double. Sarsefield "renewed his importunities for me to fly with him. He dragged me by the arm, and, wavering and reluctant, I followed where he chose to lead. . . . It was indeed Clithero whom I now beheld, supine, polluted with blood, his eyes closed, and apparently insensible. This object was gazed at with emotions that rooted me to the spot. Sarsefield, perceiving me determined to remain where I was, rushed out of the house, and disappeared" (pp. 241–42). Father Sarsefield gone, Edgar kindly falls to his knees and puts Clithero's bloodied head in his lap, a gesture that must remind us of the gory pillow on which Edgar had swooned earlier beside Queen Mab's hut. How deeply here Edgar has joined forces with Clithero would be hard to say. Brown works these scenes with almost cinematic distance, and all attempts to explain sound lame. Clithero is carried to the bed Edgar has just occupied, and Edgar goes to explain Clithero's behavior, at least to tell his story, to Sarsefield. Sarsefield accepts Clithero's version of events, but that acceptance does not mean that Clithero can be reinstated in everyone's goodwill. I submit that he cannot be reinstated because the ostensible story still hides the natural and unavoidable antagonism between Clithero and Sarsefield.

Why natural and inevitable? The answer may be buried in two of the most easily ignored passages in the book, the bizarre adventures of Sarsefield and Weymouth. Both have undergone incredible experiences around the world, but neither story has to be told. Brown squanders material for two more romances in these pages, yet he does so in such short compass that I am unwilling to suppose he is merely padding the story. The episodes are long enough to compel our attention. Sarsefield, it turns out, has much in common with Edgar and Clithero. He, too, has known prisons and escapes and has wandered the world "by a long, circuitous, and perilous route." His subsistence has indeed been perilous; he has been reduced to poverty, hunted and waylaid by bandits, and even forced to live among outlaws before escaping to America (p. 76). Weymouth likewise was storm driven to disaster, imprisonment, and penury. Unable to speak to and communicate with his captors, he was eventually left utterly robbed of strength by "every species of insult and injury" until it became "uncertain whether I was alive or dead" (pp. 142–45). Both men have endured the wilderness and, having done so, have deserved and earned the rewards the world can pay. Sarsefield takes Euphemia and Clarice; Weymouth takes the money for which he has struggled so long.

Similar though their stories are, the consequences are quite different for Weymouth and Sarsefield. Weymouth returns with an open admission of powerlessness, lacking the evidence either to compel or induce the return of what is his. No talk from him about shielding Waldegrave's grieving sister or her lover. Sarsefield returns with his marvelous gun, with the art of making secret boxes (passed on to both Edgar and Clithero), and with Wiatte in his hip pocket. He is the spirit of hostility and concealment, and consequently his position is by far the more fragile of the two. No Wiatte or Clithero travels with Weymouth, but when Sarsefield surprisingly materializes, so does Wiatte/Clithero, just as happened in Ireland. Weymouth's situation puts Edgar on an equal standing; Sarsefield's reduces him to a son.

Perhaps Clithero never deserved his bounty from Mrs. Lorimer, never deserved his superior station, never deserved Clarice; certainly Edgar does not. Violent and flamboyant as the engagement with his vengeful self has been, he has not suffered as much as the others have, and he still remains largely unconscious of the springs of his own actions. Like Clithero's box, Edgar has enough art and luck to pry himself open, but it is not clear whether he will get the lid back down. Edgar will still try to make a pact with this offer of parental power. He still sees Sarsefield as friend and benefactor. With the death of his uncle, Edgar's situation becomes truly desperate, and Clithero's story has surely made the opulence of Euphemia and the charm of Clarice attractive. That he is tempted is obvious in the coolness with which he summarily solves Waldegrave's murder and bids Mary farewell. Still he has shown an even stronger allegiance to Clithero, whom he cannot or will not abandon. But the two impulses are not reconcilable.

Brown's recourse to the exchange of letters at the end may not be the happiest of devices, but we can see why he may have chosen this way of concluding the story. The letters give the sense of immediacy, urgency, and inconclusiveness that the memoir by its nature cannot. It is peculiarly appropriate here because Brown's theme of sons and lovers is never concluded. Now forever banished from Euphemia and Clarice, although cleared of villainous intentions even by Sarsefield, Clithero has no balancing hope. He succeeds Queen Mab as the spirit of outraged and usurped place, the injured and insulted revenger. So it is more than appropriate, it is necessary that he assume her dwelling. Edgar says he has been tricked into revealing Euphemia's whereabouts to Clithero, and both Clithero and Sarsefield accuse his rashness. One must wonder, however, if Edgar's claims here are not convenient self-deception, if his information to the unbalanced Clithero is not like Sarsefield's insidious information poured into Clithero's sleepy ears about the threatening monster Wiatte. When Clithero runs off to wreak mayhem, Edgar concludes that indeed "Clithero is a maniac." This, too, may be self-serving and self-excusing under the circumstances, but it also indicates some awareness on Edgar's part that Sarsefield is right. Naked vengeance on the parents can only be maniacal.

Clithero is thus rather easily apprehended and manacled to be hauled off to an asylum. But his threat has a chilling effect, for the very thought of confronting this son's violent self-assertion directly leads to Euphemia's miscarriage. Truly Sarsefield's "fondest hope" has been blasted, that of real fatherhood. However, there is still some hope: "I persuade myself," he writes Edgar, "that my wife's indisposition will be temporary." There may yet be other sons, even other Clithero's. For there is something remarkably fluid about Clithero's end here. On the way to the asylum, the lunatic throws himself overboard. Others give chase, "but, at the moment when his flight was overtaken, he forced himself beneath the surface, and was seen no more" (p. 261). We remember that not much earlier Edgar performed the same feat, firing directly at Sarsefield and forcing himself under the water to escape the return fire. Then, too, Sarsefield believed the victim died but with mixed feelings saw him reemerge. Clithero's burial may perhaps be temporary, in Edgar's consciousness as well as in Sarsefield's rhetoric, but at least it marks a pause, a completion of one cycle of the perpetual opposition of fathers and sons. Brown wisely avoids suggesting that now everything is decided. Sarsefield's final word, "Farewell," is also the last word of the novel, but it is not as dismissive as it may seem, for that is the very word with which Edgar ended his long memoir to Mary, after promising to see her again soon. If the victory is Sarsefield's here, enough questions remain open and unanswered for us to respect Brown's realistic perceptions through all this romance.

What Brown has given us in *Edgar Huntly* is a very sophisticated fable of adolescent self-assertion and resentment against parental prerogative, along with the guilt that inevitably accompanies those gestures toward complete adulthood. The impulse to define oneself against the parent is so basic that it seems part of our nature. In its rawest forms it is deadly and dumb—best drawn in the condition of that captive girl's ordeal at the hands of the silent savages. But attempts to clothe, to lath-and-plaster it over, to civilize it by burying it in polite letters and manners, can never entirely succeed. Nor, as Sarsefield's behavior itself suggests, is it ever conclusively destroyed. Ancient Deb is possessed by the need to identify her place in the world as much as he or the young Edgar is. Nevertheless, if the real salvation from this perpetual competition and hostility lies in the social commerce of language, in the stories we tell, Brown seems convinced that no fictive burial is so deep or dark that we will not see in it those livid eyes of the panther.

FOUR

Arthur

What is Arthur Mervyn? He tells us himself, near the end of this book: "childishly unlearned and raw; a barn-door simpleton; a plow-tail, kitchen-hearth, turnip-hoeing novice."[1] Good enough, for a start. But many a reader will gladly take the hint and fill out the picture—a double-dealing, smug, lying, self-serving, smiling villain. A sanctimonious sly manipulator; a cunning and shrewd con man, sadistic torturer, arrogant voyeur! A sponging, main-chance-minding, boorish lout! A self-drama-tizing, mischievous, meddling slickster who will sell you a Bible while he picks your pocket (and your mind) and then give you twenty good reasons why he did it. A one-man plague, who needs a Mark Twain, a Rabelais, a Joyce, a Mencken, a D. H. Lawrence to do him justice. A god-awful moralizing prig, a Benjamin Franklin with only his cynicism left, a moral fop! An impolite, insensitive, presumptuous, calculating, and heartless Satan with "an honest front and a straight story." A sharpster whose pretence is innocence and honesty, an altruist who always profits personally, a man whose chief disguise is his openness, his willingness to tell all.

Arthur is a ripe subject for the kind of analytical drama we have seen in the previous three books, but such drama just is not here. By settling into the minds of Clara, Constantia, Sophia, and Edgar, we discovered characters who reluctantly, semiconsciously—even unconsciously—

manifested essentially unacceptable aspects of their basic natures. Each of these fictions relates the discovery of what was either unknown or unknowable, or both. Pierce Arthur Mervyn and all you find is Arthur Mervyn. He is not threatened by an encounter with or accommodation of his inner self. One might say that Arthur is all and only inner self, that he knows himself quite well, such as he is. He has read and he has thought. He has lazily lounged with his own soul. He knows what is right and good, and he has the world's reasons behind him: the reasons of the ancients, the scriptures, and even common sense and William Godwin. This means, of course, that he knows why he acts as he does—always. He is a creature who fully understands his motives, whereas Clara and Edgar are very clear-headed about their actions but only indirectly and dreamily conscious of their muffled motives. Arthur's problem is the obverse of theirs; he does not understand behavior or action. He remains obtuse to Wallace's tricks, to Thetford's intrigue, to Welbeck's false front, to Mrs. Villars's anger, to Achsa Fielding's blushes and tears and averted eyes. But more important, he remains throughout ignorant of why his own actions create the negative impressions they do. His story is thus a series of shocks, surprises, explanations, excuses, justifications, and agile hindsights. In other words, his story is thus a series of stories; in *Arthur Mervyn* Brown's attention shifts from the analysis of *what* events mean to an examination of *how* they mean.

This is not to say that Brown surrenders all interest in what may loosely be called psychological events and character but that he looks more directly at mechanism and at social rather than private implications. Architecture, for example, functions differently in *Arthur Mervyn* than it does in the other romances. It is still symbolic, of course, but it is also more simply scenic. The result is that we see it and visualize it more clearly in its own nature—stairways, windows, alleyways, closets, attic ladders, and the like. Burials still occur in the cellar and insight in the study, but Brown here gives us images as much for their own sake as for their mental analogues. Also the number of characters zooms, giving us the sense of a full and rather crowded society in a way the previous books have not. There are many incidental characters in *Ormond*, of course, but one senses even more of them here, both in city and in country. Perhaps these characters gain more importance because each one is given an opinion, a point of view, or even a story, and because the network of their stories, implicit and explicit, constitutes the character of Arthur. So although elements from the other books—twinning, reflections, mirrors, symbolic inwardnesses, talismanic details—all appear again, they do so in a context of profusion that makes the mazy ways of *Edgar Huntly* look as straight as Fifth Avenue on a Sunday morning.

For this reason, I am not going to summarize the story here, as I did the others. Instead I will let Brown's synopses remind us of the main action. He made three of them, each from a slightly different angle or vantage. The first summary appeared in "Walstein's School of History" shortly after the publication of the first part of *Arthur Mervyn*. A historian named Engel has composed an instructive tale called "Olivo Ronsica." In retelling that story, Brown in effect rehearses his own tale, substituting the names Olivo Ronsica for Arthur Mervyn and Semlits for Welbeck. He begins with Olivo:

> Olivo is a rustic youth, whom domestic equality, personal independence, agricultural occupations, and studious habits, had endowed with a strong mind, pure taste, and unaffected integrity. Domestic revolutions oblige him to leave his father's house in search of subsistence. He is destitute of property, of friends, and of knowledge of the world. These are to be acquired by his own exertions, and virtue and sagacity are to guide him in the choice and the use of suitable means.
>
> Ignorance subjects us to temptation, and poverty shackles our beneficence. Olivo's conduct shews us how temptation may be baffled, in spite of ignorance, and benefits be conferred in spite of poverty.
>
> He bends his way to Weimar. He is involved, by the artifices of others, and, in consequence of his ignorance of mankind, in many perils and perplexities. He forms a connection with a man of a great and mixed, but, on the whole, a vicious character. Semlits is intro-

duced to furnish a contrast to the simplicity and rectitude of Olivo, to exemplify the misery of sensuality and fraud, and the influence which, in the present system of society, vice possesses over the reputation and external fortune of the good. . . .

[Olivo's] talents are exerted to reform the vices of others, to defeat their malice when exerted to his injury, to endure, without diminution of his usefulness or happiness, the injuries which he cannot shun.

Semlits is led, by successive accidents, to unfold his story to Ronsica, after which, they separate. Semlits is supposed to destroy himself, and Ronsica returns into the country.

A pestilential disease, prevalent throughout the north of Europe, at that time (1630), appears in the city. To ascertain the fate of one connected, by the ties of kindred and love, with the family in which Olivo resides, and whose life is endangered by residence in the city, he repairs thither, encounters the utmost perils, is seized with the reigning malady, meets, in extraordinary circumstances, with Semlits, and is finally received into the house of a physician, by whose skill he is restored to health, and to whom he relates his previous adventures.

He resolves to become a physician, but is prompted by benevolence to return for a time, to the farm which he had lately left. The series of ensuing events, are long, intricate, and congruous, and exhibit the hero of the tale in circumstances that task his fortitude, his courage, and his disinterestedness.[2]

Even before writing that—in fact, within two weeks after he finished the last chapter of the first part—Brown wrote enthusiastically to his brother James a summary of the second part, yet to be written:

The destiny of Wallace and of Mr. Hadwin is not mentioned in the present work. I intended that Mr. Hadwin, on returning to his family, should be seized with the fatal disease. That the task of nursing him, while struggling with the malady, and of interring him when dead, should, by the fears of their neighbours, be assigned to his daughters. Wallace, by his unseasonable journey, is thrown into a relapse, and dies upon the road. Mervyn, in preparing to leave the city, is accidentally detained, and his fortitude and virtue, subjected to severer trials than any hitherto related.

The character of Wallace is discovered to have been essentially defective. Marriage with this youth proved to be highly dangerous to the happiness of Susan. To prevent this union, and to ascertain the condition of this family, he speeds, at length, after the removal of various impediments, to Hadwin's residence, where he discovers the catastrophe of Wallace and his uncle, and by his presence and succour, relieves the two helpless females from their sorrows and their fears. Marriage with the youngest; the death of the elder by a consumption and grief, leaves him in possession of competence, and the rewards of virtue.[3]

Between these two readings of the story we have Brown's essential skeletons for both parts (even though, as we know, he changed his mind about Arthur's "marriage with the youngest" as he finally shaped his story). But there is yet a third, composite summary very near the end of the second part of *Arthur Mervyn*, as Arthur himself is made to muse upon his predicaments:

> To indulge an adventurous spirit, I left the precincts of the barn-door, enlisted in the service of a stranger, and encountered a thousand dangers to my virtue under the disastrous influence of Welbeck. Afterwards my life was set at hazard in the cause of Wallace, and now am I loaded with the province of protecting the helpless Eliza Hadwin and the unfortunate Clemenza. My wishes are fervent, and my powers shall not be inactive in their defence, but how slender are these powers! [p. 332]

Each of these summaries is accurate in its way, and all of them are complementary. However, the first summary is put to the service of a rather complex demonstration of a particular literary theory; that is, Engel has written "Olivo Ronsica" to demonstrate the power of fictitious history to act as a model for the moral improvement and emulation of its readers. Arthur is thus presented almost exclusively in terms of his moral firmness and energy to do good. Brown's second synopsis is primarily mechanical; it is concerned with the action that will resolve matters opened in the first part of the story and expressive of at least the structural necessity for Arthur's happiness and success at the end. But the third précis goes beyond either of the others in its organization of actions, not according to purpose or end, but according to significant pattern, namely, a sequence of hazards and threats followed by a sequence of responsibilities and duties. This sequence leaves Arthur and us with the question: will he find the means and the powers to effect these responsibilities?

By far the most obvious aspect of these summaries is their complete failure to correspond with what we read. By retelling his story this way, Brown unscrambles the persistent falsifications, confusions, and indirections that mark its telling. It is as if Sophocles were to begin *Oedipus Rex* with the story of Oedipus' birth and flight from the oracle or as if Faulkner were properly to straighten out Benjy's section in *The Sound and the Fury*. For *Arthur Mervyn* begins in the very middle, in some expanded present between past horrors and future hopes where Brown creates a space for telling. So the narrative moves forward by moving back. Arthur's story contains Welbeck's story; Stevens's narrative in turn encloses Wortley's, which contains Williams's, and so on, until a very complex rhythm of past and present emerges. Each story takes us further into the past, more deeply into events and characters, until the narrative present is so jammed with detail and conflicting evidence that we share Stevens's fundamental worry at the beginning of the second part, that we have been deceived by a pleasant face and a plausible explanation. What indeed is true in all this complexity? Who is to be trusted? Is Arthur what he says he is? And what is that? It is well past midway through the book before we begin to discover possible answers. I would suggest that if we are going to consider the action of the book rather than the story, we have to focus on the manner of its telling. If we follow Brown in his synopses and merely unscramble the order of incidents, we shall be very misled.

Should we be so misled, moreover, we are likely to continue the misplaced emphasis on Brown's artistic carelessness, his inveterate sloppiness, and his haste. Evidence of those qualities in this book are especially marked, and though I do not want to enter into a detailed discussion of the composition of *Arthur Mervyn*, which is handled thoroughly elsewhere,[4] a list of some of the problems will not hurt. The first nine chapters were published in nine weekly installments, Brown apparently writing as he went. It was months later that he took up and completed the first part. There was no notion of a second volume until he was writing the last chapter of the first part, and nearly a year passed before he could turn to the composition of the second part. There is no evidence outside the book that he attended to its production with loving care and a good bit of evidence inside the book that he did not. Names get confused or even changed, significant details are planted but disappear forever, and the sudden appearance of Mrs. Fielding as the solution to Arthur's problems and to the various narrative strands is uncomfortably swift, no matter how logically necessary. *Arthur Mervyn* gives the impression of rather uncontrolled improvisation; Brown seems to have written himself into corners from which he only sometimes emerges unscarred by leaps of narrative desperation. One admits that all this is true but need not conclude therefore that the work is unconscious and running at will. I should think that our previous examinations of *Wieland*, *Ormond*, and *Huntly* have shown the coherent matrix of ideas and purposes behind such careless appearances.

What is more, one can see from the first nine chapters that Brown knows in general and in some detail where his story must go. We are only midway through Welbeck's tale by the end of that chapter and have before us Clemenza and her problems, Clavering and Lodi, Watson's death, and the elaborate intrigues of the Thetfords. Brown's purposefulness in these chapters overwhelms the incidental oversights, I believe. But if the incidents are purposeful, so too is the elaborate structure of narratives themselves. There are clear alternatives to this way of proceeding with a story, and Brown has used them before, so I find it only perverse at this stage to avoid looking at the book as if it offered a conscious artistic structure. Let us at least begin with the possibility that, insofar as this book is improvisatory, it is improvising on a central purpose.

For the first time there is no specific auditor for this tale: no involved friend, as in *Wieland*; no ill-defined I. E. Rosenberg whose interest has been previously engaged, as in *Ormond*; no very interested Mary Walde-grave, as in *Edgar Huntly*. Indeed, it is some time before we learn much about the narrator of the outermost frame narrative, even his name. So we begin with a totally undefined reader and a memoirist whose first act is the trusting and generous one of taking a sick stranger into his house. He does so even in opposition to the views of his neighbors, who find such action imprudent and rash and who suppose without evidence that the victim "most probably was worthless" (p. 8). The sick stranger is, of course, Arthur Mervyn, and how he has come to be at this lip of death will be the substance of the first part of this narrative.

Almost at once we encounter a kind of irony in this story that we have not seen before. Arthur, recuperated from his illness, wonders what he will do for a living. Stevens recommends that he become a copyist. "To this he objected, that experience had shewn him unfit for the life of a penman. . . . He had tried the trade of a copyist, and in circumstances more favourable than it was likely he should ever again have an oppor-tunity of trying it" (pp. 10–11), but found it not conducive to his health. Is this Stevens's little joke, or Arthur's? It is certainly Brown's. For almost immediately thereafter we are launched into the tale of Arthur's service to Welbeck as amanuensis or writer, which has led to the sick condition in which Stevens first found him. What prompts this tale is the strong negative reaction to Arthur by Stevens's friend Wortley. Wortley tells Stevens of Arthur's involvement with Welbeck, who proved a con-summate fraud. Stevens is inclined to put a more favorable construction on events than Wortley is but needs to hear Arthur's version.

Arthur begins with the reasons for the move from the farm to the city. A dissolute father and an overprotective mother both drive Arthur into himself until the mother dies and the father marries a conniving slut to whom Arthur is an offense and an inconvenience. Arthur gets the mes-sage that he is unwanted, and makes his way off the farm for the first time in his life. Economic reality confronts him for the first time as he discovers not only that his total fortune of six bits barely gets him to the city, but also that people involved in economic relationships seek advantage without regard to principle or need. Overcharged and underserved, broke and lonely, compelled to bend social rules at the outset by crossing the tollbridge without paying, Arthur finds his introduction to city life crushingly rude. Tired, hungry, confused, and everywhere frustrated, Arthur is quite ready to surrender and to leave the city even without any specific goal in the country. Into this emotional situation steps a young stranger, who smilingly provides him with food and kind treatment, conversation, and even the promise of a night's lodging.

As it turns out, the promise is part of an elaborate practical joke that gets out of hand. What the joker does not know is that another babe has also been deposited secretly in the same dark upstairs bedroom. Arthur's (dare we call him the jokee?) discovery of the sleeping child is his clue to his own predicament here. His alarm triggers a natural and yet significant action on his part. His first impulse is to hide or to escape and the sound of approaching footsteps plunges the frightened and betrayed Arthur into a convenient closet. "What a condition was mine!" he laments. "Immersed in palpable darkness! Shut up in this unknown recess! Lurking like a robber!" (pp. 37–38). Once in, however, there is no easy getting out, and Arthur knows it. How could he explain being in someone's upstairs bedroom in the dark and in the presence of a strange infant? What if they call the police? "I was deeply impressed with the ambiguousness which would necessarily rest upon my motives, and the scrutiny to which they would be subjected. I shuddered at the bare possibility of being ranked with thieves" (p. 43). Arthur begins with behavior, with an alert if generally untested sensitivity to the difficulty of reconciling motives with appearances. He knows himself to be innocent of any wrongdoing, but he also senses that his actions must instantly generate suspicion in others. Instinctively he shrinks from the test and buries himself in the closet. His concealment has been natural, if not wise.

But his education in concealment is proceeding faster than he can handle. For, when locked in the closet, he overhears Thetford's scheme to pass his bastard child off on his wife, in lieu of their own recently dead child. He also hears talk of some duplicity, some swindle involving "the Nabob," as well as the justifying opinion that the Nabob himself deserves to be bilked because he must himself be "a grand imposter" (p. 41). Arthur's education into the world has become a crash course in deception and wickedness. His money has gone faster than his appetite, he has lost his prized possessions by leaving them unguarded in the streets, he has been flimflammed into a stranger's bedroom, and he has been exposed to a scheme of dark intent that can only mean injury to someone. It is enough to scare the very shoes off a good country boy. The next stage in Arthur's education will further his awareness as well as his complicity, but my point here is that this opening episode is more than a singular event; it is a rough paradigm for what will follow.

When Welbeck encounters Arthur outside his house, an elaborate series of concealments begins. Arthur enters into some of them consciously and reluctantly, others quite unconsciously though willingly, and some in purely instinctive recoil from circumstances. From the outset these two men conceal things from one another. Welbeck does not indicate that he sees in Arthur a chance to impose on Mrs. Wentworth; Arthur does not tell about his previous night's adventure in the closet. So when Arthur dons Lodi's clothing, he happily transforms himself into Welbeck's moral family, imagining himself the changeling for Welbeck's supposed lost son (like the strange infant in the previous bedroom predicament). This unintentional concealment of his own personality seems to promise great advantages, particularly wealth and marriage. With his mind filled with those possibilities, Arthur allows himself to be drawn into a promise to keep his own past history and his family secret. Once made, the promise becomes slightly uncomfortable for the voluble young man, but there is a part of Arthur himself that responds to it. He is not completely frank and detailed in telling his own history to Welbeck and is conscious of his evasion by generality (p. 61).

But Arthur's first act upon giving his word is to break it, telling Mrs. Wentworth just enough about Clavering to break his promise, but not enough to satisfy Mrs. Wentworth. The experience is painful for Arthur, who begins to change his mind about Welbeck and his new position as Welbeck's copy-er. The situation parallels that in the first episode. Again an act of kindness and generosity leads Arthur into an unhappy predicament, or at least into an uneasy recognition that he would be happier elsewhere. But this situation is much more complex than the bedroom problem, because Arthur is not aware of how much more in the dark he is here. Mrs. Wentworth has become rightfully suspicious of Arthur in this process, and the following night Wortley will find Arthur identified socially as Welbeck's protégé. In short, Arthur is metaphorically climbing into another closet, extrication from which is likely to prove much more difficult.

His discomfort is intensified when he accidentally encounters Welbeck emerging from Clemenza's bedroom in the middle of the night. "Though not conscious of having acted improperly, yet I felt reluctance to be seen," he explains (p. 74). Indeed, his whole imaginary structure of hopes turns on that occasion. Welbeck he now sees as depraved and Clemenza as ruined. He corrects these inferences (p. 76), but clearly he is growing in suspiciousness, in the conviction that everyone is concealing mean truths from others. His suspicions are only accentuated and confirmed by his errand to Thetford, where he again overhears the name Nabob and realizes that Welbeck is the object of the swindle he previously learned of. Pieces start to fit together here for Arthur, but there is so much he does not understand, and all he can do is be curious about the concealments of others. For instance, he is exceedingly curious about Welbeck's study: "What then was the nature of his employment over which a veil of such impenetrable secrecy was cast?" (p. 81). Arthur approaches the door to this forbidden sanctuary stealthily, full of fear and wonder. Doors are certainly important, because the narrative is full of them—doors opening into rooms and out to escape, doors to shut behind one or to fling open searchingly, doors with keyholes to listen at or peek through, doors for exposing and concealing. So it is significant that Arthur sneaks into the room on this occasion, concealing himself while he tries to disclose another's concealments.

When he penetrates the room, he discovers a marvelous object (p. 82). First there is a mirror before him, in which he sees himself. Next he spies a miniature portrait whose resemblance to himself "was so great that, for a moment, I imagined myself to have been the original from which it had been drawn." Shades of Picasso! But whose portrait is it? There is reason to suppose it is Vincentio Lodi's, a fact that would support Clemenza's start upon first seeing Arthur in his clothes. But it is also possible that the portrait is of the young Welbeck, for what follows immediately is "a stunning report" from the floor above; this report is both the sound of a gunshot and Welbeck's own long story of his youth and education into chicanery and murder. Over Watson's body, Welbeck describes himself as a destitute and indolent youth who is ambitious and "the slave of sensual impulses and voluntary blindness" (p. 87). The result is concealment, delusion, and deception; its fruits, shame and remorse. Perhaps here the parallels between Welbeck and Arthur begin to diverge. Arthur knows neither shame nor guilt, whereas Welbeck has drunk their bitterness full and long. Brown's implication, I suggest, is that Welbeck—for all his villainy—is a fuller human being than Arthur, but whether that is why Arthur's identification with the portrait and the mirror reflection of himself is so transitory (giving way to the conclusion "merely of similitude") must remain tentative.

Of course, Welbeck is confessing in a situation of intense stress, for his schemes for a fortune have risen and fallen with the bullet in Watson's heart. To him this is "a deceitful and flagitious world," which he promises to disclose to Arthur even while securing another promise of secrecy from the confused and curious youngster. Welbeck's own learning process began with the concealment of his poverty from his father-in-law. Just as the Stevens have taken Arthur in, so was Welbeck received by the trusting Watson family in Charleston. There Welbeck hid himself from himself and hid his passion behind his lust for Watson's married sister. Once she is seduced, he again hides the fact that he is already married. Welbeck is driven to thoughts of suicide but, even when most despairing, he finds the urge to live stronger than his shame. At times this urge appears to be an uncontrollable instinct; at others, simple cowardice. The awareness that it is weakness as well as strength on his part only increases the anxiety in which he lives. Above all, Welbeck wants to be respected. His reputation, "the esteem of mankind," the ease and "respect attendant upon opulence I was willing to purchase at the price of ever-wakeful suspicion and eternal remorse; but, even at this price, the purchase was impossible" (p. 90). His aversion to menial labor persists (in all this the likeness to Arthur is quite marked), but behind him constantly looms the shadow of Watson's avenging spirit.

Suddenly, and quite accidentally, Welbeck's salvation seems assured by the meeting with the dying Vincentio Lodi. At once he is possessed of money and a young lady, Clemenza; he has a chance for a new life, for the opulence and the esteem of men that he so hungered for. "My birth and previous adventures it was proper to conceal" (p. 95), he explains, but finds Clemenza such a weak young lady that he does not even have to conceal from her his married state, although it is not long before he has to conceal her pregnancy from the world. To solidify his fortune he invests heavily with Thetford, ignorant that he is being used by Thetford and his associates in an insurance swindle and will lose his entire investment. The news of that ruin comes through the agency of Captain Watson himself, who now seeks Welbeck out. Welbeck muses:

> I dreaded not his violence. The death that he might be prompted to inflict, was no object of aversion. It was poverty and disgrace, the detection of my crimes, the looks and voice of malediction and upbraiding, from which my cowardice shrunk. [p. 103]

But there is more, apparently, for Welbeck seems to be genuinely concerned with Clemenza's fate. Like Arthur later, he thinks that perhaps Mrs. Wentworth will take Clemenza in and protect her (p. 104). While on his way to write to Mrs. Wentworth for this purpose, Welbeck meets Watson and, as he tells it, negligently kills him (p. 106).

For Arthur, Welbeck's story is both illuminating and devastating. His first experience with city trust and generosity had proved a sham and an embarrassing cheat. But this time he has been elevated higher only to be cast down further. "The curtain was lifted," he exclaims, "and a scene of guilt and ignominy disclosed where my rash and inexperienced youth had suspected nothing but loftiness and magnanimity." What can one believe? "The very scene of these offences partook, to my rustic apprehension, of fairy splendour, and magical abruptness. My understanding was bemazed, and my senses were taught to distrust their own testimony" (p. 107). In such a state Arthur becomes fully complicit in Welbeck's character and activity, silently consenting to help in this most symbolic burial of Watson's body. Arthur becomes progressively locked into Welbeck's will and plan as they lug Watson's body to the cellar, a body that will not keep its eyes closed even in death. Or, to put it another way, Arthur in this scene surrenders completely to that Welbeckian element in himself.

In assisting Welbeck, Arthur is not responding wholly instinctively, as he was when he hid in Thetford's closet; but though he is conscious of what he is doing, he is certainly not clear-headed about it. He is now locked in, and believes at one point that Welbeck "had fled and barred every door behind him" (p. 110). Almost as disoriented as Edgar Huntly, he rushes to freedom, only to damage himself by bloodying his own nose and giving himself the appearance of a murderer. Suddenly the intensity of Welbeck's concern with public esteem takes on greater force and reality for Arthur: "shall I not be pursued by the most vehement suspicions and, perhaps, hunted to my obscurest retreat by the ministers of justice? I am innocent, but my tale however circumstantial or true, will scarcely suffice for my vindication. My flight will be construed into a proof of incontestable guilt" (pp. 111–12). In stupefaction, in shock, Arthur yields yet again to Welbeck, follows him to escape, and accepts the admonition: "All I shall ask from you will be silence, and to hide from mankind what you know concerning me" (p. 114). These are Welbeck's last words before he sinks in the midnight river waters. So end five days in Arthur's life and the first night of his storytelling. Dressed again in his rustic clothes and rustic identity, Arthur treks across the Schuylkill bridge (again without paying), bearing only Lodi's manuscript and a treasure of experience.

At this point Stevens resumes the narrative, to assure us of his firsthand confirmation of at least the last part of Arthur's story. Mrs. Wentworth has confirmed Welbeck's disappearance and has also described Arthur's strange behavior regarding Clavering's portrait. Arthur's story has, apparently inadvertently, cleared up those matters. But the second major phase of the first part of *Arthur Mervyn* is yet ahead of us. In very rapid order Arthur relates his return to the country and his coming to work for another surrogate father, Mr. Hadwin, who, unlike Welbeck, has two daughters, neither of them pregnant. Arthur realizes that marriage with the younger, Eliza, is unlikely and he then controls his passion by study of the Lodi manuscript, in which he luckily finds $20,000. Again the connection with Welbeck is quite consciously made; like the villain, Arthur finds a saving treasure, but also like him, he is obliged to return it to Clemenza. In a way, he has now joined Welbeck in the fullness of opportunity for wickedness, but before he can do anything, rumors of the yellow fever epidemic increase in number and in vividness. Despite these horrid rumors and the panic that throws hundreds upon the roads in their flight from the city, Arthur determines to return, largely to determine the fate of Wallace (Susan Hadwin's fiancé), who, as it happens, is clerk to a Mr. Thetford. Surely he is the young man who first led Arthur astray, and here he occurs again, connected with the wholesome Quaker family.

Arthur's return to the city is not so much different in kind as in degree. The trivial deceits he encountered the first time, the self-seeking of the inn-keepers, are now downright hostile. Rudeness and inhumanity are everywhere. Brown's recording of these graphic details of a city in panic and sickness immediately became his trademark. But if one focuses on those details, one may overlook their function in Arthur's narrative, namely, the intensification of the deceptions and concealments and distrusts of the first phase by paralleling them in the second. That is to say, Arthur is very conscious that the search for Wallace brings him back to the very house in which he was first bilked and buried: "This chamber, as far as the comparison of circumstances would permit me to decide, I believed to be the same in which I had passed the first night of my late abode in the city. Now was I, a second time, in almost equal ignorance of my situation, and of the consequences which impended exploring my way to the same recess" (pp. 143–44). Arthur calls this his "theatre of pestilence" (p. 144), the place where he too contracts the disease of the city.

Again he is boxed in—or nearly so, and quite involuntarily—as a ghoulish vandal attacks and knocks him unconscious. Passing hearse drivers are ready to put him into a coffin when he recovers and persuades them that he is not dead or even ill. From Dr. Estwick and later from Medlicote, both generous and sympathetic figures, he learns of the peculiar intertwining of avarice and disease connected with Thetford and his house. Because of business, Thetford refuses to leave the city when he might have, perhaps because of the Welbeck swindle. He cruelly dismisses his servant and Wallace to a hospital so inhumanely run that consignment there is like a death sentence. In the process, he loses his family, his wealth, and finally his life. When Arthur returns to the now deserted Thetford house, he enters the vomit- and bile-stained house of death, there to encounter his first serious deceiver:

> If an apparition of the dead were possible, and that possibility I could not deny, this was such an apparition. A hue, yellowish and livid; bones, uncovered with flesh; eyes, ghastly, hollow, woe-begone, and fixed in an agony of wonder upon me; and locks, matted and negligent, constituted the image which I now beheld. My belief of somewhat preternatural in this appearance, was confirmed by recollection of resemblances between these features and those of one who was dead. In this shape and visage, shadowy and death-like as they were, the lineaments of Wallace, of him who had misled my rustic simplicity on my first visit to this city, and whose death I had conceived to be incontestably ascertained, were forcibly recognized. [pp. 166–67]

So Wallace has been found, emerging from death and as death, a kind of intensification of Arthur's own resurrection from death the previous evening.

Arthur now becomes Wallace's guide out of the city, a precise reversal of their roles weeks earlier, but not before hearing Wallace's horrible description of the deadly Bush-Hill hospital—a death house made hellish by the callous and inhumane treatment by the staff. The story awakens Arthur's sense of social duty and gives him a purpose, no matter how naive he may be about the role he will play as superintendent of this inferno. Nonetheless, he seems caught in a pattern from which there is no outlet and of which he seems essentially unconscious. For his growing urge to expand his beneficence leads him to alter his original intentions regarding Clemenza's money. Although his purposes seem quite altruistic, they bear a disturbing resemblance to Welbeck's misapplication of her inheritance much earlier. The pattern is accentuated by Arthur's decision to find relief from his increasing illness by returning to Welbeck's house. This second part of the story thus recapitulates the action of the first phase, the movements from Thetford's to Welbeck's. Arthur now is quite consciously concealing himself. He fears he will collapse in the streets and have his sickness exposed, and therefore feels no compunction about sneaking into the house through a window: "I felt no scruple in profiting by this circumstance. My purposes were not dishonest. I should not injure or purloin any thing. It was laudable to seek a refuge from the well-meant persecutions of those who governed the city. All I sought was the privilege of dying alone. . . . My design was now effected. This chamber should be the scene of my disease and my refuge from the charitable cruelty of my neighbours" (p. 182). Thus, despite his frequent ruminations on the pernicious effects of secrecy, Arthur here consciously and purposefully conceals himself in the very place of his most intimate complicity with Welbeck.

Just as Welbeck was on his way to dispose of Clemenza's fortune when he was accosted by the unfortunate Watson, so Arthur now seeks out writing means to direct the disposal of her money in case he dies. Once again he seeks entry to Welbeck's closet, this time to find it secured from within. The voice that emerges to warn him off is the voice of one who first exposed Arthur to deceit and seduction—the schoolmaster Colvill, who seduced and destroyed Arthur's own sister, a girl with whose soul Arthur felt himself linked "by a thousand resemblances and sympathies" (p. 188). Arthur feels "self-condemnation and shame" at the abhorrence that voice generates in him, but shame changes to terror when he discovers that the voice is Welbeck's and not Colvill's. In his "feverish perturbations" Arthur witnesses the return to him of his own evil inclinations, the resurrection of Welbeck.

In the concluding catastrophe, Brown has brought most of his major motifs together: money, social duty, concern for concealment and secrecy as well as for reputation and esteem, and the resort to stories. In the comedy of errors that constitutes this scene Arthur destroys the 20,000 dollars, burning it in the candle provided by Welbeck and believing all the while that he is destroying forgeries. The scene is remarkable for its blundering. Welbeck has foxed himself out of a fortune, and Arthur has prevailed by accident rather than purpose. Moreover, their actions, which seem to have attracted passersby, threaten to bring the outside world into their secret place, an event dangerous to them both. Welbeck flees, somewhat consoled by the thought that Mervyn's discovery will surely lead to his death, while Arthur performs a final act of self-burial by hiding in a storage attic.

But hiding is now suffocating and deadly for him, and he emerges from his hideout as soon as he can. It is important to note that Arthur does not come out of the closet (so to speak) from principle but from necessity. Fever and thirst drive him out; the urge to live plus the suffocating effects of concealment bring him into public view again much as Welbeck's life urge restored him from the river. He does not reason from the ill consequences of secrecy (which he knows full well) but from expediency and terror. Back on the street, he is totally disoriented—"My perturbed senses and the darkness hindered me from discerning the right way" (p. 214); he staggers, again by chance, to where we and Dr. Stevens met him on the first page of the story. Prompted by Wortley's sincerely troubled reaction to Arthur, Stevens had said, when starting Arthur on his story, "Wortley is not short-sighted or hasty to condemn. So great is my confidence in his integrity that I will not promise my esteem to one who has irrecoverably lost that of Wortley. I am not acquainted with your motives to concealment or what it is you conceal, but take the word of one who possesses that experience which you complain of wanting, that sincerity is always safest" (p. 13). So Arthur ends his narrative with assurances that he has hidden nothing from Stevens: "every sacrifice is trivial which is made upon the altar of sincerity" (p. 213).

As we look back on the whole situation, we can find an abstract model for this complicated action. A doctor finds a young man who is physically sick and, with gentle care and considerable risk, restores him to health. Another person looks at this same restored young man and says that he may be physically cured, but he is still morally sick. The doctor's diagnosis, pretty much a guess, is that the moral sickness comes from insincerity and concealment. He prescribes openness and candor. The patient practices that regimen at complex length in the two major portions of his confession (almost a psychoanalytic strategy), in which he recounts his exposure to the moral disease of distrust, first in the benign form of Wallace, then in the virulent form of Welbeck. Finally the major source of infection, under threat of exposure, apparently subsides. Presumably the patient is now healed; at least he presumes himself to be so. Arthur's story is thus therapeutic, but by its very nature it is the story of the progress of disease, the disease whose agents are ambition for esteem, wealth, and sexual dominance. The story is a form of bleeding, namely, letting the ill humors out. This implies that they are at the same time a part of one's self, as Welbeck is an inward manifestation of Arthur's overbalanced moral system.

I do not want to work this allegory or conceit too hard, but I find it has real structural force. *Arthur Mervyn*, like the other works we have explored, is a story of the education of the self, especially the self in terms of society. That is why so much attention is spent on others, on passing strangers, on acquaintances, on public and private servants, on friends, mates, and lovers. This is Brown's most socially sensitive, socially alert, and socially distracting fiction. It is not—to reverse the critical commonplace—that city life is symbolized by the epidemic or by sickness, but that the city is itself a symbol of man's socialization. It is an intensified theater of the passions and hopes that are equally visible in every family and every rural community, no matter how small. In this novel the yellow fever is merely a symbol for social crisis, a condition that sharpens and calls into more visible contrasts those combats between ego protection and public obligation. Arthur as patient knows from the start what his public duties are, knows that his health and sanity utterly depend upon his putting himself at the mercy of others, but his knowledge is not intuitively felt. Therefore, despite his feeling of rectitude, he instinctively and constantly hides himself or information about himself whenever circumstances become stressful.

Brown refuses to let this psychological problem become uppermost in this romance, however, knowing that it is a two-sided problem, external as well as internal. *Arthur Mervyn* is the one novel where we are thrust outside in order to appreciate the specialness of the social conditions Arthur is forced to meet. I intend merely to mark these for others to expand.[5] First, Brown carefully attends to the dates and durations of his events, which were, in fact, annual. That is, the epidemic always struck in late summer (July or August) and ran until October, when cold weather removed the mosquitoes, in Brown's time still the unknown cause of the infection. Moreover, 1793 saw an incredible onslaught of the disease, which wiped out some 2,500 people in Philadelphia in six weeks. What proved especially disastrous to some of the prominent citizens was the community's unpreparedness. When in November of that year Matthew Carey wrote a citizens' committee report called *A Short Account of the Malignant Fever*, he began with a portrayal of the spirit of extravagance that prevailed in Philadelphia at that time. It was a period of reckless speculation, unsteady financial institutions, and widespread ruin. The business community naturally recoiled upon itself in understandable suspicion and occasionally attempted to shift its losses to the unsuspecting. Distrust was everywhere.

Neither the Congress, then seated in Philadelphia, nor the city government was in attendance when the disaster struck. A group of businessmen appointed themselves guardians of the city, but only after it was apparent some authority was necessary and only after a great deal of damage had been done. They confiscated a large house, the Bush-Hill mansion, and turned it into a 140-bed hospital, which almost at once proved totally inadequate. They set up tents in the circus ground, which also proved too small for the dead and dying. Only the strenuous personal exertions of a tiny group of businessmen overturned the callous misrule of the hospital by the middle of September. Wallace's descriptions, Carey would much later say, were "probably not too highly coloured."[6] At first death knells were rung, but when the victims began to multiply so quickly, the committee insisted they cease so as not to increase the panic. Vandals and looters roamed the streets, resulting in the appointment of a civil guard— like Baxter in *Ormond*—to protect property. Men were hired to lug the dead away, particularly blacks, who were supposed to be not so affected by the disease. Ports, roads, and bridges were blocked, and people in surrounding areas were urged to lock out Philadelphians seeking shelter.

Strangers and newcomers were everywhere, especially displaced French escaping from the Reign of Terror; in *Ormond* Brown lets Martinette estimate some ten thousand such Frenchmen in the city. But they were not the only French problem. The British, in a declared state of war with France, sought to cut off all French trade, and that meant blockading any shipping in or out of West Indies ports. American traders protested interruption of their trade with the islands, but that did not prevent British seizure of ships and cargoes on the pretext of contraband, military goods, or even money being sent to support the French Revolution; nor did it prevent the impressment of seamen into British service, despite their claims of American citizenship.[7] Welbeck naively invests Clemenza's money under such a circumstance, which Thetford and his associates take advantage of when their supposedly inadequately insured vessel is forfeited.

Brown is thus extraordinarily careful about the social situation in which Arthur's socialization will be tried. The question left at the end of the first part of *Arthur Mervyn*, then, is whether the storytelling therapy has worked. Is Arthur really free to protect himself from the prevailing panic? For Dr. Stevens, the answer to that question depends on whether Arthur has indeed told all. Has his story been the truth? Stevens and his wife are inclined to believe him, his wife because she is a woman of sentiment, Stevens somewhat more circumspectly because he has heard the story from Arthur himself, but also because his knowledge independently of Arthur's story seems to confirm it by a "tissue of nice contingencies." Particularly, Stevens knows the whereabouts of Clemenza Lodi, who was housed by Welbeck in Mrs. Villars's country whorehouse (even the flourishing of prostitution after the epidemic, and as a direct result of it, is thus nicely accommodated from Carey). But in terms of the story, the importance of Stevens's transmitting Clemenza's location to Arthur is that he sets Arthur upon a kind of healing role much like Stevens's own.

In other words, Stevens is sufficiently persuaded of Arthur's social possibility to offer to take him on as a medical apprentice and to give him the power the medical profession confers "of lightening the distresses of our neighbors, the dignity which popular opinion annexes to it, the avenue which it opens to the acquisition of competence, the freedom from servile cares which attends it, and the means of intellectual gratification with which it supplies us" (p. 223). In brief, it is the beginning of Arthur's chance to become a whole human being by developing his social responsibilities. Arthur's mission, however, is still in a sense therapeutic because the visit to the Hadwins and the rescue of Clemenza are both to some extent tests of Arthur's moral health. That is why, although Stevens's confidence is high, he remains open to any evidence that Arthur still contains the disease of concealment contracted in the first part.

Once again, the honorable Wortley points up the unanswered questions of Arthur's behavior. So the second part begins with the same pattern of events the first part did. Wortley

> suspected that Mervyn was a wily imposter; that he had been
> trained in the arts of fraud, under an accomplished teacher; that the
> tale which he had told to me, was a tissue of ingenious and plausible
> lies; that the mere assertions, however plausible and solemn, of one
> like him, whose conduct had incurred such strong suspicions, were
> unworthy of the least credit. [p. 226]

Wortley argues that Welbeck had stolen from him and two others substantial sums of money by acts of forgery, a story Arthur had not disclosed to Stevens. Stevens's own acquaintance with Mrs. Althorpe also leads to information that discredits Arthur's story and his character. She describes him as freakish, queer, having an affair with his stepmother, and plotting the ruin of his own father—an unbookish, illiterate, and effeminate young man of impetuous and odd impulses. Mrs. Althorpe feels she has full evidence of Arthur's moral corruption. Before she can provide that, however, Stevens is subjected to another assault upon Arthur's character and story.

Wortley informs him that a warrant has been issued for Arthur's arrest as an accomplice to Welbeck in the supposed murder of Watson. Watson's brother-in-law Williams has been trying to trace Watson, mainly because of personal anxiety, but also because Watson had with him a substantial amount of money in negotiable bills when he disappeared, money that belonged to Mrs. Maurice. Wortley points the issue for Stevens:

> It was time, replied my friend, that your confidence in smooth features and fluent accents should have ended long ago. Till I gained from my present profession, some knowledge of the world, a knowledge which was not gained in a moment, and has not cost a trifle, I was equally wise in my own conceit; and, in order to decide upon the truth of any one's pretensions, needed only a clear view of his face and a distinct hearing of his words. My folly in that respect, was only to be cured, however, by my own experience, and I suppose your credulity will yield to no other remedy. [p. 249]

Wortley also points out that Arthur's story about Clavering has been quite confuted by a reliable witness, who has seen Clavering in Charleston. "Now," says Stevens, "for the first time, I begin to feel that my confidence is shaken" (p. 251). Yet very shortly before this tremor, Stevens tells us that he is quite aware of Wortley's philosophy of suspicion, musing, "yet, what are the bounds of fraud? . . . A smooth exterior, a show of virtue, and a specious tale, are, a thousand times, exhibited in human intercourse by craft and subtlety. . . . But the face of Mervyn is the index of an honest mind. Calm or vehement, doubting or confident, it is full of benevolence and candor. He that listens to his words may question their truth, but he that looks upon his countenance when speaking, cannot withhold his faith" (pp. 229–30).

Brown very cleverly dodges the epistemological question he has so carefully drawn for Stevens through four chapters—certainly an unnecessary length unless he wanted us to take careful note of the problem—by having him suddenly summoned to debtors' prison. Stevens leaps to the supposition that an unfortunate friend, Carlton, had been hounded to prison, a man who "shrunk, with fastidious abhorrence, from the contact of the vulgar and the profligate" (p. 254). When Stevens enters the prison, he is almost overcome by the change of atmosphere, just as Arthur was on first reentering the Thetford house (p. 144). Like Carlton, Stevens seems to have "an exquisite sensibility to disgrace" (p. 254). Indeed Carlton is there, but he did not send for Stevens; Arthur himself, now tending the dying Welbeck, has called him.

This scene is structurally very significant. Arthur's reputation has been more fiercely assaulted than at any previous time. His disgrace is embodied in the debtors' prison itself, from which men of more delicate principles recoil in disgust. Carlton is effete and helpless. Stevens is sickened but strong. Arthur breathes its dank atmosphere without quailing, indeed, with a significant disregard. And Welbeck tosses in the throes of ultimate misery. Here for the first time Stevens recognizes the conspicuous need for esteem and reputation that constitutes Welbeck. In fact, it occurs to Stevens that Welbeck's drive to conceal is directly proportionate to his need of good opinion. Before Stevens Arthur confesses that he has told the doctor everything, has disclosed all Welbeck's darkest secrets. This perfidy leaves Welbeck incredulous, horrified, and then hopeless. He accuses Arthur of inhumanity, of cruelty, of killing him—all of which seems quite true. Arthur's forthright exposure is cruel and hurtful, but it gives Stevens a firsthand eye-and-ear view of what his cure of Arthur's malady might amount to: a crushing openness, a malicious beneficence, a cunning sincerity.

Before Stevens can unravel all the ambiguities of this meeting, he is obliged to console Carlton's sister, a person of remarkable equanimity who, though obviously distressed by her brother's shameful situation, is in no sense destroyed by it. Her buoyancy and fortitude will become models for right dealing with misfortune, but here we see just enough of her to record Stevens's admiration and approval. Her openness comes across as superior even to Stevens's delicacy in approaching the news of her brother's imprisonment; she will prove more than a mere diversion in this story of Arthur's recuperation.

As Arthur resumes his account of what has passed since he parted from Dr. and Mrs. Stevens, we realize that a great deal of time has elapsed. Indeed, we know several months have passed because several occasions are given specific dates. Although we must jump somewhat ahead in the story while tracing this chronology, this is probably the most convenient place to do so. Filled with hopes of saving Clemenza by moving her to the Hadwins, Arthur had made his way back to the country. But on his way he discovers news of Wallace's shallow character and his relapse from the yellow fever. Wallace has again disappeared, leaving behind only a bad memory. By the time Arthur reaches Malverton, "the second month of frost and snow" (p. 272) has already arrived, which puts us in late November or December. Mr. Hadwin is by now long dead.[8] Arthur goes to seek help for the two sisters from a neighbor, Ellis, but is there refused. This scene is interesting because it shows the extent to which the interests of others have come to dominate Arthur's activities. The Ellis refusal to care for the Hadwin girls is only the first in a series of exertions and setbacks on Arthur's part. Arthur's steadfast efforts for the Hadwins are at once a witness to his newly won generosity and a lesson in hardening. When Susan dies, for example, he undertakes to bury her, despite the unconventionality of his method and the disapproval of the old retainer, Caleb. What he does, he believes, is reasonable, and if "reason acquires strength only by the diminution of sensibility, perhaps it is just for sensibility to be diminished" (p. 281).

But one does not simply bury bodies and have done with them. One must deal with passionate, unreasonable, and often irresponsible actions on the part of others. Thus, when Arthur and Eliza discover Hadwin's will, Arthur is fully ready to carry it out, despite Eliza's impetuous burning of the document. That act is clearly foolish, by Arthur's values, and contributes to Arthur's cooling of emotions for the young Eliza. Critics have become fond of smirking at Arthur's renewed interest in the possibilities of marrying the orphaned girl, but that seems to me a very shortsighted view of Arthur's position. The lessons of Wallace and Welbeck are still with him. Stevens has pointed out the disadvantages of subtlety and concealment and the ill effects of reacting to circumstances instinctively, of wincing and cringing whenever threatened. Arthur's new role is that of the man of reason who has to take account of his feelings but will only act according to them by the dictates of knowledge and reason. Perhaps he senses in Eliza much of his own earlier vulnerability. When, for example, they rather foolishly leave Malverton in the blizzard, Eliza suffers a violent accident that badly bloodies her nose. The scene of course reminds us of Arthur's own bloodied nose in part one. Should he play Welbeck to Eliza's Arthur? Self-gratification says yes, but genuine affection and clear thinking say no.

Once he has Eliza clearly established with the Curling family, once, that is, the crisis is over, it is natural that he consider how far his responsibilities extend to the young lady. He must evaluate his feelings, his sexual attraction, and her helpless reliance upon him. They have left Malverton with no inconsiderable amount of money. Surely if this were Arthur's main motive, we could predict his action: it would be identical with Welbeck's. But Arthur now sees, as he did not a few months previously, that the world has more to offer than a beautiful youngster whose only claims are emotional. He considers that he is still growing and changing at eighteen or nineteen and that Eliza at fifteen is subject to even greater changes of character and growth.

> Might I not gain the knowledge of beings whose virtue was the gift of experience and the growth of knowledge? Who joined to the modesty and charms of woman, the benefits of education, the maturity and steadfastness of age, and with whose character and sentiments my own would be much more congenial than they could possibly be with the extreme youth, rustic simplicity and mental imperfections of Eliza Hadwin? [p. 292]

One winces at the phrase "mental imperfections," as Shelley and others did, but what can be argued against it? Arthur is right, and this makes him quite a dodo in most readers' eyes. He so completely ignores the affective side of human relationships that we resent his logicality regarding his country girl. But it is also clear from this passage that Brown is looking for some alternative to his original scheme for Arthur. There will be no marriage with the youngest, because Arthur has developed a vision of something better. The "objects of rational study" (p. 293) have led Arthur to value something beyond the nubile girl. He is preparing for an older, experienced, emotionally settled and educated woman. When he in effect explains this to Eliza, it is not because he has better prospects in mind.

Eliza's response, apart from feeling hurt, is very powerful. She points out that her situation is not much different from Arthur's and that her shortcomings can only be cured by worldly experience and growth, just as his must be. Arthur counters with a statement about a basic difference between men and women that would choke any modern feminist, namely, women are subject to reputation more than men are. "A fair fame is of the highest importance to a young female, and the loss of it but poorly supplied by the testimony of her own conscience" (p. 300). Such a thought completely contradicts Arthur's values for himself, of course, but he seems quite innocent of the contradiction, despite Eliza's driving it home to him.

In fact, Arthur's reputation is not doing terribly well at this stage. Caleb informs him of Philip Hadwin's visit to Malverton. Caleb has his suspicions about Arthur's manners and purposes; so has the Hadwins' neighbor, Mr. Ellis, who has heard rumors about Arthur's unsavoryness prior to leaving home. The story Mrs. Althorpe reported to Stevens has indeed traveled. Arthur is perturbed by Caleb's report, but not so much that he does not take the initiative toward Philip Hadwin. Rather than wait to be accosted, he seeks out Hadwin himself and outfaces him in one of the better scenes of the novel. But he leaves convinced that Phil Hadwin will prove no substantial help for Eliza.

Does his success against the crude and bullying Hadwin remind him of his responsibility to Clemenza? He does not say so, but the juxtaposition seems significant. For on his return from the Hadwins he resolves to visit Mrs. Villars to rescue Clemenza: "Doors and passages may be between her and me," he is aware, but "with a purpose such as mine, no one had a right to close the one or obstruct the other" (p. 313). (He actually stopped off to discomfit Eliza with a report of the interview with Hadwin but left the next morning on his way to the Stevens's home; p. 312.) Thus, at so unseemly a time for entering a brothel as 9 A.M., Arthur crowds his way into Mrs. Villars's country house. Warner Berthoff has noted Brown's instinct for the comic in this scene, and although we must admit his comedy is not that of Virgil and Fonzo in Faulkner's Memphis, having Arthur enter the brothel with "an erect spirit" comes pretty close. "Be Bold," say Busirane's doors to Britomart; "be not too bold," says one iron door,[9] a lesson Arthur might well have learned. For he now begins to play the bold fool, armed with innocence and chastity, with good thoughts and noble motives; he will pursue passages and open doors unannounced, armed with Stevens's lessons on openness. If in the first part he recoiled from circumstances and closed himself in, locking doors behind him, he begins to err here in the opposite direction, bursting in upon others quite without regard for their feelings, wishes, or will. When Mrs. Villars shoots him in the head, he deserves it.

The results of his new boldness also pay off. He exposes Mrs. Villars, finds Clemenza, learns the whereabouts of Welbeck, and, most important, meets his ideal mate in Achsa Fielding. But the meeting is not very auspicious. Arthur has entered with expectations of sin, and Mrs. Fielding's presence brings him up short: "I had brought with me the belief of their being unchaste; and seized, perhaps, with too much avidity, any appearance that coincided with my prepossessions. Yet the younger [Mrs. Fielding] by no means inspired the same disgust; though I had no reason to suppose her more unblemished than the elder. Her modesty seemed unaffected, and was by no means satisfied, like that of the elder, with defeating future curiosity" (p. 318). What he hopes to gain by putting the question to her directly is unclear, but he does: "Under this veil, perhaps, lurk a tainted heart and depraved appetites. Is it so?" (p. 320). She does not, quite sensibly, respond, but Arthur succeeds in conveying the idea that prostitution is a form of dastardly concealment (p. 322) and worthy of exposure.

The most interesting feature of this meeting is the fact that both Mrs. Fielding and Arthur are in the same situation. They meet in a whorehouse. Each has reason to suppose the other base and immoral. Arthur can say of Achsa what everyone says of him: "I depend only on your looks and professions, and these may be dissembled" (p. 328). Fortunately, her discretion guards her, no matter how ambiguous her situation or pure her motives.

Arthur, on the other hand, has undergone an unsavory transformation. His sense of the overwhelming rectitude of his motives does more than make him regardless of others' sensibilities; it gives him a sense of superiority and a delight in others' misfortunes. With even greater assurance than that with which he penetrated the Villars household, he descends in vampiric purity to suck satisfaction from Welbeck's misery. Having overcome the Welbeck in his own soul, he can now safely linger over Welbeck's changed condition: "Let me gain, from contemplation of thy misery, new motives to sincerity and rectitude" (p. 334). Ugh! It may well be that Arthur's new strength is Welbeck's death. After all, Welbeck does confess to having seen the notice of the money Watson was supposed to have about him, as well as to having gone to exhume the body to recover that treasure, which he passes on to Arthur at his death. But Arthur stalks this winter landscape like the very yellow fever itself, in his new erectitude. "An honest front and a straight story" (p. 349) is now Arthur's motto, and his overweening insistence on acting accordingly is both comic and dangerous. When one thinks of Brown's major fictions, one always remembers the identifying oddities that occupy them—Carwin's biloquism, Edgar's somnambulism, Ormond's disguises. Insofar as *Arthur Mervyn* has any similar feature, it is the yellow fever itself. The yellow fever is Arthur, the victim and agent of moral righteousness who is caught in the grip of unmodified sincerity and impulse and devastating in his effects on others. Once again in Stevens's company Arthur visits Welbeck; the combination is too much for the old deceiver, who seems to dry and fade away like Roger Chillingworth, lost in assurances that he will soon be well and perhaps in equally illusory concerns for Clemenza's welfare. Brown's anticipations of Melville's Bartleby in this scene are almost unnerving, but Welbeck does break his silence and does, finally, seek to benefit others, making his last act the recovery of the money Watson owed the Maurice family.

Upon Welbeck's death, Stevens's narrative ceases, and Arthur takes it up himself. Chapters 16 through 22 are a coherent story told by an Arthur who has regained his reputation, moved ahead with his medical studies, found relief for Clemenza and Eliza, and turned both Mrs. Wentworth and Wortley into believers. Except for one major scene, Stevens essentially fades from the story, and so we have an interesting inversion of the narrative procedure in *Ormond*. There the narrator usurps the story of her chief character; here the main character usurps the narrative function, one of several ways in which Arthur is shown to become Stevens. This is Arthur triumphant! But it is not Arthur complete.

Because Arthur has triumphed by the time of this telling and because he knows it, he declares himself somewhat less circumspectly about his actions. For example, earlier on, when he buried Susan's body, he was conscious that his actions were unusual and was at some pains to justify them to himself and perhaps especially to his auditors. When he reentered Thetford's house, and Welbeck's, and even Mrs. Villars's, he was acutely conscious that entering without being admitted was unusual, although justified in the circumstances. Now he refers his unconcern about doors to his "usual carelessness of forms" (p. 354). Nonetheless, he does apologize to Mrs. Wentworth, when she discovers him in her parlor (p. 355), and soon wins half her confidence at least, though she tells him quite frankly: "till [his] character be established by other means than [his] own assertions," Arthur can expect only half trust.

The following visit to Miss Carlton's again chastens Arthur's simple views of the world. He is certain that he could show her brother's creditor the folly of imprisoning another for debt, until Miss Carlton rather condescendingly and ironically corrects his "very abstract view of things" (p. 365). Again the scene shows us Brown's awareness of Arthur's simplemindedness, although Arthur remains, like Pippa, blessedly untouched by the conversation. Such a persistent abstract view remains through the interview with Mrs. Fielding, where with the righteousness of youth he fails to see that forms are protective devices that weld society, not simply guards for isolating individuals. At the end of the conversation, he is quite sure that Mrs. Fielding's reluctance to bow immediately to his desire to aid Clemenza derives from selfish fears:

You are rich, and abound in all the conveniences and luxuries of life. A small portion of your superfluity would obviate the wants of

a being not less worthy than yourself. It is not avarice or aversion
to labor that makes you withhold your hand. It is dread of the
sneers and surmises of malevolence and ignorance. [p. 369]

Impetuous candor overrules all circumspection for Arthur, even in the
most delicate situations, as he discovers in Baltimore.

There he calls on Mrs. Watson, but only after being detected peeking
through the night window of her house. When Arthur returns the packet
of money that belongs to her, he has done all duty requires of him. But
that is somehow not enough, and the unvoiced urge to say or do something more overpowers him while it also confuses him. "I cannot explain
why my perplexity and the trouble of my tho'ts were greater upon this
than upon similar occasions" (p. 374). Arthur's awkwardness is only
momentary, however, and he unceremoniously (though not undramati-
cally) crashes Mrs. Watson to the floor by blurting out the news that
Watson is dead. Now a man who believes that knocking at doors is a silly
convention certainly ought not to have stuck at declaring right out that
Watson had cashed in his chips. But Arthur hesitates and stammers,
sensing in himself a "sort of electrical sympathy" with Mrs. Watson.
Nonetheless, blurt he does and then ducks out as soon as he can, reasoning to himself, or to us, that "more information would be useless to her,
and not to be given by me, at least, in the present audience, without
embarrassment and peril" (p. 375).

The eight or ten miles to the Maurice estate Arthur traverses in a trice,
designing to bring the Maurice family the same glad tidings with which
he bludgeoned Mrs. Watson. But Mrs. Maurice and her daughters are
not long-suffering Agathas like those who appealed to Melville and Haw-
thorne. They are narrow, private, guarded, and enclosed, but only by
doors. We know, however, how fragile doors can be before Arthur's
goodness. What Arthur does not know is that the family is being hounded
by creditors to a point where they cannot afford to be open or respon-
sive to anyone. Curiously enough, Arthur, even with the means in his
pocket, avoids revealing the reason for his visit when he might. He is
apparently offended because they do not immediately accede to the good

he intends to bring them, the good he himself is. For the first time Arthur becomes conscious that there is something wrong with his behavior. By sheer boorishness he has prevailed over Mrs. Maurice and her guardian daughters—evasive Polly and two Black Panthers guarding the gate. But though he has restored righteousness, he suffers an unusual letdown:

> I walked to the window absorbed in my own reflections. I was disappointed and dejected. The scene before me was the unpleasing reverse of all that my fancy, while coming hither, had foreboded. I expected to find virtuous indigence and sorrow lifted, by my means, to affluence and exultation. I expected to witness the tears of gratitude and the caresses of affection. What had I found? Nothing but sordidness, stupidity, and illiberal suspicion. [p. 382]

"By my means." Obviously, Arthur's means are not yet enough, and this sequence of encounters comes close finally to driving home to him the source of his own sickness.

But Arthur is still a buoyant and irrepressible spirit. Under the charitable counsel of Mrs. Watson's brother, Williams, he begins to sort out the factitious from the genuine. Not all the Maurices, however, are sordid, stupid, and illiberal, only the mother and elder daughter. Fanny, the younger, is generous and charming. She and Mrs. Watson completely reverse Arthur's temporary crestfallenness, bring him out of his shell, so to speak. The rapidity of Arthur's recovery and his enjoyment of these ladies (both now wealthy and eligible spouses) clearly invite confirmation of that self-seeking aspect of Arthur's character. But though he dallies for two or three weeks with them, he finally responds to the call of duty regarding Clemenza. The dalliance itself is important. Arthur is slowing down and, perhaps without full consciousness, growing up. Stevens relieves him of his concern for Clemenza, persuading both Mrs. Wentworth and Mrs. Fielding to contribute to her support, while he and Mary take the distraught young lady under their own roof.

But Arthur does more than slow down. He undergoes a kind of subtle feminization and simultaneous liberation from his own past. This odd interlude of Arthur among the ladies is striking, until we remember that the whole second part of *Arthur Mervyn* turns on his relationships with women—Mrs. Wentworth, Mrs. Althorpe, Mrs. Villars, Mrs. Fielding, Clemenza Lodi, Miss Carlton, Eliza and Susan, Fanny and Mrs. Maurice, and Mrs. Watson. Stevens the authority figure has effectively disappeared from the foreground in this part, and the extent of his absence is thrown into significant relief when we remember who most strikingly occupied our attention in the first part—Stevens, Wortley, Wallace, Watson, Welbeck, Medlicote, Thetford, and Estwick. We realize that Brown, intentionally or not, has given us Arthur in two kinds of education: the first into the possibilities of fatherhood, the second into the possibilities of mothers and wives. Part one is a book of masculine cunning, deceit, and sickness; part two the exposure to forces of healing and wholeness. Sons and lovers? Exactly. But before Arthur can enter fully into his own health, he has to relinquish the hold he has upon his numerous fathers. Stevens has made room for him in his house, his life, his profession, and his narrative. Welbeck has sinned himself out of existence, and now Arthur's actual father goes the same way, dying of drink in prison (p. 393). "I was now alone in the world," announces Arthur, "so far as the total want of kindred creates solitude. Not one of my blood, nor even of my name, were to be found in this quarter of the world. . . . The scenes of my childish and juvenile days were dreary and desolate. The fields which I was wont to traverse, the room in which I was born, retained no traces of the past" (p. 394). No traces of the past!

As I have noted previously, Arthur is still not completely cured at this stage of his experience. If women are to be his healers, he knows them in essentially three forms—whores and sisters and mothers. There is no health in Betty Lawrence, the slut-mother; there is no wholeness in Mrs. Wentworth or his own dead mother; there is no fullness in Eliza or Fanny or Miss Carlton. How does an erect spirit like Arthur's learn to bend, to flex in the world? Brown's solution to this question is at once bold and clever. In Achsa Fielding he gives Arthur the wholeness of woman, a wife. In her we understand all at once—whore, mother, sister—a marvelous invention.

Achsa is utterly foreign to Arthur, in spirit, sex, experience, even race.

She knocks before she enters. She observes forms. She has wealth. She has the mystery of knowledge, particularly sexual knowledge. She is not beautiful but prepossessing. Candor and circumspection sit easily together in her. Most of all, she is dark, Jewish, and feminine. Achsa Fielding is Arthur's Orient, much as Ormond was Constantia's, and she juxtaposes the adult against Arthur's adolescence. To put it another way, Achsa is Arthur's potential for full manhood, her companionship a necessary though hitherto missing dimension to Arthur's education. She is the aim as well as the meaning of his sexual maturity, the counterpoise to the Welbeck in him. This is important, I think. Brown's men tend to be vile and violent seducers who yield to lust and brutality in their sexual relations, with no more regard for an intact hymen than Arthur has for a closed door. In Brown's world, such behavior shows weakness and fault, masculine perhaps, but not manly. A wholly adult manliness would incorporate the feminine aspect of human nature as well. Achsa represents Arthur's possibility to do just that.

But Arthur appears to be unequipped to accept Achsa as his own wholeness, so his relationship to her is a series of distancing evasions. Arthur sees Achsa in her feminine aspect first as a woman of pleasure, another Mrs. Villars perhaps, who is dressed negligently and lounging in a brothel. She is shocked when the impetuous youth bounds in, but so is Mrs. Villars. At their next meeting, this time in the company of motherly Mrs. Wentworth, Achsa blushes at the recollection of their first meeting, and Arthur finds himself almost completely confounded: "Certain tremors which I had not been accustomed to feel, and which seemed to possess a mystical relation to the visitant [Mrs. Fielding], disabled me at once from taking my leave, or from performing any useful purpose by staying" (p. 363). Only later with Mrs. Watson does a similar discomfiture occur. Arthur records these, pretty clearly without understanding. But Brown understands, and so do we. Arthur needs another strategy for handling this woman, a strategy he develops after the visit to Baltimore:

Achsa Fielding's countenance bespoke, I thought, a mind worthy to be known and to be loved. The first moment I engaged her at-

tention, I told her so. I related the little story of my family, spread
out before her all my reasonings and determinations, my notions of
right and wrong, my fears and wishes. All this was done with sincerity and fervor, with gestures, actions and looks, in which I felt as
if my whole soul was visible. Her superior age, sedateness and
prudence, gave my deportment a filial freedom and affection, and I
was fond of calling her "*mamma*." [p. 397]

What "mamma" thought of that he does not say, but we can imagine. We
do know, however, what she thought about his next attempt to characterize Achsa as his sister. "A sister: [Eliza's] *elder* sister you should be.
That, when there is no other relation, includes them all. Fond sisters you
would be, and I the fond brother to you both" (p. 398). Achsa's momentary confusion disappears as she tries to focus his attention on reality, on
nature, by having him read Lacépède's description of a snake! Surely this
is one of Brown's best fictional ironies.

Arthur is teasing Achsa here and she may suspect it, but how can
anyone be sure with Arthur? It is doubtful that Arthur knows. But she
has her fill when Arthur produces Eliza's pleading love note. Arthur is
quite explicit about his brotherly love for Eliza and equally urgent in
asserting that what he seeks in a wife is the model, the picture, the coun-
terpart of Achsa herself. To this cloudy proffer of love Achsa responds by
agreeing to take Eliza as a sister. Arthur agrees to get her from the
Curlings immediately and does so. Surely Achsa is aware of her own
passion for Arthur at this point. Possibly Arthur knows that and is toying
with her emotions as he has done elsewhere, but the evidence for that
does not exist. Arthur seems unable to accept his own passion for her. He
can call it love and see her as a paragon but not envision her as the direct
object of his love. Why then does Achsa send for Eliza? Partly to test
Arthur's mettle, one must suppose, partly to see just how deep Arthur's
love for Eliza is, partly perhaps to demonstrate her own superior merits
by having herself and Eliza in direct and visible comparison. Achsa,
though smitten with her strange young man, is no novice about such
matters. Eight years a mother, she watched her father commit suicide in

recoil from financial ruin, watched her mother go violently mad, and witnessed her husband running off with her best friend even while Ascha was in childbirth a second time. Her long diligence in caring for her mother and her son, even for her runaway husband, has now come to a close. She wonders at the effect such prolonged suffering has had upon her:

> I have often reflected with surprise on the nature of my own mind. It is eight years since my father's violent death. How few of my hours since that period, have been blessed with serenity! How many nights and days, in hateful and lingering succession, have been bathed in tears and tormented with regrets! That I am still alive with so many causes of death, and with such a slow consuming malady, is surely to be wondered at. [p. 425]

Arthur will do more than wonder. What story of accumulated woes could be better designed to wrest commiseration from this young feeder upon misery? "None will be surprized," he remarks, "that to a woman thus unfortunate and thus deserving, my heart willingly rendered up all its sympathies; that as I partook of all her grief, I hailed, with equal delight, those omens of felicity which now, at length, seemed to play in her fancy" (p. 427).

Like Arthur, Achsa is now alone, cut off from her past, her husband executed in France at the end of 1793, her son away at school. Achsa needs ease; Arthur, a woman to serve. Yet he tortures her with his conviction that she is "the substitute of my lost mamma" until Stevens jollies and teases him into realizing that he not only loves Achsa as a woman, but she also loves him. The scene is very unusual in Brown's fiction—ironic, humorous, sarcastic. It is appropriate that the doctor diagnoses the case here (Mrs. Wentworth could have served the same purpose, as could young Eliza). For by making Arthur see the possibility of joining with this fascinating woman, Stevens completes the cure that was only partially effected in the first part. It is not enough that he see good, right, and duty, and act upon them; nor is it enough that he abandon concealment in his own behavior. Moreover, it certainly is not right that he violate the wishes and privacies of others in his determination to make them better. He must embody the sensibilities that anguish and guilt and pain and remorse alone teach, the complex of sensibilities that women primarily seem to represent in Brown's psychology.

We remember that Miss Carlton accused Arthur of having too abstract a view of things. We can see now how right she was and how her view applies to what I have called Arthur's strategies of evasion with Mrs. Fielding. We might say that in many ways Arthur has fallen in love with Achsa's tale. It is a love of ideas, of categories such as mother or sister, of abstractions to be served, not married. Arthur is moving to some consciousness of this on his own, as we see in his contrast between books and conversation. "Books are cold, jejune, vexatious in their sparingness of information at one time, and their impertinent loquacity at another. Besides, all they chuse to give, they give at once; they allow no questions; offer no further explanations, and bend not to the caprices of our curiosity. They talk to us behind a screen. Their tone is lifeless and monotonous. They charm not our attention by mute significances of gesture and looks. They spread no light upon their meaning by cadences and emphasis and pause" (p. 427). This curious little essay, Baconian in its trenchancy, argues what Stevens realized at the beginning of the second part, namely, that the story by itself is dead and unconvincing, whereas the personal presence of the teller generates conviction and confidence. That Arthur can voice the concept without appreciating its full application to himself is a common enough human failing. So is the shock with which Arthur responds to Stevens's prescription. Forget your idolatries, he says. Here is a living woman in front of you. She loves you; join with her.

This is easier to say than to do, of course, as Stevens knows and Arthur discovers. The effect of Stevens's curative judgment is to awaken in Arthur more fears and personal uncertainties than we can easily believe him to have, certainly more than he has exhibited throughout these two volumes. In the excellent dream sequence where Fielding returns to claim his wife and stabs Arthur in the heart, Arthur finally encounters a door that will not open at his will. Fled is the boldness that has led him through others' houses and souls. In its place is a sense of infamy and guilt. Arthur feels unworthy, guilty of wanting what he does not deserve.

He is also jealous, first of Fielding, then of young Stedman; he is thrown into all-night distresses and melancholia during which he wanders "embarrassed and obscure paths" and weeps in the forests for reasons he cannot fathom. In short, Arthur the man of reason has learned to play Romeo; if Arthur's righteousness is not precisely thrown upon the thorns of life, it is nonetheless substantially and effectively humbled. When Achsa accepts him and forgives him, he can suffer that acceptance gently and take the woman in place of her story; he can indeed at last be himself instead of his stories. Arthur has found that to be a whole man requires more than the courage to resist one's fears and the intimidations of others, that it means more than clumsy beneficence and dutiful aggression, that it demands surrender, vulnerability, yielding, gentleness. Arthur is now ready to be a father himself.

In coming to this direct confrontation with life, Arthur has learned both the limitations of sincerity and the need not for deception but for a gentle construction of experience. Achsa is terrified by the omens signaled in Arthur's dream. Arthur's gentle reasonings with her aim to reassure and to console. How different is this man from the youngster who only a couple of months before broke the news to Mrs. Watson of her husband's death! Having faced living directly, Arthur also knows the triviality of the abstractions by which he formerly lived. Stories and writing no longer have the sustaining force they have been invested with earlier in this narrative. Now he can say, "I merely write to allay these tumults which our necessary separation produces; to aid me in calling up a little patience, till the time arrives, when our persons, like our minds, shall be united forever" (p. 445). Stories, Brown seems to have discovered in writing this book, do not ultimately matter, and Arthur is not the only one who concludes with a Prospero-like abjuration of his art in the very last words:

> But why am I indulging this pen-prattle? The hour she fixed for my return to her is come, and now take thyself away, quill. Lie there, snug in thy leathern case, till I call for thee, and that will not be very soon. I believe I will abjure thy company till all is settled

with my love. Yes: I *will* abjure thee, so let *this* be thy last office, till Mervyn has been made the happiest of men. [p. 446]

Arthur may abandon his pen at this point but we cannot. For Brown has explicitly tied at least the first part of this story to a particular literary theory, which obliges us to ask whether and to what extent our reading of the story corresponds to Brown's stated intentions. The critical problem is complicated by the fact that Brown presents the theory as the invention of a fictitious writer, Walstein of Jena, and distances the theory even further from himself by pretending that the story of Walstein and his school is a translation from the German of Krants of Gotha. So, to be precise, we have for Brown's intentions an anonymous publication, allegedly translated from a fictitious original, about a cogent but equally fictitious literary theory, represented by a précis of a nonexistent book. But that book exactly parallels *Arthur Mervyn* and thus brings the cycle of fictions back to reality. I have no difficulty whatsoever in taking "Walstein's School of History" as a reliable index to Brown's concept of the function of fiction, at least at the point when he wrote it.

For Walstein the purpose of learning is the promotion of human happiness. His purpose is to write history so that others will learn from the great champions of intellectual vigor what the possibilities of noble and heroic behavior are. Moral heroes are everywhere the same, no matter what the scope of their actions, whether they involve the fate of kingdoms or the adventures of country boys in the city. Walstein has chosen to write of two historical personages whose lives and actions and principles are universally acclaimed—Cicero and the Marquis of Pombal. Cicero needs no further identification, but in our time the Marquis of Pombal does. In the eighteenth century, Pombal, the minister of Portugal under Joseph I, was acclaimed as a wise political philosopher who managed to improve the public welfare of his country even while serving a monarchy that he also strengthened. Pombal died in 1782, full of years and international acclaim. What differentiates Walstein's histories of these men from other histories is his writing of the story from their point of view. He has them tell their own stories and in the process permits us to penetrate beyond their actions to their motives, their passions and private understandings, the very roots of the intellectual vigor that most fully illustrates their virtue even when they fail. In short, Walstein writes fictional memoirs of actual persons, achieving models of virtuous action by a means that would be otherwise unattainable. It is a risky approach, as Brown acknowledges in an article appearing in *The Monthly Magazine* (September 1799):

> To assume the person of Cicero, as the narrator of his own transactions, was certainly an hazardous undertaking. Frequent errors and lapses, violations of probability, and incongruities in the style and conduct of this imaginary history with genuine productions of Cicero, might be reasonably expected, but these are not found. The more conversant we are with the authentic monuments, the more is our admiration at the felicity of this imposture enhanced.
>
> The conspiracy of Cataline is here related with abundance of circumstances not to be found in Sallust. The difference, however, is of that kind which result from a deeper insight into human nature, a more accurate acquaintance with the facts, more correctness of arrangement, and a deeper concern in the progress and issue of the story. What is false, is so admirable in itself, so conformable to Roman modes and sentiments, so self-consistent, that one is almost prompted to accept it as the gift of inspiration. [pp. 337–38]

Walstein is, in brief, a master of fictitious history and fictitious biography. His followers are so caught up in his technique that their efforts can hardly be separated from his: "The same minute explication of motives, the same indissoluble and well-woven tissue of causes and effects, the same unity and coherence of design, the same power of engrossing the attention, and the same felicity, purity, and compactness of style, are conspicuous in all" (p. 335). Of these features, the one supreme mark of Walstein's "school" is its "minute explication of motives," which only the teller can know.

But Walstein himself takes us only partway toward *Arthur Mervyn*. It is his eldest disciple who makes the crucial move. If semifictitious narratives are good, how much better will totally fictitious memoirs be as models of human behavior, when not limited by the particulars of historical circumstance? Moreover, few people are in the position of historical giants such as Cicero and Pombal and few of us stand in relations of political authority to each other. Nonetheless, reasons Engel, we all do stand in relation to each other, and surely in such relations lie worthy examples of justice and virtue. The writer who concentrates on those relationships as most men experience them will find ample ranges of similitude by which to provide wholesome moral lessons for the benefit of others. Engel retains, therefore, Walstein's notion of fiction as a moral instrument, and presumably his fictions will be first-person narrations designed to move past external actions into an exploration of motives. But without relationships of political authority, what relationships will most reveal models for virtue? About this Engel has clear ideas:

> An extensive source of these relations, is property. No topic can engage the attention of man more momentous than this. Opinions, relative to property, are the immediate source of nearly all the happiness and misery that exist among mankind. If men were guided by justice in the acquisition and disbursement, the brood of private and public evils would be extinguished. . . .
>
> Next to property, the most extensive source of our relations is sex. On the circumstances which produce, and the principles which regulate the union between the sexes, happiness greatly depends. The conduct to be pursued by a virtuous man in those situations which arise from sex, it was thought useful to display. [pp. 408, 409]

This being so, Engel argues that every man has the obligation to find a way of life, a livelihood, that will permit him to blend property and sex in the most useful way. "We are bound to chuse that species of industry which combines most profit to ourselves with the least injury to others; to select that instrument which, by most speedily supplying our necessities, leaves us at most leisure to act from the impulse of benevolence" (p. 409). The two most suitable professions are law and medicine.

Engel's "Olivo Ronsica" is the embodiment of this theory, and because it is simply a summary of *Arthur Mervyn*, I believe we have to take seriously Brown's judgments that his novel, at least through the first part, is based on Engel's principles. But if we do take these seriously, we have to surrender certain pleasing ironies in our reading of the story. Arthur's good fortune is not the result of connivance or self-seeking but that of basic honesty, a sense of justice, persistence in rectifying others' wrongs, and lots of good luck. In the first part, then, Brown's basic concern is with the distribution of property, especially its negative aspects. Property is falsely distributed through greed, deceit, robbery, and forgery; moreover, it is distributed in so complicated a way that it will take Arthur most of the second part to set things to rights. But Brown contends in "Walstein's School" that Arthur is just exactly what he claims to be—so upright that no one believes him but the man of medicine, the married whole man whose profession has given him the leisure at least to trust in virtue. When we readers yield to disbelief in Arthur and characterize him as a subtle huckster, the self-serving creature I described at the outset of this chapter, we have put ourselves in the position of Mrs. Wentworth, Wortley, Mrs. Althorpe, and Mrs. Maurice. In our distrust we betray our own sickness.

Like them, of course, we have good reason. Brown has complicated his point very effectively by making Arthur such a naïf. He is not faultless, although he behaves as if he were. Welbeck turns Arthur's own virtue against him by swearing him to secrecy, and Arthur is so ignorant that his judgments of others are steadily wrong. Even when he overcomes his impulse to concealment he goes overboard in the other direction, and in both cases he manufactures reasons to account for his obnoxiousness. So Brown gives us plenty of reason to suspect Arthur but through Stevens tells us to stick with him and not finally condemn him. Moreover, the second part is designed to modify Arthur's abstract commitments by developing his sexual awareness. In his choice of profession and marriage partner Arthur both enacts Engel's principles and grows toward normalcy. By the end, Arthur may still be too much the Prince of Abyssinia for modern cynicism, but he is learning. In fact, Arthur Mervyn is the only major character in Brown's fiction to be changed by his experience, to understand even partially what his adventures mean. His readers should understand even more, but whether we do or not, whether we can abide Arthur any better at the end than we could earlier, whether the experience of reading this book has made us healthier, we should now be able to appreciate somewhat better how Brown could believe in Arthur as a moral model without sharing Arthur's naiveté.

Jane and Clara and Steve

When inspiration—or whatever it was that produced the four major romances—deserted Brown, he discarded it like a splat of wet clay. The major narrative interest of each of the stories we have examined so far lies decidedly in a contrast between the stories one lives by and the facts of experience. Perhaps a better distinction is that between the stories one tells and the more satisfactory story one lives. Clara Wieland, we saw, was a character in search of a story she does not find. Huntly tells a tale he cannot himself fully penetrate or understand. Sophia relates a story that is not the real story at all. And Arthur endures so many stories that he can finally assert his reality only by abjuring stories altogether. If we infer that Charles Brockden Brown is thus a storyteller without much faith in stories, can we be very wrong? Yet the fact that we persist in telling our stories interests Brown very deeply, as does especially the way in which the disparity between satisfactory and unsatisfactory stories operates. I want to say this again, because it is so easy to pass it by without appreciating its importance. Brown's major aesthetic concern is with the breakdown of forms, with that point where two or more structures intersect, with that crack where two planes of experience or understanding collide. Each of these books breaks (nearer the end than not) and each major break is our clue to the significance of the book. Hence it is only when Clara tries to pass herself off as another threatened heroine

J ANE AND CLARA AND STEVE 129

that we sense how much her character in the preceding part of *Wieland* has been a forced and unsatisfactory creation. When Sophia emerges in *Ormond*, we learn the triumph that has lurked gloatingly behind all of Constantia's misadventures. When Edgar pauses to celebrate Queen Mab, we see the numb blindness from which he is operating, the blindness that will terminate the story in the exchange of letters with Sarsefield. In Arthur's case, we watch him struggle through the tales until he not only forces their coalescence into one sweeping view (his own) but also puts his pen to rest with imperious confidence. These changes, these breakdowns of prevailing structures, do not so much clarify the stories as they open to view the complexities and ambiguities playing beneath the obvious surfaces and conventions.

Such complexity and ambiguity claim our interest and respect. Their presence, even when we perceive it dimly, is why we remember these books, why we often enjoy them despite their many failings. When complexity and uncertainty exist without a contrasting plane, when the surface is all there is, no matter how complicated, the results are only trivial and silly. A chief case is *Clara Howard: or, the Enthusiasm of Love*,[1] an especially pointed case because it is a reworking of the *Edgar Huntly* material, a recounting of only one strand in that story, with bathetic effects. Formally the book signals its own defeat; that is, it fails to establish any central point of view as the other romances do and therefore provides no coherent structure on which to work a collapse or breakdown. It is not a memoir, but a packet of thirty-three letters exchanged between Philip Stanley (initially named Edward Hartley), Mary Wilmot, and Clara. The book progresses as if we had each of the separate stories about Arthur presented without the unifying sensibility of Stevens to react to them. It is all breakdown; the only things left to collapse are the characters and our interest. And they do.

The central situation is this. Philip has fallen in love with Clara, but only after having promised to wed Mary, whom he does not love but to whom he now feels duty bound. Clara will not have him until he does right by Mary. Mary will not have him because she knows he does not love her. Philip stands to lose all around. Eventually the predicament is resolved when the condition that created Philip's obligation (Mary's poverty) is relieved and when her affections turn to another man. She helps Clara calm her own scrupulous conscience, and between them they prevail upon a sick and sullen Philip to say he is sorry for even thinking of running away from the whole mess and going to California. It is a story with no risks, no heroism, almost no action. No one deceives anyone else. Everyone is entirely honorable, even punctilious. No one has a sense of humor and there is hardly a motive worthy of the name in the entire story.

Some complications do occur, almost all of which are revealed in the longest letter (no. 13, pp. 314–51), in which Philip writes to an otherwise unidentified friend named Francis Harris and explains how he got into this predicament. Here the *Edgar Huntly* material is most obvious. Philip and his sisters live with his uncle in a small village. There he meets Mary Wilmot and her brother, who ekes out a meager income as a schoolteacher. When the brother dies, Mary and Philip are amazed to find $5,000 in his bank account. She has meanwhile fallen in love with Philip, and he, rather vaguely, finds himself proposing to her (the prospect of financial independence is not entirely outside Philip's consciousness). They decide to wait six months to make sure Philip's offer of marriage is sincere, and he finds a comfortable place for her to say in Abingdon. Before that time has arrived, a stranger named Morton presents himself to Philip and explains how some years earlier he had sent a note for 5,000 dollars to his friend Wilmot to hold for him. Like Edgar, Philip concludes the money must be Morton's and informs Mary that this seals their misfortune, making marriage impossible. Moreover, like Edgar, Philip bears a strong responsibility, for the uncle with whom Philip and his sisters live is aged, and his son bears no love for the orphans.

In addition to these resemblances, yet another emerges. Philip has long been the protégé of a Briton exiled in America, a generous, worldly man named Howard, who has treated Philip like a son. Howard returns to England, just as Sarsefield did, to marry a woman he has loved for eighteen years. She, Clara Lisle, had married Howard's cousin but through his death is now free to join with Howard. They return to make their life in America, and Howard is now sufficiently moneyed to offer Philip a true sonship through marriage with their daughter Clara. Philip quickly comes to love both the mother and the daughter, delighting in the fortune that whipsawed him from weal to woe and now back to weal again. Philip's relish for his new situation is spiced by the feelings of undeserving peasantry that, like Clithero, he has been unable to shake. Charmed by this new situation, Philip neglects to mention his obligation to Mary, but when Howard calls him to come to New York, he uses the occasion to visit Mary. But he finds that she has fled, presumably in the company of Sedley, an honorable young man who loved her as Philip did not. In New York he learns that Morton has never received the money that presumably belongs to him. When he finally relates this entire story to Clara, she concludes that his first duty is to Mary and sends him forth to carry that duty out.

These story strands so match the domestic episodes in *Edgar Huntly* that one cannot hurry past the connection. But what is the connection? The two most obvious explanations seem quite opposed. First, this is a preliminary sketch for the later, more truly complex *Edgar Huntly*— perhaps a proto-*Sky-Walk*, the original version of *Edgar Huntly*. The second possibility is that Brown still felt the power of the Weymouth incident after *Edgar Huntly* and wanted to play with another resolution, so he retold the story, eliminating the entire savagery theme. Evidence being so scanty, only speculation can induce a decision between these, but I find it so much harder to believe Brown could have come to the sophisticated formal and thematic accomplishments of the major romances first and then backed off to this. Instead I am strongly inclined to believe *Clara Howard* was a kind of pilot study mainly written before the major works we have reviewed. In either event, however, Brown made a mistake in publishing the work.

It strikes me, however, that *Clara Howard* marks the beginning of several ideas later developed in the other fictions rather than derived from them. Thus Philip, like Arthur, lets himself into doors without announcing himself: "I approached my friend's door, and lifted the latch without giving any signal of my approach" (no. 2, p. 292). His later reasonings with Clara about a passionless marriage with Mary anticipate

Ormond's arguments with Constantia when she pleads for Helena Cleves (no. 24, p. 378). But the most telling display of the preliminary nature of this material is Philip's impulse to get away by plunging into the Louisiana Territory (no. 26, p. 382): "I at this moment anticipate the dawn of comfort from the scenes of the wilderness and of savage life"—an impulse that Philip himself recognizes to be essentially a juvenile fantasy. Mary is perturbed and rather astonished by this evidence of the enthusiasms to which love has driven Philip: "I cannot comprehend his intimations of a journey to the wilderness; of imbruting his faculties; of exposing his humanity, his life, to hazard" (no. 28, p. 402). This is in response to Philip's threats to hurt himself if Mary will not accept his proposal: "If you refuse this gift, I shall instantly vanish from society. I shall undertake a journey in which my life will be exposed to numberless perils. If I pass them in safety, I shall be dead to all the offices and pleasures of civilized existence. I shall hasten to imbrute all my faculties. I shall make myself akin to savages and tigers, and forget that I once was a man" (no. 28, p. 398). Philip is no savage or tiger, however, but a very domesticated pussycat. He is no Edgar Huntly either; that Brown could have created this insipidity after exploring the nightmare wilderness is nearly inconceivable.

In 1811 William Dunlap was trying desperately to dry out his drunkard friend, the actor George Frederick Cooke. Dunlap's treatment required lots of sleep, a bland diet, and the reading of *Clara Howard* and *Jane Talbot*.[2] The cure did not take. If Cooke's diet was as bland as *Clara Howard*, one can see why. But in *Jane Talbot* the problem is different. There is scarcely an idea worthy of the name in the misfortunes of Clara and Philip, but in *Jane Talbot* there is an ethical, religious, and psychological concept of considerable potential.[3] Here the failure is primarily formal, and that in two senses. First, we have here nearly double the number of letters (seventy) and double the number of correspondents; second, the correlation between ideas or principles and characters is entirely different from those correlations in the major romances. I will return to this problem, but first let me describe the story.

Jane Talbot writes to her lover Henry Colden, who is absent attending a dying friend. She tells him of her early life, especially about the death of her mother and being sent to be raised by a surrogate mother, Mrs. Fielder, at the age of five. Jane's mean, impetuous, and greedy brother Frank worsens as he grows older, wasting his father's fortune and bringing him eventually to ruin through unwise business speculation. This wastrel brother has no compunction about borrowing half his sister's legacy, which increases her dependency upon Mrs. Fielder and also demonstrates her own weakness in the face of strong personalities and her sense of obligation to please those close to her. During the protracted destruction of her father, Jane meets and marries Talbot. While Talbot is absent in Europe, she meets Henry Colden. Her attachment deepens and eventually turns to love after the death of Talbot. Mrs. Fielder, however, strongly disapproves of Colden and, when she gets wind of their possible marriage, threatens very seriously to disown Jane, refusing either to see her or to receive her letters.

Jane begs not to be abandoned. "What heinous offense has he committed, that makes him unworthy of my regard?" she begs of her mother. Mrs. Fielder relents, at least so far as to reveal that at best Jane's seeing Henry while she was married was indiscreet and that there is good reason to believe that Henry seduced Jane during her marriage. Talbot himself— a good burgher in his forties, an unintellectual, not particularly attractive, and philosophically unspeculative man—knew all before his death, having come upon a letter from Jane to Henry that indicated they spent a night together during one of Talbot's excursions. What alarms Mrs. Fielder is partly Jane's susceptibility to the romantic and poetic alternative of Henry and partly her conviction that Colden is a dissolute Godwinian, a freethinking hypocrite who will absolutely corrupt Jane by "counterfeiting a moral and pious strain" (no. 15, p. 71).

Jane is moved by concern for her mother, even to the extent of agreeing to give up Henry. Mrs. Fielder attempts to pay him to leave town, but he refuses very politely. He urges that Jane show all their correspondence to Mrs. Fielder, and is so straightforward and constant that Jane cannot but commend his excellence. Yet, wanting a force and passion from him that he does not show, she detects a kind of coldness in his response. Confused, she reverses herself again, claiming that she can never give up Henry. The incriminating letter that Talbot had given to Mrs. Fielder is partly forged, but how it came to be so is inexpressibly mysterious. Despite his coldness, his holding back too much, Henry is severely depressed by these events. He is attending the deathbed of his friend Thomson, the very young man who revealed Henry's outrageous speculations about the irrelevancy of vows and such conventions as marriage to Mrs. Fielder, out of Christian concern for Henry's soul. If they do marry in six weeks, as they intend, and if Mrs. Fielder turns Jane out, how will they manage? They will not even be able to afford to live together.

Henry's discouragement produces two fine and strong letters from Jane, cheery and loving. She knows of a way to manage to live contentedly and virtuously, she argues in one. In the other she wonders how she and her mother can see the same person so differently, remarking on the irony that it has been Henry's freely expressed doubts about religious principles that wrought in her a renewal of her own Christian faith. "In no respect," she assures him, "has your company made me a worse— in every respect it has made me a better—woman" (no. 34, p. 136). Nonetheless, in a fortnight she calls off their engagement having learned from Mrs. Fielder that her proposed marriage has driven Henry from his father's love and protection also. She will not hurt him so. Painfully he accepts her decision and bids her "farewell—*forever*" (no. 39, p. 150). Mrs. Fielder renews her offer of money, but he returns it to her, admitting to having done no wrong. With his brother-in-law James Montford he arranges to make a voyage to the Northwest and goes to Philadelphia to await the departure of the ship.

But Henry's curiosity will not let slip the mystery of the incriminating letter. By chance and the discovery of some misplaced letters, he learns that Polly Jessup, an aging coquette and regular visitor to the Talbot's, had been desperately in love with Talbot before Jane married him, despite Talbot's scornful rejection of her. Artfully and persistently he browbeats Jessup into confessing that it was indeed she who forged the letter and got it into Talbot's hands. She sends him a full and damning written confession. Meanwhile Jane's changeableness continues; she knows he is in Philadelphia and urges their elopement. Henry is irresolute. But he gets Polly Jessup's letter to Mrs. Fielder; she calls on Jessup to confirm the letter, but Jessup airily denies all. Henry has shortsightedly surrendered the only evidence, the only club he held over Jessup, and he sees his case is now hopeless. He had already become conscious that the more he urged his innocence, the more it would look as if he were primarily after Jane's marriage portion (no. 43). Mrs. Fielder suspects that he is indeed after Jane's fortune and makes this perfectly explicit in their uncomfortable interview. The events plunge him into suicidal despondency, from which he is in some sense relieved by a chance encounter with Harriet, sister of the now dead Thomson. She returns to him the damaging letters he had written his friend and also strongly advises him to overcome his religious and moral doubts. Any certainty, she says, is better than perpetual doubt, and Henry's best course will be to accept things as they are with Jane Talbot and to amend his moral principles. It is now ten days prior to the start of his voyage. During that period an undated letter is sent from Jane to Henry (we do not know if he received it), urging him to let her know whether he and his father have been reconciled.

The remaining twenty letters are primarily between Jane and Henry's sister, Mary Montford. A year passes as Henry takes a slow boat to China. Two or three more years pass. Jane is courted by an old friend, Cartwright, but cannot promise more than "a brotherly affection." Henry, meanwhile, goes literally around the world. He is overtaken by pirates, abandoned on a Japanese island, lives for a time in Japan, makes his way to Germany, and eventually returns to America, just as Jane is about to expire from lost wits and lost hope. He returns a changed man, quite converted to Jane's religious principles, although a carriage accident has him laid up in New Haven. The final letter is from Jane to Henry: she is coming to join him. Their marriage will be immediate. Mrs. Fielder has died, but not before being apprised of the truth of Henry's character by Polly Jessup's deathbed confession. Love is now "authorized."

No one can be more aware than he who tries to do it of how impossible it is to make a précis of an epistolary romance. Much of the original effect depends upon the manner and the order in which information is revealed. Letters miscarry or pass each other in the night. Information is necessarily disordered and out of sequence. Emotions and motives among the correspondents are constantly unsynchronized. What is known to one character is not known, or not known at the right time, to others very involved in the action. Thus Jane can write to Mrs. Fielder a letter of complete acquiescence. Mrs. Fielder immediately leaves New York for Philadelphia to join her errant daughter. But Jane changes her mind and sends another letter indicating so. Mrs. Fielder, of course, is by now on the road and cannot receive the second letter. Letters are contained within letters and thereby given a context that "explains" them one way while unexplaining them another. Brown is quite conscious of his method of storytelling here but exacerbates its problems by misdating and misnumbering several of the letters. The last twenty letters also fail to communicate the long duration of time between 1797, when Jane and Henry first met, until 1801, the reader's present, when they come together again. In addition, it more likely results in confusion rather than the kind of complexity Brown attained in the memoir form. Without a central and sustained narrative point of view, it appears that Brown could not work the kind of artistic magic he succeeded with in the major romances. There are too many letters, too many voices; no one is in charge.

Yet one has to admit that this is good material for a major romance; its failure does not reside entirely in the structural problem of the letter form. All the right elements are here—the foster parent, the purposeful intertwining of material and moral problems, the epistemological uncertainties, the stresses that affect decision and action. There are also the apparently self-conscious parallels between characters, the traditional doublings, that made the other stories so insightful. Jane and her brother Frank set up one possibility. Thomson and his sister Harriet constitute another. The mutual disowning of the children by Mrs. Fielder and the elder Colden is one more. The major romances invite us to entertain the possibility that Jane and Henry are soul twins, sharing enough of each other to make their eventual union mystically right if not entirely psychologically so. Jane's moral stability is complicated by her social instability; Colden's steadfastness throughout ought to be in contradiction to his unsound moral principles. But by the time of *Jane Talbot* Brown seems to have lost his artistic energy to entertain real ambiguity, and having lost that, he loses all.

Instead he gives us a heroine who never finally acts from the principles she supposedly espouses. From the outset Jane is a weak person. Her will is the plaything of the strong and demanding persons she is closest to— her brother Frank, her "mother," even Henry. Her husband is just that— a "husband," a status situation—as if Constantia had accepted Balfour. But Constantia refused on principle, a principle that Brown can no longer muster for simple Jane. Jane has some real problems: her love for Henry is apparently going to come into conflict with her Christian marriage vows—how could it not? But Jane's flightiness is never really put to a test. Talbot is conveniently removed, so Brown does not have to tangle with the problems of romance in conflict with duty. Even Jane's main problem, the conflict between her duty and love for Mrs. Fielder and her passion for Henry (which is also spiritual and intellectual), also goes unresolved. Her vacillations are resolved only by Henry's long absence and, finally, by Mrs. Fielder's removal from the scene. In short, her principles have nothing to do with right action and even less to do with her good fortune at the end. One looks for Brown's ordinary perception that this is so, but it nowhere appears.

Likewise with Henry. If his morals need repair, that fact is hardly visible in his behavior. He treats everyone fairly, understands Mrs. Fielder's concern to protect Jane's reputation, and is not upset by Jane's little jealousies. He forgives Thomson's having communicated Henry's radical moral statements to Mrs. Fielder, even though they were privately expressed, because he knows Thomson acted out of virtuous concern for his spiritual condition. He spends weeks at the dying Thomson's bedside. He experiences no outbursts of rage or bliss. He patiently endures misunderstanding and abuse and hardship. He does not complain. He does not assign blame to others and he tends to keep some problems, such as his unhappy relationship with his father, to himself. He is diligent in seeking out truth and willing to undergo physical danger and great risk. Where is his fault? Even the indiscretion that has brought Mrs. Fielder's ill judgment upon him is more Jane's fault than his. No, he behaves as a staunch and responsible young man for all his alleged romantic speculations. Perhaps the most one can say is that his radicalism offers too little solace under stress, and so he is inclined to melancholy as events seem to conspire against his happiness. If one had to choose between Jane's flibbertigibbet morality and Henry's honest questioning, the nod would have to go to Henry.

Jane blames him for holding back, for a kind of defensiveness and coldness in his relationships, especially with her. Perhaps her perception is right. But when he forgets to hold back, we see what happens— he enthusiastically talks a stormy night away with Mrs. Talbot, only to give cause for scandal, to seriously damage Jane's relationship with her mother, to provide an occasion for the forgery of the incriminating letter. He opens himself unguardedly to Thomson in expressing his radical view of things and Thomson, well-intentioned though he is, spills the beans to Mrs. Fielder. Having secured Polly Jessup's confession, he returns to her the only real evidence he has to insure her sticking to her story. With the damaging evidence back in her hands, she promptly denies the story altogether, which reconfirms Mrs. Fielder's judgment that Henry is primarily after Jane's marriage portion. No, all the evidence clearly shows that to be entirely open is to light the bomb in your own pocket. But restraint comes at a price as well.

Thomson, for example, is so sure that Henry's spirit is lost to atheism that even until his death the subject of Henry's spiritual condition excites him dangerously. To keep from agitating his dying friend, Henry avoids discussion of religious and moral questions, implying that Thomson has at least overread the case and has taken Henry's speculations as evidence of confirmed atheism when they were only skeptical musings, serious but not final. It almost seems that Henry has been trying on extreme positions to see if they might fit. The implication, of course, is that Henry's mode of skeptical speculation is as efficacious for him as it has been for Jane and that a strong Christian conviction underlies even his most extreme musings. By sparing Thomson religious discussion, Henry has also denied him the comfort of knowing that Henry may not be irretrievably lost.

This may be less important than the fact that, by committing his intellectual jousts with Thomson to letters, he has opened himself to criticism from a bluenose like Mrs. Fielder or Talbot himself, people who confuse social respectability with personal righteousness. Mrs. Fielder relates the incident of her discovery of Henry's scandalous opinions in a letter to Jane. She writes:

> Thomson is an excellent young man: he loves Colden much, and describes the progress of his friend's opinions with every mark of regret. He even showed me letters that had passed between them, and in which every horrid and immoral tenet was defended by one and denied by the other. These letters showed Colden as the advocate of suicide; a scoffer at promises; the despiser of revelation, of Providence and a future state; an opponent of marriage, and as one who denied (shocking!) that any thing but mere habit and positive law stood in the way of marriage, nay, of intercourse without marriage, between brother and sister, parent and child! [no. 15, p. 70]

Henry's commitment to Godwin's *Political Justice* is held to be both the model and the source of Henry's pernicious opinions:

> A most fascinating book fell at length into his hands, which changed, in a moment, the whole course of his ideas. What he had before regarded with reluctance and terror, this book taught him to admire and love. The writer has the art of the grand deceiver; the fatal art of arraying the worst poison under the name and appearance of wholesome food; of disguising all that is impious; or blasphemous, or licentious, under the guise and sanctions of virtue. [no. 15, pp. 70–71]

No wonder Mrs. Fielder was shocked. But she is not alone in misreading Henry's zealous advocacies.

Thomson's sister Harriet watched with Henry during the protracted death of her brother. She saw Henry's kindness and restraint. But she has also read Henry's letters to Thomson. Instead of concluding like Mrs.

Fielder that they evidence his irretrievable turpitude, Harriet reads them as the record of a persistent doubter, erring perhaps herself by taking the written record as evidence of a permanent state. But her conclusion produces at least a more generous view of Henry's spiritual condition than Mrs. Fielder can imagine. She sees him as one in search of a certainty he has not yet attained; and Henry takes some comfort in the rather odd advice that any certainty is better than doubting. So there is considerable evidence that Henry is not the spiritual scoundrel he has been taken to be, that indeed his principles and Jane's have been similar all along, and that his ultimate approval is less a conversion to Jane's religious principles than an abandonment of a fruitless skepticism that drives him around the world without teaching him anything. He does not change his principles, he accepts them. By ceasing to doubt, he enables himself to join Jane in the union they both desire. Another view of the matter, however, is simply that three years of mutiny and mayhem have beaten the spunk out of him. He returns a happily beaten man, able to accept the changeable Jane as at least preferable to servitude in Japan.

Now this is potentially the stuff of good fiction, but somehow it eludes Brown. One reason is, of course, the complication of the epistolary form. The major lack, however, is the element that proved so fruitful in the major fictions, namely, characters who are somehow split in themselves and whose doubts truly express aspects of their inner nature that training and circumstance have made improper to own, let alone make visible. Brown makes rather rudimentary gestures in that direction, but they never develop. Jane, for example, is conscious that she is of two minds regarding Henry. As she understands him, he is disturbingly selfless, whereas she is disturbingly self-concerned (nos. 24 and 25, pp. 92–94). In both views she is acknowledging a split in character, an essential dichotomy between private motive and public behavior—not merely difference, but opposition. "I am very often on the brink of hating myself," she wails, while complaining in the same letter that Henry does not seek his own self-interest with sufficient passion. Henry's response almost willfully evades Jane's point. He practically confesses to Jane's accusation, pointing out at length the universal ambiguity of appearances and justifying her mother's attitudes given her information and her point of view (no. 27).

In a later letter to his brother-in-law (no. 40), Henry implies an ability to see himself from a distance, possessing a split view of things:

> I have sometimes given myself credit for impartiality in judging others. Indeed, I am inclined to think myself no blind or perverse judge even of my own actions. Hence, indeed, the greater part of my unhappiness. If my conduct had always conformed, instead of being adverse, to my principles, I should have moved on tranquilly and self-satisfied, at least; but, in truth, the being that goes by my name was never more thoroughly contemned by another than by myself,—but this is falling into the old strain,—irksome, tiresome, and useless to you as to me. [p. 152]

He expresses the same view, however, when he contemplates confronting Polly Jessup with the forgery: "Let me sever myself *from* myself, and judge impartially" (p. 167). Something like this is also asserted in an earlier letter to Jane, in an image anticipatory of William James's famous opening to *Pragmatism*—the man circling a squirrel that simultaneously circles a tree:

> One of my faults, thou sayest, is a propensity to reason. Not satisfied with looking at that side of the post that chances to be near me, I move round and round it, and pause and scrutinize till those whose ill fate it is to wait upon my motions are out of patience with me.
>
> Every one has ways of his own. A transient glance at the post satisfies the mob of passengers. 'Tis my choice to stand a while and gaze.
>
> The only post, indeed, which I closely examine, is myself, because my station is most convenient for inspecting *that*. Yet, though I have a fuller view of myself than any other can have of me, my imperfect *sight*—that is, my erring judgment—is continually blundering. [no. 25, p. 137]

But even here, despite the implications of doubleness, we see that Henry
is really talking about point of view, the slippery vantage from which one
perceives, not about the fractured nature of the perceiver.

Again, as with *Clara Howard*, there are hints of the source of power
and fascination that marks the major romances, but no realization. Without such realization, the story remains extraordinarily banal, despite the
essentially good ideas with which it works. Both stories have a primitive
quality about them.

I suggested that *Clara Howard* may well have been written before
Edgar Huntly and will speculate further that *Edgar Huntly* is probably
the stunning marriage of Brown's missing *Sky-Walk* with *Clara Howard*.
Speculation of such sort is happily easy in the absence of hard fact to the
contrary. It also gains some plausibility from Brown's obvious canni-
balizing tendency. Thus, although Dunlap testifies everywhere to Brown's
haste and others support that impression of compulsive hurry, it is also
true that story elements sometimes tumbled about in his consciousness
for years before they found what he took to be a satisfactory form. Priority in time among these stories is thus almost impossible to sort out.
The order of conception and composition and publication is impossible
to establish with certainty, despite the partial hard evidence offered by
Dunlap's *Diary*. But priority in time is less interesting than the priority in
sophistication of insight and workmanship. In that sense, *Clara Howard*
stands at the very bottom, with *Jane Talbot* a mere half step higher. The
fact that they were the last published does not affect this view. Their failure as fictions resides partly in their epistolary form but mainly in their
psychological obtuseness. They are more easily comprehended as incomplete steps toward the realization of the major fictions than as later
fallings off. Although it is possible, therefore, to see Brown's ultimate
rejection of fiction in Henry Colden's worn-out return to Jane Talbot and
in his complete repudiation of youthful deviations from right Christian
principle (deviations so like those expressed in *Alcuin*), it may be more to
the point to see Brown's artistic career ending when Arthur Mervyn shut
up his pen to marry Achsa Fielding. When he turned his back on the mul-
tistoried world of man's inner guilts and chaos, Brown in effect repudi-

ated his art. Both *Clara Howard* and *Jane Talbot* resemble those wavelets that beat against a seawall after the main wave has shot its strength.

Before he surrendered his pen, however, Brown had launched two other stories, both published in the first two volumes of *The Monthly Magazine* in 1799 and 1800. Warner Berthoff has praised the short story, "A Lesson on Concealment," for its strength and subtlety in terms very similar to my claims for the major romances. Because of its brevity, I will not discuss that story. But Berthoff sees the other work, *Memoirs of Stephen Calvert*, as an instance of Brown riding his unruly imagination headlong into insoluble confusion, of writing himself into corners from which no escape is possible.[4] But, let's see. I am inclined to believe that only its incompleteness places it among Brown's losers and that it is a work of great importance in appraising Brown's art and laying to rest a number of critical commonplaces about Brown. But first to the story.

Stephen Calvert is a continuous memoir unbroken into chapters or other formal divisions.[5] It contains only two embedded stories: one the story of past experiences told to Stephen by another character, the other a series of three letters in the very last episode that we are permitted to view just as our title character does. These letters are all by the same person and thereby escape the formal difficulties of epistolary exchange that mar the other stories we have looked at in this chapter. The only formal breaks are the eight installments in the magazine, where there is a kind of episodic integrity but where we cannot be sure Brown would have made chapter divisions. I pause over this because, purposeful or not, *Stephen Calvert* exhibits a real difference in form from the other stories. We are also back to Clara's narrative situation in *Wieland*, with the narrator apparently in complete control over his own story. Moreover, from Brown's point of view, *Stephen Calvert* might be described as a western story, told at some distance in time from the events described (we do not know how long) and also told from the shores of Lake Michigan, where Stephen has become "the recluse of Michigan" (1:192) in an effort to withdraw from temptation and to escape guilt and remorse (1:191). Occasional Indian and Canadian traders are his only society, but he is apparently telling this story (rather than writing it) to a friend he has invited solely for this purpose. The question of whether the story is written or spoken is probably not important here; the inclusion of telling letters suggests a written memoir, but in this story Brown seems much less conscious of the act of writing itself than he has been in others.

Stephen begins with his ancestry, particularly with Sir Stephen Porter, who had two sons—the older, Henry, and the younger, Stephen. Sir Stephen is a fierce Jacobin and antimonarchist, as well as an anti-Catholic. Unknown to him, the younger son secretly marries a Catholic girl and converts to that religion. Sir Stephen ignorantly invites young Stephen to lead a suicide mission to assassinate the king, at which the young man secretly recoils. But he is concerned for the safety of his wife, a Calvert, and their infant twin sons and, with the advice of his brother Henry, puts one of the boys under the foster parentage of a family named Thurston. The other twin, our Stephen, accompanies his parents to Philadelphia, where Stephen Porter assumes his wife's family name of Calvert. Meanwhile, Henry Porter dies, and Sir Stephen takes the child Felix into his own care from the Thurstons, partly as a hostage to insure secrecy regarding the plotted insurrection. The plot is discovered nonetheless, and Sir Stephen and others assume that Stephen Porter has been responsible. Stephen disappears one stormy night, turning up dead days later. He can be identified only by his clothes and was presumably the victim either of his father's agents or of his own suicidal impulses derived from the anxiety of his situation. At this time our Stephen is but three years old and is given the name of his English brother, Felix. His cousin Henry, who inherits the British estate of Sir Stephen, proves to be an open and generous man, but the English Felix has disappeared.

Our Stephen's maternal uncle, Ambrose Calvert, who early came to America, had meanwhile made himself master of a large estate that included both land and black slaves. He has two daughters, legitimate Louisa and illegitimate black Althea. In his dissolution, he eventually beats Althea to death, sending Louisa scurrying for protection to Stephen's mother, now a widowed schoolteacher. When Ambrose dies, he leaves Calverton to Stephen. Stephen does not need the property or its value, so he easily persuades himself to return the estate to Louisa, whom he has not seen for some years. Quickly he imagines himself master of the girl's gratitude and then of herself. Her friend Sydney shares with Stephen his four years' correspondence with Louisa, which cements Stephen's devotion to her as well as to his own sense of self-worth.

Upon seeing her in person, he is shocked to find her small, dark, drab, plain if not ugly, pockmarked and crushingly verbose, but savingly honest and virtuous. The jolt to Stephen's feelings makes him begin to question the motives for his love. He is now less willing to be her benefactor, persuading himself that he can keep the property and gain a virtuous wife in the bargain by marrying Louisa. He makes the offer, but before their conversation can proceed very far, shouts and the other sounds of a city fire startle them both. Louisa urges Stephen to help. He finds the fire and makes a daring rescue of a sleeping woman from the upper story of a burning building. Her beauty strikes him deeply, and his romantic interest is pricked until he gathers that she is merely a servant girl. Rumor regarding the character of the young hero rages for days following this exciting exploit, until the newspaper finally identifies him as "Felix Calvert, a young gentleman lately from Europe." Well, at least they got the name right. The following morning Stephen, putting aside his own anxieties about their proposed marriage, calls on Louisa to make wedding plans. But all is suddenly changed. The wedding is postponed indefinitely on Sydney's insistence that Stephen's character is not yet sufficiently formed for so serious and irreversible a connection.

Stephen may not have been so sure he wanted Louisa himself, but he is furious at being denied her by Sydney. He rages and sulks rather badly for some time, becomes quite impossible company, and refuses to accept Louisa's advice to acquire a philosophy of self-denial (an idea that has become for her a steady theme, 1:281–354 passim). Finally Stephen threatens to run off to Europe, an alternative he only partly desires. He resolves to give Louisa one more chance to accept him and arranges to offer her an ultimatum.

Awaiting the time for their crucial interview, Stephen makes a duty call for a friend. He is startled by a shriek that rings through the streets on his approach but makes nothing of the incident. When he returns to his rooms, he finds a note inviting him to call at the very neighborhood where he heard the shriek. He tries to pick up information from a talkative shopkeeper, Mrs. Rivers (1:426–28). After he is admitted to the nearby house, however, he learns that his hostess is Clelia Neville, the very woman whose life he had saved from the fire. Stephen is utterly smitten by the lovely Clelia and now finds his intentions regarding Louisa quite inverted.

He pretends to have decided to stay by virtue of Louisa's and his mother's arguments but gets progressively deeper in dissimulation, not telling Louisa about Clelia, nor her about Louisa. His evening visits to Clelia become regular and intense, as her charms stand in beautiful relief against Louisa. Within five weeks he is madly in love, a feeling Clelia confesses for him also, though she remarks rather strangely, "Long have I known you, and can bear witness to that unparalleled magnanimity which makes you worthy of the devotion of a pure heart" (2:28). But when he impulsively proposes marriage, she collapses in terror and tears. Once again Stephen is rejected, but this time because Clelia Neville is "*a wife already!*"

Louisa, whom he blames for this misfortune also, tells him he is the victim of books, especially of the Scudéry variety. He tries to defend his relationship with Clelia and indeed to defend Clelia herself as never having hidden that she was married. But even here he allows falsehood to creep into his defense. He promises soberly never to see Clelia again, but a letter from her leads him to another interview. Clelia then tells her story (2:263–68) of abuse by her husband Belgrave, who misappropriated her property and her good name only to further his insatiable and monstrous homosexuality. Stephen is at once compassionate and convinced, although he still cannot understand how Clelia could have supposed him to know of her married condition. On one visit he detects her hiding an object, which proves to be a drawing of him, a portrait with some odd discrepancies in hair and eye color and entirely missing a conspicuous scar. Clelia tells him that she is writing a secret history of their relationship that will someday explain all.

Again Stephen calls on Louisa, who reveals that all his backsliding is known, again through the intelligence of Sydney. She takes him apart mercilessly (2:274–75), pointing out that he has only Clelia's testimony to rely upon. Sydney has discovered her to be beyond doubt a wanton woman who deserted her husband to run off to America with her paramour. Sydney strongly confirms the story that Clelia is involved in illicit nightly rendezvous with her lover. But Stephen knows that only he has been with her nightly and says so. Sydney is so disgusted by what he supposes to be the ultimate lie (because Stephen has been observed elsewhere) that he rejects Stephen on Louisa's behalf.

Stephen undertakes some detective work of his own, which proves fruitless and which leads him back to Clelia. But she is in private conversation with someone who turns out to be Sydney. To avoid accosting them together he throws himself into an adjoining room (shades of Arthur Mervyn!) until Sydney leaves. But Clelia then coldly shuts him out after asking some curious questions about his life prior to their first meeting. Bewildered, he calls on Sydney, who seems pleased to have somehow settled everything, who forgives Stephen's deceits, and who even persuades Louisa to take Stephen back into her good graces. Stephen returns to his mother's farm, brooding on the oddities of his couple of months in the city. There are two unanswered questions that especially confound him: "Two incidents, particularly, at this time, arrested my attention. The first was the charge urged, with so much confidence, against Miss Neville, by Sydney, of nightly admitting the visits of a paramour, with whom she had intercourse in her native country. The next was the imputation of lying, which he had fixed upon me, in relation to the manner in which I had spent a certain evening" (2:337). He writes his suspicions to Louisa but receives in response a bitter and angry letter. Her response hurries him back to the city, where a very bitter interview with Sydney ends with Stephen throwing himself impetuously upon a ship bound for Ireland (2:340).

Heartsick and seasick, he quickly repents of his desperate action. The ship sinks in a violent storm, and he is providentially picked up and returned to Philadelphia. This whole episode takes some five weeks; yet when he sees Sydney again, that good gentleman behaves as if nothing unusual had happened, as if Stephen had never gone. Conversation only increases both Sydney's and Stephen's perplexities, until Sydney leaves for a short time, asking Stephen to read over three letters he had earlier sent to Louisa. They indicate that in Stephen's absence Sydney had met another Felix Calvert with the same name and the same features (excepting a scar, the color of eyes and hair, and a more composed manner), until reader and characters alike come to see this new Felix Calvert as Stephen's long-lost twin brother: "The suddenness of this occurrence, the meeting with a brother so long severed from my side, and whose mode of birth made him, in some sort, an essential part of myself, seemed like passage into a new state of being. My suspenses were quickly at an end: for Sydney returned in a moment, leading in the stranger" (2:422).

Here the story ends, except for a short postscript:

> P. S. Calvert's story is a five-act drama. Here ends the *first* act; and this being in itself complete, the links connecting it with ensuing acts being only afterwards unfolded, it is thought best to stop the peace-meal [sic] publication of it here. The reader's fancy has now a clue to all that has heretofore bewildered him, and will easily image to itself the consequences of such a meeting as is now about to take place. [2:423]

Well, Berthoff is right; it is a busy story, but no busier than some of the others. Also, compared to *Clara Howard* and *Jane Talbot*, this story exhibits Brown's powers at their strongest. Brown has hardly written himself into a corner or into so many complications that he had to give up in confusion. If he really intended to extend the story, he has planted a number of possibilities capable of interesting development. First, he has raised the possibility of international intrigue and the prospect of re-engaging that at a later turn. In addition, he has underscored Stephen Porter's Catholicism early on, in opposition to Sir Stephen's Protestantism, as a possible line of development. Was it really his father's body that was discovered years ago? There also remain two estates to settle—one in England; the other, Calverton. The real story of Clelia and Belgrave remains untested. Felix's story has not yet been told, and a good deal of mystery about his relationship with Clelia remains to be cleared up. For example, Clelia is accused of having left her husband to join Felix in America; he is supposed to be her paramour, but when she first meets Stephen—also called Felix, remember—her behavior with him is anything but intimate. Indeed, she hints that she has only seen him at some kind of masked occasion. This matter will surely have to be set straight in Brown's crooked way. Then how will Sydney emerge from his meddling orchestration of events and emotions? As Brown typically works, he could well emerge as the crucial figure of the book. Will Louisa and Clelia bring their contrasting characters and reputations into clearer adjustment? Will the new brother Felix prove to be Louisa's true soul mate? Will she accept a young man who squanders his time in seedy inns playing draughts? No, I should say that though there are possibilities aplenty, they are merely hints for the kind of complications Brown could work out in four more volumes. Brown has also demonstrated exquisite skill in not bringing the twin brothers together until the very last page. Now, no such possibilities even suggest themselves, at any stage, in *Jane Talbot* or *Clara Howard*.

With the slave issue and miscegenation already prepared as part of Calverton and therefore Stephen's ultimate responsibility, to say nothing of Belgrave's alleged homosexual adventures, Brown has some shockingly good prospects before him. But in the long part that we have, these are only hints, foreshadowings. Two essential issues really matter here. The first is that all the twinning and doubling I have called attention to in the major fictions here tend strongly toward their natural, or at least logical, conclusion—a story of real twins. In other words, *Stephen Calvert* brings to the foreground at a completely conscious level (potentially) what has intrigued Brown through all the previous stories. That he did not work it all out is perhaps a mixed blessing, but it at least substantiates many of the relationships I have urged in the preceding chapters.

The second important matter also concerns consciousness, and this time it is worked out quite satisfactorily. *Stephen Calvert* is the only instance in Brown's major fictions where the storyteller is fully conscious of his own moral and emotional splits. Edgar and Clara Wieland never know, never perhaps allow themselves to know, the others they contain. Constantia never knows (though Sophia does). And with Arthur nobody knows. But here there is no mistake—Stephen knows, both at the time of his actions and at the time of his telling about them. One way or another, this is Brown's most subtle analysis of self-deception; it deserves some attention.

We begin with a narrator looking back at his youth, at least back from some later time to his nineteenth year (roughly the same age as Arthur Mervyn). Perhaps he prides himself on his noble ancestry; that is difficult to judge. He is certainly intrigued by its romance, at least sufficiently so to retain it as part of "his" story. When he surprisingly inherits Calverton, he apparently is not rich, but financially secure. His impulse to give the property to Louisa because of her greater need and deserts has therefore nothing heroic or self-sacrificing about it, although it is a genuinely generous gesture. But the gesture is somewhat entangled in his own self-generated enthusiasm that the gift will be greater if he accompanies it. He first thinks rather abstractly about marriage, but then with increasing ardor for this cousin whose letters reveal a beautiful and virtuous soul. When he first encounters her as an ugly chatterbox, however, he recoils—not merely from romance, but from the just gift as well:

> The thoughts which had occupied me most, related to herself. My design of gaining her love had been thwarted, or, at least, discouraged by first appearances. The transfer of her father's property, had been recommended by a sense of justice, but I will not deny that I was also influenced by other motives. These motives had governed me without my being fully conscious of their force. I had desired, by bestowing this benefit, to advance myself in her esteem; and I could scarcely conceal from myself that marriage would restore to me what I should thus have given away. . . . It was difficult to stifle my conviction of being actuated by selfish and ignoble views. I saw that I had formed this design upon improper motives, and had relinquished it from motives equally sordid. [1:269]

Of course, in his enthusiasm for the good opinion of others, he has indicated so much of his original intention to permit word of it to get to

Louisa. She puts the question directly to him. Has he changed his mind from fickleness of temper or because he sagaciously sees she is faulty?

> This incident led my thoughts into a new direction. It seemed as if the option of doing or forbearing was taken away. My reputation was made to depend upon my conduct, and the rebukes and contempts of my mother, of Sydney, and of the lady herself, were to be shunned at a greater price than this. I was determined, with whatever reluctance, to execute my first purpose. [1:270]

Slowly he persuades himself that beauty is not everything, and resolves to marry her. But, he thinks, "to proffer money and love, in the same moment, is ridiculous. It would appear like bribing her affections, and is absurd, since it would be equivalent to taking back with one hand what we bestow with the other" (1:271). On the other hand, if she loves him, her acceptance of his proposal will automatically solve the property problem; in which case, why delay?

Stephen rushes impulsively to propose, finding her at her window, singing. But singing very badly:

> My expectations of seeing Louisa at the window were fulfilled. Her voice was coarse and monotonous, and wholly unadapted to music; but she was, nevertheless, fond of the art, and, when alone, was accustomed to sing. This, at present, was her occupation, and though its influence was unpleasing, inasmuch as it reminded me of her deficiency in an art, upon skill in which my imagination had been used to set the highest value; it likewise delighted me, by denoting her presence at the window. [1:272]

Clearly Brown has gone past simple irony here to real comedy, at which he is talentless. But comedy is a new dimension in his fiction and is only part of a buildup to the real howler to come. We may note in these passages that not only does the older Stephen report back on his mixed motives, even with some sense that he was a joke, but the actor himself is also conscious of his double role even as he acts. This proves typical of young Stephen throughout the story.

Despite Louisa's monotone, however, Stephen is determined to propose, and he does so to his own disgust. Louisa may be a sharp young lady, but she is clearly affected by the gesture, whereas Stephen blames himself for what he knows to be his own profound indifference. Just then the fire breaks out and Stephen is propelled into heroics that can only enhance him in his lady's eyes, though of course she remains ignorant of his fixation upon the fire victim's "features, and neck, and bosom, which were stampt upon my memory and fancy, in eternal characters. Though seen for an instant, they refused to disappear, and the image was so vivid that I almost stretched forth my hand to discover whether it were not really before me" (1:274). Clearly this luscious phantasm cannot sit easily on a youngster who has just confessed his love elsewhere, and Stephen is both relieved and disappointed to get the popular report that this "nymph whom my imagination had deified, and whose presence I was to shun with as much care as Ulysses shut his ears against the song of the syrens, proved to be nothing more than a waiting-maid, who, though not an unsightly girl, was affirmed to be illiterate and coarse in manners and sentiments. I was sufficiently disposed to question the truth of this intelligence; but these facts were not equally liable to misrepresentation and mistake, as those which related to me; and were supported by no unplausible evidence." Stephen draws a useful lesson from this discovery: "I learned to contemn the vagaries of my fancy, and to place more reliance on experience" (1:276). Of course, he has learned no such thing.

Indeed, Stephen is a creature of fancy at once extreme and typical. He expects all women to be coy about love and is shocked when Louisa jumps at the proposal of marriage and wants to carry it out immediately. He would gladly be out of it, until Sydney implicitly accuses him of being exactly what he is—enthusiastic, impetuous, fanciful, and unformed in character—and so breaks off the marriage plans. He resents the description violently, knowing all the time that it is true. Of course he then blames Louisa for giving him the way out he wanted essentially all the while. Through all of this Stephen the narrator remains sufficiently close to Stephen the character to keep us sympathetic even when we cluck our tongues at his perversities or laugh outright. As he lies and evades and hides the truth (always ineffectually) from Sydney's "intelligence," we have to be impressed with the complex way in which truth inevitably emerges from all the falsehoods in which it is couched. Thus, when Stephen gets involved with Clelia, we know that Ulysses has managed to leave his mast behind. Not only does she sing beautifully, she accompanies herself on the viola d'amore. She is the siren beyond compare, and sirens are bad, but it is not entirely clear that her "song" is false, though it certainly seems to be. That is why, I think, the central joke of Clelia's rejection of Stephen works so well. She is so fully in contrast to Louisa that her repudiation of his self-seeking ambitions, though covered and colored entirely by his utter devotion, is so right. Stephen's courtship of "Miss" Neville is the obverse reflection of his courtship of Miss Calvert, and he is no more ready for one than for the other.

But the point is not that Stephen deserves all the discomfiture he gets. Nor is it that he is peculiarly a creature of fancy, although it would be easy to conclude this from several passages in the book. Everyone who has roared with outrage at Terence Martin's brilliant typical early American novel[6] knows the trope of innocence corrupted by the reading of novels, and Brown gives us that as the most easy and ostensible explanation of his predicament. Stephen believes this himself, as he tells us:

> I scarcely know how to convey to you just ideas of so motly a character as mine was, in my juvenile days. I was the slave of phantasies and contradictions. My preceptors were books. These were of such a kind as to make me wise in speculation, but absurd in practice. I had blendid [sic] the illusions of poetry with the essences of science. My mind was fertile in reasoning and invention, and my theory was not incorrect; but my practical notions of happiness and dignity, were full of imbecility and folly. [1:275]

But it is one thing to know you are a fool and quite another to do anything about it. Stephen realizes, for example, how quixotic it is of him to have fallen in love with Louisa solely through her letters: "I regarded my feelings with wonder and mortification. They reminded me of what I had read in the old poets, of heroes who wept away their lives for love, though the object of their passion had never been seen, and sometimes did not exist. These pictures, which Cervantes had taught me to ridicule or to disbelieve, I now regarded with altered eyes, and perceived that they were somewhat more than creatures of a crazed or perverse fancy" (1:267–68). Later Louisa upbraids him sternly for modeling his passionate yearnings for Clelia upon the characters in a precious novel by Madeleine de Scudéry. "'Do you know the book?' asks Louisa with mock innocence. 'Full well,' I answered. 'If I ever grow old and reflect upon the events that formed my character, I shall mark out this book as the most powerful of all the agents who made me what I am. If I am fickle and fantastic, not a moral or rational, or political being, but a thing of mere sex, *this* it was that fashioned me'" (2:258). Of course, by placing a letter from Sydney concerning Stephen's naughty relationship inside the book for Stephen to find—a little gesture straight out of Lyly's *Euphues* —Louisa is endorsing Stephen's judgment.[7]

Louisa uses this view of Stephen, that he is the creature of the precious fictions he loves, later when she unmasks his continuing enchantment by Clelia. Louisa has him so pegged, anatomizes his secret motives so mercilessly, that he is astonished:

> I was overpowered with confusion. I shuddered as if a witness
> had really been present at our interviews. I was astonished and
> abashed at so faithful a picture. [2:275]

But Brown has done a rather clever thing here. He has used Sydney's and Louisa's certainty that they "know" their man because he fits their labels and has even convinced Stephen that he is what they take him to be, only to turn everything topsy-turvy. As it turns out, they are wrong about a good many things, even though they are right about others. Stephen is indeed a bundle of romantic expectations and Clelia is likewise a seductive wanton. But Stephen is also hard-headed; he cannot shake his awareness of the anomalies that exist between his firsthand knowledge and what others say. Even Clelia's behavior belies the mean opinion others have of her. If her supposed paramour indeed were the English Felix, surely her treatment of him would be different. Nor would she be so shocked at her discovery that Stephen is the wrong man. The fact is, their friendship remains precisely that, a friendship, despite Stephen's secret lusts and Clelia's mysteries.

So again we see that Brown's characters are the victims of the stories told about them, the constructions we make in our minds of what other people are. His chief vehicle for treating that concept in this story is the episode of Stephen's daring rescue of Clelia from the burning house. For the first time in his romances, Brown renders the texture of city life with care and appreciation. It is clearly a post-Franklin society, with fire engines, clanging bells, neighbors sitting on the front-porch steps on hot summer evenings, newspapers, lamp-lighted streets, and closely packed houses across the street from stores, with narrow ways between them. Nowhere is the surrealism of the streets in *Arthur Mervyn* or *Ormond* visible. One gets the sense of city society as a quite ordinary condition of human experience here. Part of that city texture is the intercourse of reputation, report, and rumor.

Now, Stephen's exploit is strangely passive, what we would call a knee-jerk kind of heroics. Stephen climbs a ladder that others had placed against the burning building but were afraid to mount. He carries a hysterical Clelia down the ladder even as the flaming roof of the building crashes around him, forcing him to leap the remaining few feet. The lady passes out and is trundled off to recover, while our hero goes to change his cinder-eaten clothes. The feat is all done in the most public and conspicuous manner imaginable, in plain view of dozens of watchers. Despite this no one recognizes the hero, which rather pleases Stephen:

I withheld the knowledge which I possessed, being much amused with the speculations and comments that were made in my hearing. I could not but remark the numberless deviations from truth which the story exhibited in passing from one mouth to the other. A score of eye-witnesses communicated each a different tale, and a different description of my person. I was sometimes a youth, sometimes middle-aged. To no two observers was my garb precisely of the same colour and form; and one person solemnly maintained, on the evidence of a pair of eyes whose acuteness had, in this instance,

been assisted by spectacles, that I was a negro man, about forty,
who was formerly a slave of his own, and whom he had sought out
and *handsomely* rewarded for his courage. It must be added,
indeed, that this witness had not acquired much reputation for
veracity. [1:275–76]

The treatment is heavily humorous, but that does not qualify its serious
function as an encapsulation or allegory of the story as a whole.[8] Indeed,
the passage looks forward to the very conclusion of this segment of the
Memoir where the local gazette carries the following item:

We learn that the person who so bravely exposed his life for the
sake of a fellow creature, at the late fire in High-street, is Mr. Felix
Calvert, a young gentleman lately from Europe. [1:276]

Stephen comments, "This paragraph put an end to my concealment; and
my narrative of this transaction afforded to Louisa and my friends a
topic of much curiosity and congratulation. The assertion of my late
arrival from Europe was a new proof of the fallacy of rumour; and I took
no pains either to confute this error, or to detect the means by which my
concern in this affair had been discovered" (1:276). Nonetheless, from
this odd fallacy we may surmise the presence this early of the lost twin,
though Stephen suspects no such thing. We also can see Felix here being
credited with Stephen's actions just as later Stephen will bear the blame
for Felix's.

It is Brown's instinctive attraction for this point at which the mixture
of truth and falsehood becomes significant that makes possible his better
fictions. Whether they were early or tentative essays or simply burned out
after-shocks, neither *Jane Talbot* nor *Clara Howard* manage to locate or
recognize that point. The result is decidedly weak fiction. The advantage
of considering the incomplete *Stephen Calvert* alongside the last two published romances is that it highlights the real difference between Brown's
successful and unsuccessful work. In 1820, James Kirke Paulding opined
that Brown was the chief exponent of what he called "Rational Fictions,"[9] which over the years have come to stand for fictions of ideas, in

the sense of intellectual themes or topics. Politics and the Illuminati, religious fanaticism, Lockean sense-psychology, Godwinian freethinking, the rights of women, and such concepts as concealment, secrecy, forgery, and dreams are typical examples. Subtly the concept has developed that the greater the presence and the greater the mix of such ideas, the better and more interesting Brown's books are. This is of course true, but it is not the truth that matters. *Stephen Calvert* is almost as conceptually vapid as *Clara Howard*, but it works, whereas *Jane Talbot*'s concern with the cost of skeptical inquiry in the deepest reaches of morality—certainly a worthy and rich idea for exploration—fails almost miserably. No, *Stephen Calvert* demonstrates that the important difference is formal rather than thematic. Or, to put it more accurately, it lies in those creases in imaginative space where concept dictates formal consequences. By bringing to complete consciousness the doubleness of nature and experience and self in *Stephen Calvert*'s twins, Brown has made explicit the relationships I have described in the previous chapters. He has also made it necessary for us to rethink the matter of "Rational Fictions."

Patterns of Purpose

RATIONAL FICTIONS

The first man to take a serious gamble on Charles Brockden Brown's literary talent was a French entrepreneur who arrived in New York in 1797. M. Hocquet Caritat was in the book business. It was he who secured the copyrights for *Wieland* and *Ormond* and who acted as Brown's agent with the Minerva Press in England. And it was Caritat who established a reading room and circulating library in his bookshop at No. 1 City Hotel, on Broadway.[1] John Davis, a traveling poet and translator, writes of seeing Brown in Caritat's rooms one cold wintry morning, huddled in a great coat and worn-down shoes, busily "embodying virtue in a new novel, and making his pen fly before him."[2] Imagine the scene had Davis been able to see the parade of Brown's inventions in that busy room of books! Young Stephen Calvert (or is it Felix?) flips happily through the pages of La Calprenède (or is it Scudéry?). Philip Stanhope and Henry Colden check maps of the Northwest Territory with Edgar and Clithero. Miss Howard and Mrs. Talbot pass notes around aimlessly, while Mrs. Lorimer and Mrs. Fielder watch their young charges anxiously, quietly discovering that they have much in common. The wild looking young man in the corner is Theodore, collating more texts of Cicero; his sister meanwhile concentrates on Dr. Samuel Latham Mitchell's latest speculations on dreams and delusions of the senses. The very well-dressed redhead, a promising physician from Philadelphia, pores with concerned fascination over Matthew Carey's dismal report of the famous yellow fever epidemic of 1793. Ormond and Welbeck try to cheat each other at a game of double solitaire, while the man with the striking profile seems to be trying to bounce his voice off the ceiling. Sarsefield and Martinette argue over the merits of various fusils and other engines of destruction, while Helena Cleves and Clelia Neville, both astonishing beauties, read aloud together the climactic scene of Nathaniel Lee's *The Rival Queens*. Henry Pleyel tries to engage Mr. Dudley in a comparison of Paine's *Age of Reason* with Godwin's *Political Justice*, but Dudley is too absorbed in his book of Italian engravings. Neither even notices the old Indian woman barking to her troop of silent savages as she dog-ears corner after corner of the pages of Cadwallader Colden's *History of the Five Indian Nations*. Young Constantia glances around the room with apprehensive eyes; her companion, Sophia, soothingly holds her hand. All the conversation is uncommonly rational—indeed, it all sounds like one voice. Despite the differences of dress, one has the distinct impression that everyone in the room somehow looks like everyone else, and all bear an uncanny resemblance to their inventor. But above all, one senses something inescapably odd about them all, the feeling that M. Caritat's establishment is a madhouse, the Green Room for a drama to be written by Poe.

Perhaps "madhouse" is too strong a term. Perhaps their intensity and strange resemblances give them the air of unreality or at least unnaturalness that every reader of Brown senses. The conventional explanation for this oddness is that Brown simply could not break loose from the Gothic grotesqueries of the fiction of his day, despite his efforts to do so.[3] Surely this explanation is correct, but it does not finally tell us much about the nature of Brown's accomplishment as a fabulist and tends instead to discourage examining him more closely. Brown's avuncular friend William Dunlap did his share of locking Brown into inappropriate categories by pointing out early and often Brown's shared interest in William Godwin's *Caleb Williams*.[4] Dunlap as painter, dramatist, and historian was capable of penetrating insights into intellectual and aesthetic matters, but there was an overcompensating obtuseness about the man that discouraged his pursuit of his own insights.[5] He was prolific and punctual, a Babbitt of the art world when America sorely needed one. However, his encouragement of the Godwin connection with Brown has been very damaging. But it was also very natural, because Dunlap saw less of Godwin's radicalism in Brown than he saw of Godwin's model of psychological and moral power relationships between major characters in *Caleb Williams*. Indeed, the earliest English reviewers of Brown's fiction were most taken with his treatment of "character," although probably not in a sense we would be quick to acknowledge.[6] In the past twenty years or so, the perception that Brown was a psychological novelist in some sort of a direct line with Hawthorne, Poe, Melville, James, Faulkner, and Flannery O'Connor has become commonplace. But once made, this observation has been generally passed over rather hurriedly.

To some extent all these observations are true and worthy, but they share a common defect that I believe my readings of Brown's work render conspicuous. That is, they all proceed from an assumption that Brown was working novelistically or mimetically and was concerned with character much as F. Scott Fitzgerald or James Gould Cozzens is. Once that assumption is made, however, incredible embarrassments arise to choke the reader. We know Brown was a hasty writer and a careless one, but that can hardly explain such unbelievable lapses as the Maxwell-Stuart-Conway anticlimax to *Wieland*, the train of convenient coincidences on which major actions depend in all the stories, the undifferentiated voices, and the confusing complexity of narrative structures. By the mimetic model these are all glaring faults, largely because they are inexplicable. No, as depictions of the folks next door, Brown's fictions just will not do. But if they are not next door, surely they are inside us, and that of course returns us to another kind of psychological fiction, essentially nonmimetic. Criticism this past fifty years has carved out just such a genre by isolating the literature of doubling; this genre illuminates a number of our observations about Brown's typical procedures.

If we take this too strictly or too narrowly, we shall merely substitute another genre category for the Gothic, sentimental, or psychological genres that prevailed before. Reasons for doing so are very compelling, however. In the first place, stories of doubling, which involved duplication or multiplication of the narrative self or the central consciousness, exploded into prominence exactly at the time of Brown's creative outburst. The chief catalyst was Jean Paul Richter's *Siebenkäs* (1796) and his *Titan* (1800). By 1815, in *Die Elixiere des Teufels*, E. T. A. Hoffmann had turned the phenomenon of the divided self into a stock formula of German romantic writing. Indeed, the literary consciousness of the double had become so explicit by that time that Clemens Brentano parodied the device in *Die Mehreren Wehmuller* as early as 1817. In story and poem, the Germans cranked out episode after episode of bartered shadows and mirror reflections, of phantom selves who sprang into existence with the protagonist's commitment to some significant action or thought. Jean Paul himself had dubbed the appearance of such phantasmal existences doppelgänger, a name that has stuck. By the time of Poe's *William Wilson*, the literature of the double—the encounter with an aspect of oneself, either evil or good, that is normally repressed or simply not visible to the protagonist or the central consciousness of the story—was more than conventional; it was hackneyed.

Was Brown aware of such concerns of popular and influential fiction? Apparently not. Caritat's catalogues do not reflect it. Dunlap, who was an eager follower of German writing, especially the dramas of Schiller and Kotzebue, also gives no indication of acquaintance with this mode and its possibilities.[7] Indeed, it seems that Brown and Jean Paul came upon the possibilities of the doubling device independently, but at just about the same time, though I believe that Brown explored those possibilities with greater subtlety than the more famous German did. Insofar as the basic experience of separation and projection of one's self into some other apparently independent and totally realized person is a real experience, such stories fall under the expectations of any mimetic fiction. If I can stand outside myself and watch myself do something I would not ordinarily do, or act from motives I could never consciously acknowledge and accept, my actions and my interactions with myself could be described with all the accuracy and point of any natural action. In fact, some people can do exactly that, although the experience is generally accounted to be neurotic and abnormal. It is nonetheless natural.

Undoubtedly it is this appeal to abnormal experience that has attracted most critics to the phenomenon of literary doubling. Otto Rank identified the basic texts and set the underlying tone of most of this critical literature in *The Double: A Psychoanalytical Study*, which assumed various forms between 1914 and 1925.[8] Rank goes beyond the German romantics to look at Dostoevsky, Wilde, Kafka, and R. L. Stevenson. In 1949 Ralph Tymms systematized Rank's enthusiastic discovery of the doubling mode and broadened the literature in his *Doubles in Literary Psychology*.[9] Perhaps the culmination of such studies is Robert Rogers's *A Psychoanalytic Study of the Double in Literature*,[10] where Conrad, Poe, Nabokov, and Borges join Rank's group. These books have demonstrated the broad and international scope of the doubling genre but by and large have been seen as a convenient model of Freud's superego-id-ego structure and the general evidence of the effects of repression. The studies by Rank and Rogers in particular have revealed the excitement of the genre so that we have a chance to study the artist's personal neuroses, insofar as each projected or divided character reflects some aspects of the writer's own psyche. Were we to pursue this line of inquiry, we would derive at least a partial psychoanalysis of Brown and thereby jump past the stories more quickly than I wish to jump.

I do not wish to imply that there are no inspired literary guesses and perceptions in these books, merely that one feels the writers are too eager to find in every incident of doubling support for a generally Freudian analysis. None of them performs the intriguing feats of sustained literary analysis that John Irwin does in his *Doubling and Incest / Repetition and Revenge* (Baltimore: Johns Hopkins University Press, 1975), where Freudian perceptions are folded back into the analysis of both purpose and effect in Faulkner's stories. Nor do I intend to suggest that these writers are so narrowly Freudian that they are ignorant of other dimensions—mythological, folkloristic, anthropological—for Frazer's *Golden Bough* and ancient myths are referred to much more frequently than psychiatric records. Let me illustrate the point with a rather long quotation from Rogers:

> It must also be insisted that when a man sees an image of himself a
> few paces away and when an artist doubles or splits up a coherent

psychological entity into two or more seemingly autonomous characters, both the neurotic and the artist are "thinking" archaically,
that is, their mental operations in this matter are not logical and in
accordance with objective reality. This kind of mental activity is
what Todd and Dewhurst call "archetypic thinking" in their discussion of autoscopy in life and literature. They mean that the mental
processes of neurotics and psychotics who see visions of themselves
resemble in their content the magical conceptions of "primitive"
superstition as seen in myth and folklore. In psychoanalysis such
mental processes, occurring characteristically in neurosis, psycho-
sis, narcosis, extreme inebriation, dreams, and in the fantasies of
children, are known technically as "primary process thinking."
While artistic creation, in literature and other media, may involve
critical, ratiocinative, ego-oriented thinking (the secondary process), it should be borne in mind . . . that id-oriented primary
process mentation in the artist is largely responsible for the con-
creteness of symbolic representation which so distinguishes the
literary imagination from that of the analytical, discursive thinker.
Where a philosopher might speak of conflicts between body and
spirit, for example, a literary artist would be likely to conjure up
representative characters: a Sancho Panza and a Don Quixote, let
us say. In short, autoscopy and decomposition always involve
archaic thinking.[11]

The passage nicely demonstrates the psychopathological interest in the
main line of thought about doubling; it exhibits the quasi-technical language, the process of dividing or multiplying and the acknowledgment
that it is a real human process, the Freudian terminology, and especially
the allowance for mythical and anthropological primitivism, for archaic
thinking.

Between Tymms in 1949 and Rogers in 1970, critics in increasing
numbers resorted to the concept of doubling, often disagreeing in details
of analysis, until Carl F. Keppler protested in 1972 that most critics had
not the slightest notion of what they meant by doubling and that a view
of the various ways in which so-called doubles function would go far to

straighten out the genre. In *The Literature of the Second Self*, Keppler begins by distinguishing true "second selves" from fuzzy doubles, shadows, reflections, and outright hallucinations. In throwing out what he calls spurious second selves, however, Keppler has purchased clarity at the expense of many familiar examples. Although his morphology of second selves threatens to rigidify his categories beyond critical usefulness, his energetic prose and clear thought obviate that threat. Keppler's second selves appear in these primary forms as Twin Brother, as Pursuer, as Tempter, as Vision of Horror, as Savior, as the Beloved, and as the realization of past or future Time. Two or more of these functions may operate simultaneously, of course, and one's imagination leaps quickly to the obvious connection between these types and Brown's characters— Felix and Stephen the twin brothers, Edgar and Clithero the pursuers, Theodore as Clara's vision of horror, Sophia and Arthur as two kinds of savior, two kinds of beloved. Undoubtedly a close look at Brown's characters against Keppler's major examples will be instructive about Brown's mind and art. But a more telling contribution to the genre of Brown's fiction seems to lie in a number of other speculations Keppler makes.

First, he pays more serious attention than others do to the ancient and mythological and indeed universal origins of the interest in second selves or doubles. Second, more Jungian than Freudian, he is impatient with the urge others feel to see doubling as pathological. Third, he entertains the philosophical implications of this literature more thoroughly and seriously than others do and finds ramifications in the areas of time and change and knowing that seem remarkably pertinent to Brown. Finally, he offers a reason for artistic resort to the techniques of doubling that does not require a neurotic personality at its base. My purpose is not merely to squeeze Brown's characters into Keppler's various stencils but to point out that Keppler expands the conceptual possibilities of the genre in such a way that we appreciate the complexity of Brown's creative imagination. Thus the comparisons from which Keppler begins— the Narcissus and Echo myth, say, or the stories of Jacob and Esau, Jesus and Judas, Romulus and Remus, the Greek Dioscuri, Ahriman and Ormuzd, and the legends of Parsvanatha or of Gilgamesh and Enkidu[12]—

establish a dimension to Brown's doubling that may seem grandiose and pretentious for the chilled young writer in Caritat's library ("What's Hecuba to him, or he to Hecuba," wonders the skeptical Hamlet, but players may play at being kings). But I see no overwhelming reason to conclude that because Brown was both a political and a cultural provincial, he could not respond to the timeless myths of human civilization. Indeed, the Jungian commitment that Keppler makes here to the principle that men discover and announce their individual intimations of a racial unconscious in symbolic forms is at least as satisfying and as generative of meaning as Freudian analyses or the propositions of cultural history.

Perhaps the fault with this mythic context is not its scope but its defensiveness. Tymms begins his germinal study with the statement, "Superficially, doubles are among the facile, and less reputable devices of fiction," a judgment that Rogers underscores.[13] But I do not see that comparison of a less honorific nature (say to Clark Kent and his second self, Superman) invalidates the connection. The question of the level at which the pervading pattern is grasped and propounded is simply another question, one to which we shall return with Brown.

More important are Keppler's ruminations when he turns to "The Second Self in Time." In most instances of legitimate doubling, different as they may be in detail, the dichotomies are all spatial. "The essential paradox of the relationship is achieved by the fact that the two participants in it are simultaneously separate from each other in Space and continuous with each other in personality" (p. 161). But in other instances, when a person meets himself in a previous state or a future one—as in James's "The Jolly Corner" and *The Sense of the Past*, Poe's "A Tale of the Ragged Mountains," and Walter de la Mare's *The Return*—there occurs a conflation of times, the meeting of past and present or of future possible and actual that in effect negates Time. Brown, of course, tells no such stories, although one supposes some dim consciousness of their possibility when Edgar and Clithero crudely recreate the Wiatte/Sarsefield antagonisms, as if the rivalry were not merely recurrent but static. Nonetheless, Brown does create the effect of time escaped, as R. W. B.

Lewis pointed out in *The American Adam* (1955), which presents Arthur Mervyn as the first American hero out of space, out of time.[14] For Lewis, however, this is a metaphor, ineluctably time-locked because it is culturally locked, and so can be explained or described in terms of historical conditions themselves. On the other hand, Keppler points out that if Time is negated (or transcended, if you prefer), its normal consequences of causality, chance, and change disappear with it. All possibilities are actualized in some vital present under the condition we normally call fate.

Keppler has difficulty with this category; his examples admittedly fail him. But I would suggest that he has surmised quite well. In making Space and Time the two necessary conditions of all experience and of all knowledge, Immanuel Kant did not suppose their necessary separateness. Consider, for example, the Einstein explanation of astronomers' black holes, which argues that when matter exceeds the speed of light it ceases to be visible. Velocity in this case (speed in time) constitutes spatiality. But one needs no fancy theories to recognize that Brown's fictive world is a closed and fated one. Nothing happens really by accident. Carwin has to appear in Clara's closet, Edgar must also be a sleepwalker. Arthur must be a reflection of Mrs. Wentworth's young relative as well as of Lodi, just as he must meet Achsa in a brothel. And Martynne must purchase the miniature portrait that leads Constantia to Sophia in his rooms. These are all fated acts in Brown's universe, where chance, accident, fortuitous circumstance, and even coincidence simply do not exist any more than they could if Brown had sought to conflate times past and present.

Admittedly, Brown's control over this surprising concept appears to be very tenuous, though it is at the same time astonishingly tenacious. Brown was always profligate of invention. He did not, like Jack London, need to buy plots from a Sinclair Lewis.[15] Indeed, he at times throws away whole novels in the space of a page or two—Weymouth's history, for example, or Sarsefield's, Welbeck's and Martinette's, even Henry Colden's adventures from Alaska to Japan to Germany. We know of his youthful ambition to write epics on Columbus, Pizarro, and Cortez. Undoubtedly he knew the technique of squeezing endless complications out of historical episodes in the manner of Mlle de Scudéry and La Calprenède, who wrote forerunners of today's comic strips and television soaps. Want of incident is not the problem of his incredibly tedious "Sketches of a History of Carsol" and "Sketches of a History of the Carrils and Ormes."[16] These are perhaps farfetched stories, but perfectly causal and time-bound. They represent an opposite extreme from the equally fatal epistolary form of *Clara Howard* and *Jane Talbot*, with which they share an apparent mimetic intention in a time frame; that is, they simultaneously compel our acceptance of a normal sense of causation and probability and fall to utter paralysis of interest in the process. Brown is clearly at his literary best when he steps, leaps, falls, or stumbles into Keppler's time-negated world of second selves.

When Keppler asks finally why Brown or anyone else bothers to create such second-self stories, his answer is both intriguing and disappointing. The roots of our fascination with second selves lies precisely in their uncanniness, in their paradoxical blend of our selves and our otherness, our desire for benefit and our fear of harm. Doubles in this sense are embodiments combining our desire for differences with our fear of loss of what we are: ". . . there is evidently within us a dissatisfaction with our normally strict division between the objective and subjective worlds . . . as well as a deep-seated need to fuse them together while still keeping them apart, to preserve the twoness but to expand it with a simultaneous oneness; and such dissatisfaction is therefore the first thing that the student of this literature must try to understand."[17] This perception seems to me quite true, although its force lies largely in Keppler's very fine analyses of many stories. But it disappoints, I think, by its abstractness, by the leap into a single explanation that, although very complicated and suggestive, is as valid for Bellows's *The Victim* as for *Edgar Huntly*. It deepens our sense of the genre without helping us to see Brown's place in it, although it certainly helps define the neighborhood where Brown resides.

Keppler is apparently willing to see a kind of archetypal thought process at work here, but not a primitive one. He values symbolic expression of such thought but rather curtly dismisses such primitive forms as fairy tale (the place where alone happy endings exist, p. 193) and allegories (that world of mechanical connections between signifier and signified, where translation is the only mode of discourse, pp. 200, 227). Yet Bruno Bettelheim gives at least a courageous demonstration of the possibility that fairy tales mainly function to help children attain maturity, that they are vehicles for integrating personality and for bringing the superego, ego, and id into a balanced, functioning relationship.[18] To do so they must of course disrupt and meaningfully threaten that temporary balance we call identity. Bettelheim's crude Freudianism is discouraging, but even Keppler would see value in his analyses of " 'Brother and Sister': Unifying our Dual Nature" (pp. 78–82) and "Tales of Two Brothers" (pp. 90–96), stories that Bettelheim sees as preliminary to more sophisticated fantasy forms such as *The Faerie Queene* (pp. 23–24).[19]

Angus Fletcher also sees Keppler's literature of the second self as one of many features of a larger literary concept, locating that concept squarely where Keppler appears to feel least comfortable. Thus in *Allegory*, Fletcher musters a powerful intelligence and astonishing learning to re-align the relationship between symbolism and allegory.[20] Contra Cole-ridge, Fletcher argues that allegory and symbolism are not opposed modes of expression distinguished by the relative fixity of the referents, but that allegory is one kind or, better yet, one *mode* of symbolism. "In the simplest terms," begins Fletcher, "allegory says one thing and means another. It destroys the normal expectation we have about language, that our words 'mean what they say.' When we predicate quality x of person Y, Y really is what our predication says he is (or we assume so); but allegory would turn Y into something other (*allos*) than what the open and direct statement tells the reader. Pushed to an extreme, this ironic usage would subvert language itself, turning everything into an Orwellian newspeak. In this sense we see how allegory is properly con-sidered a mode: it is a fundamental process of encoding our speech. For the very reason that it is a radical linguistic procedure, it can appear in all sorts of different works" (pp. 2–3). The list he then provides certainly demonstrates the elasticity of this concept of allegory, including westerns, romances, naturalistic novels, imaginary travels, detective stories, fairy tales, debate poems, and complaints. "All these and more, with one genre sometimes merging into another, may be termed allegorical or partly allegorical works—by which we mean primarily that as they go along they are usually saying one thing in order to mean something beyond that one thing" (p. 4). Allegory is in a sense just the capacity to be interpreted, a figural dimension that leaves the literal surface intact (p. 7). Now a garment that can cover so many and such various bodies must be a wonder indeed, and we have to be careful that Fletcher has not merely given us the Emperor's new clothes.

But substantial or not, I would like to point out how closely several of Fletcher's main observations about the allegorical mode fit Brown. First, Fletcher maintains that allegorical characters are daemonic. Second, they operate in a closed world whose hierarchy of values is clearly set and usually embodied in a central image or ornament that Fletcher calls a *kosmos*. Third, they primarily engage in symbolic actions, chief of which are progresses and battles. Fourth, the operation of causality in these actions is usually magical and ritualistic rather than natural. Fifth, without at all granting the notion that allegories spell out rather simple and moral lessons, they are fundamentally thematic in character, even didactic. Finally, there is a broad but inescapable analogy between allegorical fictions and psychoanalytic behavior usually described as obsessive and compulsive. Now most of these points we have already encountered in the criticism of the literature of the double or second self. Fletcher, however, finds these same characteristics in a much broader range of literature and so offers other explanations for their presence. What is remarkable is how exactly and satisfactorily Fletcher's account squares with Brown's practice. The points are therefore deserving of additional examination.

Would you know a daemonic character if you met one? Fletcher thinks you would. "Daemons, as I shall define them," Fletcher says, "share this major characteristic of allegorical agents, the fact that they compartmentalize function. If we were to meet an allegorical character in real life, we would say of him that he was obsessed with only one idea, or that he had an absolutely one-track mind, or that his life was patterned according to absolutely rigid habits from which he never allowed himself to vary. It would seem that he was driven by some hidden, private force; or, viewing him from another angle, it would appear that he did not control his own destiny, but appeared to be controlled by some foreign force, something outside the sphere of his own ego" (pp. 40–41). Fletcher's daemonic agent, then, is one possessed by a singleness of function. At one extreme, such an agent might appear very like the personifications of Gray's odes or even the visually restricted characters of some seventeenth-century emblem figures; at another, the agent might appear as naturalistic as Faulkner's Lena Grove. Such daemonism might be diabolical, as it is commonly taken to be, but need not be so. What matters is the single-mindedness of the character, its quality of heroic persistence, whether fulfilling the role of an intellectualized concept or not. Brown's Constantia's singleness of devotion to her own femininity is a good case. True to her name, she proves in a sense heroic in the preservation of her chastity while not having to resort to the aggressive heroics of Spenser's Britomart. We might not grant Fletcher's daemonism so readily here, but certainly we can see it clearly in Arthur Mervyn's driven sincerity and openness and in Edgar Huntly's mysterious need to do good by Clithero.

When Brown talks about daemonic possession, he admittedly does so in a more limited way than Fletcher wants to emphasize. We remember that one explanation for Wieland's butchery is his possession by a daemon, an imputation he bitterly repudiates. His tormenter Carwin also uses the term in a way that diminishes its seriousness, when he guiltily confesses to Clara, "some daemon of mischief seized me." But finally Theodore himself, although quite mad, acknowledges his being possessed: "The form thou hast seen was the incarnation of a daemon." His admission seems to point at once to himself and to Carwin. Perhaps the most one can infer from this is that daemons are part of the conceptual world of Brown's characters. Clithero, too, explains his fate as under the control of a diabolical "demon" (*Edgar Huntly*, p. 95), an explanation his "father" Sarsefield eagerly adopts: "He that could meditate a deed like this was no longer a man. An agent from hell had mastered his faculties" (*Edgar Huntly*, p. 248). In these explicit instances, the daemonic is consciously diabolical and only partially meets Fletcher's description.

But when these characters butt up against others not so conspicuously sick or mad, we see the same kind of behavior without the diabolical explanation. The chief example here, of course, is Edgar Huntly, who unlike Clithero has no conscious guilt, but who parallels and indeed becomes Clithero in his actions. Indeed, the case is clearest here precisely because, since we see everything from Edgar's telling, we have no reason for a long time to suspect any but the most obvious of declared motives for his behavior. And what is Clara Wieland's persistence in revealing her supposedly protective voice but the same desire to be in direct contact with the divine will that her brother has met so fully? So for Brown's characters benign daemonism is marked by a greater consciousness of ordinary motivation, a greater appearance, at any rate, of naturalism. Who, after all, will blame Constantia for protecting her chastity and disposing of it as she sees best and safest? Who can fault Arthur's desire to expose the kinds of diseased concealments that sicken his society? But if Welbeck is compelled by some strange inner necessity inevitably to choose devious responses to circumstances, Arthur is no less compelled to try to right them, whatever the reasons he musters to justify that compulsion.

So we may want to find some more appropriate term than *daemonic* for these characters, but there is no gainsaying their fulfillment of Fletcher's typical allegorical agents. There must be even greater difficulty in seeing Fletcher's term *kosmos* in relation to Brown's fiction, but again the perception matters more than the terminology. Fletcher points out that the term *kosmos* is offered by Aristotle as a species of verbal ornament. Its primary signification is of an ornamental or decorative object that implies a set of values that in turn symbolizes a hierarchical order in the universe. The object may be a badge, a banner, an insignia, a bumper sticker, a ring, a locket, a cross or crucifix, a scapula, a Freemason's ring, a national seal. Worn or displayed by a patently allegorical character, as Florimell's girdle is worn, it generates structures of meaning and order far beyond its physical character. At this level of meaning the only *kosmos* we have in Brown is the miniature portrait temporarily lost by Constantia in *Ormond*. Venus separated from Diana may appear to be a rather trivial mechanism for motivating Brown's characters in that story, but if those portraits function as I have suggested in my discussion of that romance, Brown is trying to present objects as significant to the moral order and fixed values of the world of this story as Homer was in the archetypal *kosmos* of the divinely wrought shield of Achilles.

But such a symbolic ornament may not be significant; it is, after all, the only such example in Brown. If we ask, however, what is the signal of moral order in Brown's fiction that establishes his world of values, our answer must be that it is not, typically, any visible object, but another kind of presence. It is the voice that sounds through all these romances, the very voice that makes all these characters sound alike. Here, as elsewhere, Brown seems to fit Fletcher's general observation though escaping his particular categories. Thus Fletcher points explicitly to that gradual generalization of the term "ornament" to include any element of style (pp. 128–29). Style as the dress of thought does more than cover the indecent nature of the human mind. It, too, may have its decorums, and they may differ from time to time. "During the Elizabethan period," suggests Fletcher by way of example, "it is apparent that the Court, with its real political power on the one hand and its ideal, moral, and aesthetic sanctions on the other, could set the standard of 'dress' that would be the pattern for rhetorical as well as actual costume" (pp. 136–37). But the style he finds typically allegorical does not sound like Brown's. It is a highly paratactic style, relatively terse and declarative because it avoids subordination.[21] Perhaps a close look at Brown's style would support this general characteristic of allegorical style, but one's primary impression is that the voice of Brown's prose escapes the general extremes of parataxis or hypertaxis. More remarkable still, the voice remains the same both in narrative and in dialogue, whether direct or indirect.

One reason for thinking Brown's fictions rational may be precisely this sense that the voice of reason is always the same voice. But this supposition does not quite hold. Wieland is patently crazy, although he speaks with the same voice as Dr. Stevens, a model of health and sanity. Characters may be troubled, frightened, hysterical, shocked, outraged, loving, ridiculing, dying, or rejoicing; they may be socially elevated, wealthy, and educated, or poor, average, and relatively ignorant. They nonetheless sound the same, with some significant exceptions. Without trying to be systematic or exhaustive about the exceptions, a few leap quickly to mind —the gross innkeeper Philip Hadwin, the sleazy creditors who swindle Jane Talbot's brother Frank, black servants and slaves generally, the hearse drivers in *Arthur Mervyn*, and the street ruffians who pester Constantia in *Ormond*. Most obviously Brown is making a crude social distinction here between acceptable and unacceptable voices.[22] He does characterize his lower speakers with dialects, slang, and some energetic coarseness. But there is no real difference, say, between the impoverished Arthur and the surly hearse drivers who describe the deaths at the Thetford house (*Arthur Mervyn*, p. 140). Nor are the Dudleys different in dress, manners, habits, employment, or spirit from any of their slum neighbors. No doubt many of those neighbors are as inwardly good and gentle as the Dudleys, but the Dudleys are dignified by Brown's voice, not the others. The voice implies a state of being to which the characters aspire or a kind of mental atmosphere inside of which only the things that Brown wants to happen can happen. It is an enabling condition, like Puritan grace; those who speak with this voice, even those who are merely described by it, become thereby worthy of participating in the story itself, without regard to either their moral or their social value.

I believe we have already seen enough of the symbolic nature of Brown's actions in the preceding chapters and need not explore that feature of Fletcher's allegorical mode directly. Nor need we dwell on the ordering principles of progresses and battles in Brown's stories, except to note that they are prominent and tend to strengthen Brown's conformity to this mode. But the magical and ritualistic nature of the action requires comment. Keppler, remember, discussed a situation in second-self stories where time is negated and causality becomes purely illusory. Fletcher observes the same phenomenon, but offers another explanation. His general statement is of interest because it implies stories very much like Brown's:

> In allegorical actions generally events do not even have to be plausibly connected. Reversals and discoveries arbitrarily imposed

on the action, the *deus ex machina* introduced to rid the action of an impasse—these do not imitate Nature, though they may imitate ideas and theories. Even so, however, allegorical actions do hold together on their own principles of unity. We shall find that these principles require a suspension of disbelief in magic and magical causation. When plots and subplots are combined in certain ways, the effect of interplay between them is a causal one, and when major characters "generate" subcharacters, fractions of themselves, these fractions have peculiar causal interrelations. The dramatis personae in allegorical fictions will not have to interact plausibly, or according to probability, as long as they interact with a certain logical necessity. This necessity in turn appears, as a result of the rhythms of allegory, to take on a magical force. The agents of allegory can help, hurt, change, and otherwise affect each other "as if by magic." [p. 182]

Such instances do strike us in the stories—Arthur's uncanny resemblance to young Lodi, Clithero's transformation into the panther, Edgar's pack of silent Indians, Wieland's illumination and angelic voice. But such obvious magic is less important than the general way in which characters multiply and generate other characters. We have multiplications throughout Brown, as I have illustrated, but I am uncomfortable in calling those projections (what Rogers calls decompositions) magic and will avoid that term. Fletcher himself provides a more natural explanation for the implausibility of such stories, when he echoes Empson to point out that as soon as one character generates another, there is a simultaneous doubling of plots, a symmetry of story lines.[23] Again, he points to *The Faerie Queene* to illustrate the effect:

Spenser creates true doubles like Archimago and Duessa, who then assume particular aspects to fit each realm of virtue in which Redcrosse may be deceived. With the Fair and the False Florimell he extends the idea of deceptive appearance to cover the realm of aesthetics. In all these cases he is able, by the generation of subcharacters, to introduce symmetrical double plots. And once again, the creation of a double plot line enforces an allegorical interpretation, since, in effect, we always want to know which is the genuine and which the false representation. [p. 195]

In Brown we have seen everywhere the symmetry of actions: Arthur's entering and reentering houses, his movements from country to city and back, and the sequence of male encounters duplicated by the sequel of females. Perhaps the most Spenserian of Brown's tales in this respect is *Ormond*, where each character seems to project into existence his or her opposite: Sophia an Ormond, Helena a Martinette, and her cousin a Martynne, with each of the pairs arranged in a hierarchical order leading to Constantia's final peace of mind. *Edgar Huntly* may be less Spenserian but is most conspicuous in this respect. Though simpler in its range of doubles, it is much more elaborate in the two plots of Clithero's attack on Mrs. Lorimer and Edgar's on Sarsefield. *Wieland* is perhaps the least conspicuous, balancing Theodore's desire for godly knowledge against Clara's desire for carnal. The symmetries, then, are plain enough. The important point is that they are necessary because the actions are designed basically to double each other. At those points where particulars are most determined, where those Lobochevskyan parallels most nearly intersect, just there do we experience the greatest implausibility, the greatest coincidence.

Edgar, for example, has to take on Clithero's life for the story to achieve its end, but he must not realize that he is doing this. Seeking enlightenment, he falls into darkness; searching for Clithero, he discovers and kills the panther. The point is that the action is necessary. Edgar must vitalize himself with Clithero's spirit, and to do that he must dispatch the panther first. So far so good. But the convenient tomahawk that he coincidentally finds bothers readers looking for a naturally plausible means. According to Fletcher's allegorical mode, however, the particular means just at hand is singularly insignificant. Martinette's purchase of Mr. Dudley's lute is the same kind of coincidence, though one less likely to offend a naturalistic reader. The most difficult of these coincidences for even very good readers to accept and at the same time the chief example in Brown's fiction of the interaction of parallel stories is the coincidence that puts Carwin the biloquist in Clara Wieland's house at the very moment that Theodore is visited by his avenging angel of God. Readers fight that with almost the strength of Clara, despite Brown's evidence that Carwin did not order the murder of Theodore's family.[24] Of course, these are probably the same innocents who believe Mrs. Macomber shot her husband on purpose.

Such observations do not justify Brown's narrative behavior, even if they may in some sense account for it. In other words, we seem to be inferring that Brown is working with some degree of consciousness in the mode of Dante and Spenser and that he will therefore tolerate deviations from naturalistic behavior exactly as they did. I will return to the question of Brown's literary consciousness but point out here that if Brown's intentions were not entirely or primarily naturalistic, we judge awry if we blame him for being a failed realist. From that point of view, the very evidence we most quickly point to, the implausible coincidences, is the strongest evidence that Brown's intentions were different.

The final characteristic that I have chosen from Angus Fletcher's much more elaborate characterization of the allegorical mode is its didactic or overriding thematic purpose.[25] In so doing, I give away a good deal indeed to the many critics of allegory who find that the connections between characters, ideas, and actions are disappointingly mechanistic and lacking the organic richness that Coleridge celebrated in distinguishing symbolism from allegory. Following Frye, Fletcher admits that naive allegory is mechanical, but he does not see all allegory, or any sophisticated allegory, as such. Insofar as his allegorical mode is defined by the capacity to be explicated, every allegory runs the risk of being thoroughly and satisfactorily explained or explained away. It is truly odd that even in the most obvious allegorical case, Spenser's dark conceits, this is clearly not our experience. Every new and inspired reading of *The Faerie Queene* seems to exhaust the possibilities, to illuminate both the whole and its details beyond all extension. This poem has been sliced literally, analogically, allegorically, and anagogically; it has been analyzed politically, spiritually, historically, psychologically, and socially. Yet each new reading generates more readings. The process is matched only by explications of ancient classical texts, the Bible, and Dante, and has only just begun with Kafka and Nabokov, with Pynchon and Mann. These allegories reside essentially in enigmas, in riddles expressed sometimes as verbal conundrums and sometimes as symbolic visual emblems—images of ambivalence and often of paradox. But where a symbolic work might present, celebrate, or succumb to the mystery of connection at its root, allegory by its very nature refuses to rest there. "Allegory does not accept doubt," maintains Fletcher. "Its enigmas show instead an obsessive battling with doubt. It does not accept the world of experience and the senses; it thrives on their overthrow, replacing them with ideas. In these ways allegory departs from mimesis and myth, and its intention in either case seems to be a matter of clearly rationalized 'allegorical levels of meaning.' These levels are the double aim of the aesthetic surface; they are its intention, and its ritualized form is intended to elicit from the reader some sort of exegetical response" (p. 323).

Surely that distrust of the senses brings us at a dead run into the world of Brown's fiction; it explains to some degree why Brown so readily invites and frustrates interpretation at one and the same time. But what advantage, what necessity—indeed, what warrant—is there for implicating Brown's fictions in this allegorical mode? In general, the answer must be that anything so resembling what Fletcher depicts in such telling detail must be that very thing. What is more, Fletcher (apparently in happy ignorance of Brown's work) has described a literary mode, and this fact tends to validate its independent though versatile character. Third, Fletcher's procedure both anticipates and goes well beyond the criticism that focuses on literary doubling, second selves, and psychoanalytic analogies. He uses and includes them, but passes beyond them to create critical descriptions that fit Brown's practice with stunning exactness. It matters very little whether we call this literary mode "allegorical," then, or whether we use any other label. What matters is that we see a literary method nonmimetic and thematically ordered, a method whose agents behave with single-minded fervor in actions that are symmetrically and purposefully patterned towards some ideal goal, a method that sometimes rests on simple moral equations of social and personal virtue or on Freudian or Jungian structures but refuses finally to be pinned by them.

Brown is fortunately not entirely silent upon the subject of allegory. In

May of 1792, when he was twenty-one, he wrote the following remarks to his closest friend, Joseph Bringhurst, in response to Bringhurst's long description of a dream-vision:

> I wish I were so fortunate a visionary, and that, during sleep, my soul could mingle at will with the beings that people the world of Allegory, but the privilege of dreaming to any agreeable or useful purpose is denied me and I am forced to be contented with insipid realities or at least with those shadowy and fleeting images which the wand of wakeful Imagination can call into existence.
>
> The morality of this Allegory is undoubtedly sublime, and in the conduct of it, all the graces of poetry are exhibited. [This apparently refers to Bringhurst's performance.] Prose and poetry are very far from being terms of opposite signification, according to the common, but erroneous opinion, and a performance may justly be esteemed a poem, though not distributed into lines or resolvable into metre, if it be pregnant with "music, image, sentiment and thought," and that any of those requisite[s] are wanting in this allegorical production, I shall not be easily convinced.
>
> Allegory appears to be the native region of the poet, and notwithstanding the severity of critical prohibition, it has hitherto and ever will continue to find a place in the most exalted species of poetical composition. That allegory is inconsistent with the nature of an Epopee has, by many critics, been obstinately asserted though, in defence of a contrary opinion, it may be observed that of the poems of this class, one of the most celebrated is merely allegorical, and that allegory is, in some degree, interwoven with the texture of all the rest. There is no performance of this kind from the Iliad to the Henriade from which it is totally excluded. With what indignation have I heard it asserted that the Paradise Lost would be more perfect, if the episode of Sin and death and the relation of Satan's *chaotic* journey were omitted or retrenched.
>
> Are you, my friend, of a different opinion? If you are, beware of attempting to defend it, until you have forgotten that *Tasso* ever had a being.[26]

Who can tell how much of this sense lasted beyond the occasion, or beyond Brown's own serious attempts at fictive composition? That he and Fletcher ever talked the same language, however, is arresting. But Brown's degree of critical consciousness (as shown, for example, in his published remarks as a reviewer) is better displayed in his creations than in his reflections about others.[27] In any event, if we can accept Brown's work as decidedly allegorical in mode, we recognize that what would be warts and disfigurements, lapses of taste and loss of direction, suddenly look like purposeful and well-judged patterns. Possibly this sense of purpose is heightened simply by the formal consequences of these stories; that is, the double structures necessarily generate meaning, even if Brown had no consciousness that they were doing so and no specific purpose in creating them. But after our review of the books, the argument that they are totally naive and unreflecting products, accidents of Brown's writing fits, seems to me too unlikely to maintain.

We must also note that the general thematic purposes of these stories are quite original and sophisticated. Brown's characters are not moral abstractions of the virtues and vices we associate with Spenser. Nor are they the clamoring libidinous abstractions of Freudian criticism. They more nearly approach full personality than either type of abstraction. Perhaps they enjoy a status somewhere between universal abstractions on the one hand and unknowable personal mystery on the other, a condition participating in the empyrean and in the unconscious at once. To say, for example, that *Wieland* is about the evils of religious fanaticism, or about the inadequacy of the human senses, or about a young girl's fear of hysterical madness may be correct, but only coarsely approximates what the story is doing. We come much closer to solving the enigma of this book when we say it is about the growing consciousness of the desire for power, the desire to be God. This force is powerful, deadly, and strangely erotic, and marrying it finally to some kind of rationality (as Clara finally marries Pleyel) is not achieved without trauma. The pull of sexual abandon with Carwin represents an erotic displacement of her real desire, which is the possession of her father's intense enlightenment. His glorious self-annihilation in the temple, however, is for Clara an ultimate taboo. We also noted earlier that Brown is equally interested in how we come to talk about such urges. Clara's rational stories are not very satisfactory, just as Pleyel's skeptical explanations rather steadily fail to grasp the reality of his experience. So Clara is conscious of the necessity to explain and to tell, and also of the inadequacy of her telling, but she is not fully conscious of her own impiety, the evidence for which only glimmers through the cracks in her narrative. Her stories cannot be perfect, because she cannot face her own impulses straight on; but survival depends on the telling.[28] This is sophisticated allegory.

Likewise Constantia Dudley, at about the same stage of maturation as Clara, hungers for knowledge, though never with Clara's intensity or presumption. *Ormond* is the story of her progress to the knowledge of her sexual identity; she passes through a series of encounters with various kinds of sex roles until she attains her own full femininity. The major characters are at once her desires (although she is only partly and occasionally conscious of these) and her disappointments. They are also a kind of guide to the destined state of at least temporary peace with herself. Again, the experience of coming to know is erotic, but it would be a mistake, I believe, to assert that Brown's subject is erotic epistemology or some other very broad category. *Ormond* resists such labeling, and we must see that it is the process that interests Brown rather than the subject. Not everyone may fight Clara Wieland's fight to reconcile one's god-consciousness with one's human limitations. But everyone has experienced the confusions of sexual maturity, of coming to terms with one's sexual character. To that extent, *Ormond* is a more accessible book, though clearly not the same story as *Wieland*, despite common features between them.

Edgar Huntly and *Arthur Mervyn* also tell closely related stories, but different ones. *Edgar Huntly* is by far the more social of the stories. Young men duplicate the age-old trek of humanity from animal ferocity and brutality to what passes for civilization. Men are not born civilized. Indeed, at the point in life when the instinct for asserting one's self as provider and sexual partner is sensed most sharply, the young man becomes most competitive, most ruthless, and most violent and potentially destructive. It is never clear that Edgar himself is aware of the track he is tracing as he traverses the dark wilderness of his own powerful urges. Surely he is not conscious of what drives him, but he is aware that he has chosen Clithero over Sarsefield, that his sympathies are less with his surrogate father than with the brother-outcast. By story's end, Edgar has not quite made the passage to civilized maturity. By unleashing Clithero's murderous attempt and by bringing about Mrs. Lorimer's miscarriage, Edgar has disqualified himself from mature society. We leave him without parents, without wife, without property, but not entirely without hope. Brown clearly does not simply pose adolescent assertiveness against mature tranquillity. Civilization in this book is not without its brutality, violence, and bloody force. But society can only work if it keeps that side of itself hidden as much as possible. Clithero thrust under the waters at the end of this story is not Clithero destroyed; but Clithero is put out of sight, which is the only way that society can keep itself going, the only way that the family, clan, and tribe can persist. Society cannot utterly expunge its Queen Mabs, those embodiments of its own Dionysian energy; from time to time they will revolt and rampage. At those times society must reassert its principles of order and value and put down its own most violent impulses. That society *should* preserve itself seems unquestioned by Brown here.

Although Edgar comes a cropper, Arthur Mervyn slides, squirms, and braves his way through life. He overcomes the instinct to recoil from contact with a sick society, first by putting on the fortitude of manly openness and then by submitting progressively to a gentler feminine aspect of himself. Brown shows that the socialization of Arthur is the successful bringing into balance of essentially contrary inclinations. Social health is balance here, and when Arthur achieves it, he is ready for its rewards—the wife, the property, and the fatherhood that Edgar forfeited. It is an anxious period, but the only way one can escape the social epidemic of distrust is to trustingly expose oneself to it.

Rational concepts akin to these are at the heart of Brown's rational fictions. At one general level they are all psychological concepts. At a broader level they are all about socialization. Perhaps most broadly they are about maturation. Each major story is an examination of a state of being coming into being, both process and static state at once. Keppler has a marvelous image for this in his discussion of timeless process.

> One's notion of oneself, in other words, is like a vastly more complicated version of Duchamp's painting, *Nude Descending the Stairs* [sic], in which the nude is at no one stage of the descent but at all. Something like this is the picture in man's mind of his own identity: not any stage in the descent of the staircase of life, not the infant on the top step nor the oldster on the bottom, but the whole series of minute alterations that have cooperated in making the journey.[29]

To some extent Brown has rather extraordinarily intuited this simultaneity of existing stages in these books. I would suggest that readers continue to be intrigued by Brown because his elementary concern with natural human experience cuts through the melodrama, the Gothicisms, the sentimental elements, and even the psychological and allegorical trappings to show us our selves. His stories are a stunning accomplishment.

I hope that if we think back now to the folks crowding Caritat's reading room they will seem less mad than they did before. They are us, really, and perhaps they can convince us that the range of normality extends more broadly than we imagined. Their intense look is largely stage make-up in the style of Brown's time, slightly overdone, one suspects, for the world of Washington Irving, but not quite qualified for the hypertense stage of Poe's.

It is not sufficient, however, to show by these readings that Brown was artistically conscious or that for whatever reasons he fell upon the devices of coincidence and doubling, multiple characters and parallel elements. One wants to know, finally, what these add up to in appraising Brown as a novelist. Merely to note that he was an allegorist is not enough. His virtues as a storyteller are indeed solid. He has a cultivated architectural sense, which the parallels and doublings formally signify. Incidents occurred to him spontaneously, no doubt, seeming to grow out of whatever preceded, but when we look back at *Arthur Mervyn* or *Edgar Huntly*, we see artistic forms controlled at some very basic level. Brown was fond of sketching buildings; we have some sketches by him that are very classical and very symmetrical. If that was a basic tendency of his mind, it is especially worth noting that his best books tend to obscure the underlying symmetry. His narrative structures are intentionally flawed. That, it seems to me, is a sign of artistic risk. His faults, like the faults geologists read, become the clues to a prevailing order; they point always to a design and a meaning that the reader is forced to supply. Coincidences and disconnections are his formal keys to right readings. They function beyond the wild grove or the carefully arranged ruin in the formal eighteenth-century garden. They are not present merely to enhance the order by contrast; only by seeing through them can we see the order at all.

Did Brown see this consciously? It seems to me he probably did not. Like all of us, he was limited by the critical and conceptual boundaries of his era.[30] When we read the complicated patterns of Nabokov's *Pnin*, say, or Barth's *Letters*, we begin by granting a conscious purpose to whatever surprising patterns may emerge. We tend to resist that in Brown, partly because he is so early, partly because he is so clumsy. But the technique had to begin somewhere, and Brown did have the stunning example of Sterne before him. At the same time Jean Paul Richter was playing with doppelgänger in his idylls. By 1818 Mary Shelley produced a classic English doubling story in *Frankenstein*. Like others of the Godwin-Shelley circle, Mary read Brown.[31] She bewailed like so many other readers Arthur's casting off of his bucolic Eliza. But how much did her exposure to Brown's multiple characters take her beyond Godwin in conditioning her mind toward the monstrous invention of her good doctor? Might Brown have recognized his own influence in *Frankenstein*? Would he have said at the end of Poe's "The Fall of the House of Usher," "Ah, but that's exactly what happened when Clara's house burned down upon her in *Wieland*"? Would he have noticed, when Spencer Bryden meets his would-have-been self in James's "The Jolly Corner," that the alter ego has borrowed Welbeck's mutilated hand? What in Brown appears instinctual became through the nineteenth century contrived and conscious, and very effective.

But let us ask other questions. Would Brown have recognized Ormond in Melville's *Confidence Man*? Would he have scented Philadelphia in Camus's *The Plague*? Would he not immediately have grasped the Picasso paintings and sketches where men, women, and beasts are variously reflected in mirrors and transformed to canvas? Would he have recognized Edgar Huntly in Ike McCaslin? To acknowledge that Brown's art was instinctive rather than analytical or totally calculated (he did not compose backwards like Poe and Godwin) certainly in no way diminishes his art or the credit due it. He had a strong architectural sense, even if he did not work from blueprints. Even the admission that Brown would have profited from some good editing after the heat of composition does not imply that he should have rid himself of his improbabilities and coincidences and unlikely resemblances. For they are the badges of his art, his passport to a world apart.

Coincidence is, after all, but a flag of the doubleness of things. Even that pesky tomahawk is a coalescence of will and fact, a simultaneity of existence joining the ideal and the material into a whole reality. This kind of coincidence supposes a continuity between mind and reality that historically anticipates, even prepares the ground for, the more philosophical and pretentious formulations by Emerson and Thoreau and Poe. To put it in less fancy terms, the moral world of Charles Brockden Brown is single and continuous. In it material objects, human behavior, feelings, and thoughts all participate equally and all belong. Being universal, that moral world holds all things simultaneously. In the *Timaeus* Plato begins the creation myth with the tension between the two motions of the Same and the Other, the mutual dependence that generates both motion and life. In the *Phaedo* he lets Socrates develop the theory of opposites that students of American literature know more familiarly through Emerson. "Let us see," says Socrates, "whether in general everything that admits of generation is generated this way and no other—opposites from opposites, wherever there is an opposite—as for instance beauty is opposite to ugliness and right to wrong, and there are countless other examples" (*Phaedo* 70D–70E). The reasoning that follows is outrageously complicated, but I lug Plato into this discussion only to remind us that theories of coincidence and doubling, elaborately wrought, were available to any bright young American in the eighteenth century. Our young goodman Brown, trained by his reading in law to seek out alternatives and opposites, was obviously fitted to bring philosophical suppositions to his artistic work, even though he may have phrased his purposes in somewhat less grandiose terms.

I do not intend to say, either, that every detail in these books is consciously planted to direct our attention to any such philosophy. E. B. White once described his mother hanging a decorative mobile every Christmas, an act done differently each time, but each time done just so rightly that her children were filled with admiration. Try as they might, the children could never hit that right arrangement. Brown's art was something like that, a response to some inner sense of design. His stories apparently artlessly unfolded as they proceeded, but were never very far from Brown's underlying conviction of doubleness. No wonder then that the patterns his words make so constantly depend upon resemblance, duplication, confused identities, ambiguity, ambivalence, and irony, all of which derive from that doubleness at the heart of coincidence.

Brown, however, does not use his fiction primarily to explore abstract ideas or philosophical absolutes. This is the direction Poe would take. Instead Brown rests in human experience, in the confused hints and uncertainties, the sufferings and anxieties that complicate all relationships of property and sex. It is young fiction, depicting the gradual awareness that we cannot play god like Theodore or savage our world like Edgar without grief and pain, that maturity is finding some way to master the desires and weaknesses in ourselves, as Constantia and Arthur in their different ways act out. Brown's fiction is a muddled process, then, by nature enigmatic and paradoxical because the process is constant and universal, and therefore timeless.

Notes

Chapter One

1. The best text is volume 1 of the bicentennial edition of *The Novels and Related Works of Charles Brockden Brown*, ed. Sydney J. Krause and S. W. Reid (Kent, Ohio: Kent State University Press, 1977). Parenthetical page references in my text are to this volume.

"A Census of the Works of Charles Brockden Brown" was published by Sydney J. Krause in *The Serif* 3 (1966): 27–55. All the works I discuss were probably composed between 1795 and 1801, several of them simultaneously. This overlapping of composition bears slightly on my argument in subsequent chapters; the illusion of an orderly progress of the dates of publication therefore tends to falsify the yeasty actuality of Brown's creative period. Nevertheless, readers may find value in the sequence of publication. *Wieland* was first published in 1798; *Ormond* in 1799; the first part of *Arthur Mervyn* later in 1799; *Edgar Huntly* also in 1799; the second part of *Arthur Mervyn* in 1800; *Clara Howard* and *Jane Talbot* both in 1801; *Stephen Calvert* in magazine form only between June 1799 and June 1800.

One may get a quick overview of Brown criticism and *Wieland*'s place in it from Donald A. Ringe, "Charles Brockden Brown," in *Major Writers of Early American Literature*, ed. Everett Emerson (Madison: University of Wisconsin Press, 1972), pp. 273–94. Robert E. Hemenway and Dean H. Keller compiled the fullest list in "Charles Brockden Brown, America's First Important Novelist: A Checklist of Biography and Criticism," *Papers of the Bibliographical Society of*

America (1966). The general contours of Brown criticism are sketched in Paul Witherington, "Charles Brockden Brown: A Bibliographical Essay," *Early American Literature* 9 (1974): 164–87.

2. In *Madness and Civilization: A History of Insanity in the Age of Reason*, trans. Richard Howard (New York: Random House, 1973), Michel Foucault says much of interest on the logicality of madness in seventeenth- and eighteenth-century accounts (see especially pp. 83, 94–95); his treatment throughout of the essential doubleness of reason and madness, of their mirrorlike relationship (p. 27), suggests the peculiar nature of the Theodore/Clara relationship here, and illuminates my final chapter on doubling in Brown. Ever since Anne Hutchinson was excommunicated and banished by taking seriously the logic of John Cotton, the fragile distinction between godliness and antinomianism had worried Americans. The logic of Jonathan Edwards's *The Nature of True Virtue* (1755) exactly duplicates Theodore's here, even though when he tried a decade earlier to distinguish between truly gracious affections (sane) and those that only seem so (insane), in his *Treatise Concerning Religious Affections* (1746), he failed utterly.

3. Larzer Ziff, "A Reading of *Wieland*," *PMLA* 77 (1962): 51–57.

Chapter Two

1. Charles Brockden Brown, *Ormond: or the Secret Witness*, ed. Ernest Marchand (New York: American Book Company, 1937; reprinted Hafner Publishing Co., Inc., 1962).

2. Page references to "Jessica" are from Paul Allen, *Life of Charles Brockden Brown*, ed. Charles E. Bennett (Delmar, New York: Scholars' Facsimiles & Reprints, 1975), pp. 108–69.

3. See Donald A. Ringe, "Charles Brockden Brown," in *Major Writers of Early American Literature*, ed. Everett Emerson (Madison: University of Wisconsin Press, 1972), p. 278.

Chapter Three

1. The earliest reviews may talk about "character" and "motive," but they are clearly talking about what we call psychology. David Stineback's introduction to *Edgar Huntly: or, Memoirs of a Sleepwalker* (New Haven: College & University

Press, 1973), is a good example of the current and persistent psychological emphasis, as is the more exciting treatment by Richard Slotkin in *Regeneration through Violence: The Mythology of the American Frontier, 1600–1860* (Middletown, Ct.: Wesleyan University Press, 1973), pp. 382–90. Page references in my text are to Stineback's edition. Arthur Kimball reads *Edgar Huntly* much as I do; see his *Rational Fictions: A Study of Charles Brockden Brown* (McMinnville, Oregon: Linfield Research Institute, 1968).

2. See Kenneth Bernard, "*Edgar Huntly*: Charles Brockden Brown's Unsolved Murder," *Library Chronicle* 30 (1967): 30–53.

Chapter Four

1. Charles Brockden Brown, *Arthur Mervyn; or, Memoirs of the Year 1793*, volume 3 of the bicentennial edition of *The Novels and Related Works of Charles Brockden Brown*, ed. Sydney J. Krause and S. W. Reid (Kent, Ohio: Kent State University Press, 1980), p. 434; subsequent page references in my text are to this edition. Warner Berthoff has been consistently the best reader of Brown in print; he announced this view of Arthur as a moral sharpster in "Adventures of the Young Man: An Approach to Charles Brockden Brown," *American Quarterly* 9 (1957): 421–34, and repeated it in his introduction to *Arthur Mervyn; Or, Memoirs of the Year 1793*, ed. Warner Berthoff (New York: Holt, Rinehart and Winston, 1962), p. xvii. Variations on Arthur as a master of convenient virtue appear in Donald A. Ringe, *Charles Brockden Brown* (New York: Twayne Publishers, 1966), pp. 80–85; in William L. Hedges, "Charles Brockden Brown and the Culture of Contradictions," *Early American Literature* 9 (1974): 107–42; and in Michael Davitt Bell, " 'The Double-Tongued Deceiver': Sincerity and Duplicity in the Novels of Charles Brockden Brown," *Early American Literature* 9 (1974): 143–63.

2. Charles Brockden Brown, "Walstein's School of History: From the German of Krants of Gotha," *The Monthly Magazine* 1 (September 1799): 410–11.

3. Letter of 15 February, 1799, in William Dunlap, *Life of Charles Brockden Brown*, 2 vols. (Philadelphia: James P. Parke, 1815), 2:98.

4. See the "Historical Essay" in the Kent State bicentennial edition of *Arthur Mervyn*, pp. 447–75.

5. The following details are from Matthew Carey, *A Brief Account of the Malignant Fever which prevailed in Philadelphia, in the year 1793: with a state-*

ment of the proceedings that took place on the subject, in different parts of the United States, 5th ed. (Philadelphia, 1830). First called *A Short Account,* four editions appeared in 1793 and 1794. The 1830 edition remarks in a footnote, "The novel of Arthur Mervyn, by C. B. Brown, gives a vivid and terrifying picture, probably not too highly coloured, of the horrors of that period" (p. 25).

6. Ibid.

7. See John D. Hicks, *The Federal Union: A History of the United States to 1865,* 2 vols. (Boston: Houghton Mifflin Company, 1948), 1:236–38.

8. The servant Caleb apparently learned of Hadwin's death as far back as October (*Arthur Mervyn,* pp. 275–76).

9. Edmund Spenser, *The Faerie Queene,* III. xi. 54.

Chapter Five

1. Textual confusions surrounding this book extend even to the title, as explained by Sydney J. Krause in "A Census of the Works of Charles Brockden Brown," *The Serif* 3 (1966): 53. It was first published as *Clara Howard; in a Series of Letters* (Philadelphia, 1801). Six years later it was published in England as *Philip Stanley; or, The Enthusiasm of Love.* A third edition conflated the titles as *Clara Howard; or, The Enthusiasm of Love* (Boston, 1827). I cite pages and letter numbers from volume 6 of the David McKay edition of *Charles Brockden Brown's Novels* (Philadelphia, 1887), where the novel occupies pages 287–410.

2. *Diary of William Dunlap* (1766–1839), in *Collections of the New York Historical Society for the Year* 1929 (reissued, New York: Benjamin Blom, 1969), pp. 432–33.

3. *Jane Talbot, A Novel* (Philadelphia, 1801). My citations are to volume 5 of David McKay's *Charles Brockden Brown's Novels* (Philadelphia, 1887).

4. Warner Berthoff, " 'A Lesson on Concealment': Brockden Brown's Method in Fiction," *Philological Quarterly* 37 (1958): 45–57. Berthoff's description of Brown's method deserves quotation: "Brown worked out his plots as he went along, and he worked roughly. He solved problems of construction, and kept his stories moving, by improvising a series of discrete episodes, each new incident being at best rather loosely analogous to the original or focal situation. There is, however, a potential element of order in this episodic method, not that of the well-made plot or of meticulously developed characterization, but of thematic repetition, of successive and cumulative analogy. Brown's novels proceed through a

chain of incidents which, though disconnected, restate and sometimes deepen, each one, the common theme. Once furnished with a focal theme, Brown's peculiar inventiveness could go on indefinitely producing expressive new enactments of it; his problem was to move naturally from one to the next, and then bring off a coherent ending, and he rarely solved it. *Stephen Calvert* is the notorious example of the novel that comes full stop when the entanglements of plot get out of hand.

"Brown's system of composition helps to explain these difficulties, though it seems as much consequence as cause. A passage salvaged by William Dunlap from Brown's journal describes the writing of what was probably the lost *Sky-Walk*: 'When [*Alcuin*] was finished, I commenced something in the form of a Romance. I had at first no definite conceptions of my design. As my pen proceeded forward, my invention was tasked, and the materials that it afforded were arranged and digested. Fortunately I continued to view this scheme in the same light in which it had at first presented itself.' In so far as Brown worked by system, it was simply that of improvising the complex pattern of action out of which the conflicts of idea were to come. And yet they do come" (pp. 47–48).

I trust that the readings so far have demonstrated more purpose to those patterns than such an improvisatory method can account for, and I will suggest in the conclusion that Brown's thematic commitments imply their own logic and therefore their own shape.

5. The only lifetime publication of *Memoirs of Stephen Calvert* was in *The Monthly Magazine and American Review* in eight installments between June 1799 and June 1800. Because this text is widely available in the American Periodical Series on microfilm, page citations will be to the magazine: vol. 1: 191–215, 267–82, 350–59, 424–34; vol. 2: 17–30, 256–84, 330–40, 413–23. See also *Memoirs of Stephen Calvert*, ed. Hans Borchers, in *Studien und Texte zur Amerikanistik: Text*, Bd./Vol. II (Frankfort am Main: Peter Lang, 1978).

6. Professor Martin calls his masterpiece *Emily Brown; or, Innocence Betrayed. An Original Novel of the American Revolution, Founded on Fact*. It appears in "Social Institutions in the Early American Novel," *American Quarterly* 9 (1957): 72–84.

7. When Stephen is first confronted with the book, he says, "I took the book, and the first words I met with were Statira, Lysimachus, Perdiccas" (2:258). It is puzzling to know what Brown intended here, for these characters do not belong to Scudéry, whose seventeenth-century novels remained widely popular throughout the eighteenth century. Clelia Neville is obviously named for Scudéry's *Clélie*,

Histoire romaine, 10 vols. (Courbé, 1654–60), translated into English as *Clelia, An Excellent New Romance* between 1656 and 1661. Statira was the wife of Alexander the Great; Lysimachus and Perdiccas, his officers. A more likely source for them might be Madeleine de Scudéry's *Artamene ou le Grand Cyrus*, 10 vols. (Courbé, 1649–53), but I do not find them there, and Professor Nicole Aronson assures me they are not from Scudéry but from La Calprenède's *Cassandre* (Courbé, 1642–60). The tragedy resulting in Statira's murder by Roxana and Perdiccas was further popularized in Nathaniel Lee's long-lived play, *The Rival Queens* (1678). It is not clear to me what recognition value these names would have had for readers of *The Monthly Magazine*; it is also not clear whether they would have recognized Stephen's "error" or what they might be expected to make of it. It could simply be Brown's mistake, of course, but I am hesitant to grant that too quickly. The run-on narrative structure of these sources, with numerous embedded tales, may well provide additional insight into the sources of Brown's narrative techniques. See Nicole Aronson, *Mademoiselle de Scudéry* (Boston: Twayne Publishers, 1978).

8. For this use of allegory as a foreshadowing or prefiguration of larger structures, see A. C. Hamilton, *The Structure of the Allegory in "The Faerie Queene"* (Oxford: Clarendon Press, 1961).

9. James Kirke Paulding, "The Wreck of Genius," *Salmagundi*, 2nd series, 3 (1820): 265–72.

Chapter Six

1. George Gates Raddin, Jr., has explored Caritat's New York activities primarily in three books: *An Early New York Library of Fiction, with a Checklist of the Fiction in H. Caritat's Circulating Library, No. 1 City Hotel, Broadway, New York, 1804* (New York: H. W. Wilson Company, 1940); *Hocquet Caritat and the Early New York Literary Scene* (Dover, N.J.: Dover Advance Press, 1953); and *The New York of Hocquet Caritat and his Associates, 1797–1817* (Dover, N.J.: Dover Advance Press, 1953). The first two are especially useful for Brown. One gets a fine sense of the centrality of booksellers to American cultural life in this period from Kenneth Silverman, *A Cultural History of the American Revolution* (New York: Thomas Y. Crowell Company, 1976), pp. 47–49.

2. John Davis, *Travels of Four Years and a Half in the United States of America: During 1798, 1799, 1800, and 1802* (London, 1803; reprint ed., A. J. Morrison, New York: Henry Holt and Co., 1909), p. 163.

3. The best quick evidence for this is Paul Witherington's essay, "Charles Brockden Brown: A Bibliographical Essay," *Early American Literature* 9 (1974): 164–87; see especially pages 174–77.

4. This was first announced in William Dunlap's influential *Life of Charles Brockden Brown*, 2 vols. (Philadelphia: James P. Parke, 1815), which can be said to have first established the categories for Brown criticism (2:15). He was repeating the same attitudes as late as 1839, in his brief biography of Brown that appeared in volume 3 of James Herring and James B. Longacre's *National Portrait Gallery of Distinguished Americans* (New York: Hermon Bancroft, 1839). Between 1815 and 1839, both American and British reviewers often did little more than echo Dunlap's sometimes rash and arresting statements.

5. I find a tendency in Dunlap's critics and memoirists to overstate the quality of his poetry and painting, as if he had to be spectacularly good himself to be so important a midwife to the arts in America. This is true, it seems to me, of Oral Coad's *William Dunlap* (The Dunlap Society, 1917; reissued, New York: Russell & Russell, 1962), Robert H. Canary's *William Dunlap* (New York: Twayne Publishers, 1970), and the passing comments in Silverman, *Cultural History*. But Jay Martin is extraordinarily subtle and convincing in arguing for Dunlap's conceptual richness as more than an accident of Dunlap's productions. See "William Dunlap: The Documentary Vision," in *Theater und Drama in Amerika: Aspekte und Interpretationen*, ed. Edgar Lohner and Rudolph Haas (Berlin: Erich Schmidt Verlag, 1978), pp. 170–93. Dunlap's treatment of Brown is in general officious and impatient; it should be used cautiously.

6. See "On the Writings of Charles Brockden Brown, the American Novelist," *New Monthly Magazine and Universal Register* 14 (1820): 609–11 and "American Literature," *The Retrospective Review* 9 (1824): 304–26, for superficially contrasting views. William H. Prescott's "A Biographical and Critical Memoir of *Charles Brockden Brown*," first published in 1834, comments: Brown "deals less in external nature, but searches the depths of the soul. He may be rather called a philosophical than a poetical writer; for, though he has that intensity of feeling which constitutes one of the distinguishing attributes of the latter, yet in his most tumultuous bursts of passion we frequently find him pausing to analyze and coolly speculate on the elements which have raised it." See volume 3 of the David McKay edition of *Charles Brockden Brown's Novels* (Philadelphia, 1887), p. 35.

7. E. T. A. Hoffmann's work popularizing this use of doubling postdates Brown's work, of course; he is not listed in Caritat's 1804 catalogue (see Raddin, *An Early New York Library*). Dunlap's *Diary*, which runs to 1834, is equally without mention of the major writers in this genre. *The Monthly Magazine* for

the year 1799 to 1800 does list New York plays whose titles suggest cases of mistaken identity, a kind of doubling increasingly dismissed by students of the subject.

8. Otto Rank, *The Double: A Psychoanalytic Study*, trans. and ed. Harry Tucker, Jr. (Chapel Hill: University of North Carolina Press, 1971). I have been selective in my sources concerning literary doubling but do not mean thereby to exclude some of the works I ignore as irrelevant to Brown. Barbara Hill Rigney, for example, who based her *Madness and Sexual Politics in the Feminist Novel: Studies in Brontë, Woolf, Lessing, and Atwood* (Madison: University of Wisconsin Press, 1978) largely upon R. D. Laing's *The Divided Self* (New York: Random House, 1969), discusses fear of engulfment in connection with images of water or fire in ways clearly pertinent to *Wieland* (p. 20). However, she concludes that doppelgänger by female writers are positive, whereas those by males are negative (p. 123), which is equally clearly not true, and certainly not valid for Brown. Robert Langbaum's *The Mysteries of Identity: A Theme in Modern Literature* (New York: Oxford University Press, 1977) offers a broader but related way into this subject, as does Masao Myoshi's *The Divided Self* (New York: New York University Press, 1969), on the cultural and social implications of such writing.

9. Ralph Tymms, *Doubles in Literary Psychology* (Cambridge: Bowes and Bowes, 1949).

10. Robert Rogers, *A Psychoanalytic Study of the Double in Literature* (Detroit: Wayne State University Press, 1970).

11. Ibid., pp. 29–30.

12. Carl F. Keppler, *The Literature of the Second Self* (Tucson: University of Arizona Press, 1972), pp. 16–25.

13. Tymms, *Doubles*, p. 15; Rogers, *Psychoanalytic Study*, p. 31.

14. R. W. B. Lewis, *The American Adam: Innocence, Tragedy, and Tradition in the Nineteenth Century* (Chicago: University of Chicago Press, 1955), pp. 90–98. I have slightly skewed Professor Lewis's language here but not, I think, his sense. In "The Hero in Space: Brown, Cooper, Bird," Lewis says, "I call such a figure the hero in *space*, in two senses of the word. First, the hero seems to take his start outside time, or on the very outer edges of it, so that his location is essentially in space alone; and, second, his initial habitat is space as spaciousness, as the unbounded, the area of total possibility" (p. 91).

15. Sheldon Norman Grebstein, *Sinclair Lewis* (New York: Twayne Publishers, 1962), p. 25. It is interesting that, with equal invention, Lewis neither invites nor rewards the kind of reading Brown does.

16. Dunlap, *Life*, 1:170, 262.

17. Keppler, *Literature of the Second Self*, pp. 198–99.

18. Bruno Bettelheim, *The Uses of Enchantment: The Meaning and Importance of Fairy Tales* (New York: Alfred A. Knopf, 1977).

19. Northrop Frye makes a similar connection in *The Secular Scripture: A Study of the Structure of Romance* (Cambridge, Mass.: Harvard University Press, 1976), p. 54: "Reality for romance is an order of existence most readily associated with the word identity. Identity means a good many things, but all its meanings in romance have some connection with a state of existence in which there is nothing to write about. It is existence before 'once upon a time,' and subsequent to 'and they lived happily ever after.' What happens in between are adventures, or collisions with external circumstances, and the return to identity is a release from the tyranny of these circumstances. Illusion for romance, then, is an order of existence that is best called alienation. Most romances end happily, with a return to the state of identity, and begin with a departure from it."

20. Angus Fletcher, *Allegory: The Theory of a Symbolic Mode* (Ithaca: Cornell University Press, 1964). There is hardly a page in this book that fails to illuminate some aspect of Brown's fiction, whether method, purpose, theme, or even style. Some of Fletcher's terms are arcane (e.g., *kosmos* and even *allegory* itself) and so generate malappropriate associations; a great many supporting examples are medieval and Renaissance and so seem quite remote from Brown. However, Fletcher also folds his psychoanalytic interests into the fine generative formal perceptions of Northrop Frye's *Anatomy of Criticism: Four Essays* (Princeton: Princeton University Press, 1957), and so creates the most ample critical mirror available in which to observe Brown's creative mind. His work implies how ripe Brown is for structuralist and neo-structuralist interpretation.

21. The most perceptive and intelligent examination of Brown's style in print is Mark Seltzer's "Saying Makes It So: Language and Event in Brown's *Wieland*," *Early American Literature* 13 (1978): 81–91, but it is only a beginning to the work that needs to be done. Good general depictions of his style and of his conscious stylistic values are found in F. L. Pattee's introduction to his edition of *Wieland* (New York: Harcourt, Brace, and Company, 1926; reprinted, New York: Hafner Publishing Company, 1964), pp. xli–xlii and in Ernest Marchand's "The Literary Opinions of Charles Brockden Brown," *Studies in Philology* 31 (1934): 541–66.

22. Northrop Frye comments on this point: "One very obvious feature of romance is its pervasive social snobbery. Naive romance confines itself largely to

royal families; sentimental romance gives us patterns of aristocratic courage and courtesy, and much of it adopts a 'blood will tell' convention, the association of moral virtue and social rank implied in the word 'noble.' A hero may appear to be of low social origin, but if he is a real hero he is likely to be revealed at the end of the story as belonging to the gentry. Even in Shakespearean romance distinctions of rank are rigidly maintained at the end. Bourgeois heroes tend to be on the industrious-apprentice model, shown in its most primitive form in the boys who arrive at the last pages of Horatio Alger working for five dollars a week with a good chance for a raise" (*Secular Scripture*, p. 161).

23. Fletcher, *Allegory*, pp. 190–95.

24. The strongest external evidence is Brown's own preliminary outline for the story, which never elevates Carwin to such a power, even as an unwitting instrument. The outline is printed in full in *Wieland*, vol. 1, *The Novels and Related Works of Charles Brockden Brown*, ed. Sydney J. Krause and S. W. Reid (Kent, Ohio: Kent State University Press, 1977), pp. 420–39.

25. Although Fletcher in effect discusses the thematic center for three long chapters (*Allegory*, pp. 220–359), his argument, put brutally, is something like this: Allegory tries to balance, and thus is constantly torn between, a fully and particularly rendered picturesque surface and a grand, vastly significant, and sublime conceptual framework. In human psychology there is a powerful analogy to this simultaneous urge to join and need to separate, namely, the experience of the *compulsive neurotic* personality. Central to both is a need to confront essential paradoxes without resolving the ambivalences essential to those paradoxes. When done well, it creates anxiety, irritation, interest, and something like Keats's negative capability, the refusal to conclude. Allegories are didactic, then, not in having pat answers and not in avoiding answers, but in the purposeful direction of our attention to precisely those questions, moral and philosophical and religious, which permit no satisfactory resolutions.

26. Quoted from the unpublished transcription by Daniel Edwards Kennedy, "Charles Brockden Brown: His Life and Works," pp. 553A–554, with permission of the Kent State University Bibliographical and Textual Center; this work is described briefly by Robert Hemenway in "Daniel Edwards Kennedy's Manuscript Biography of Charles Brockden Brown," *The Serif* 3 (1966): 16–18.

27. Marchand, "Literary Opinions," pp. 541–66.

28. Joan Didion makes the point better in her memoir of that Gothic romance called the 1960s: "We tell ourselves stories in order to live. . . . We look for the sermon in the suicide, for the social or moral lesson in the murder of five. We interpret what we see, select the most workable of the multiple choices. We live

entirely, especially if we are writers, by the imposition of a narrative line upon disparate images, by the 'ideas' with which we have learned to freeze the shifting phantasmagoria which is our actual experience" (*The White Album* [New York: Simon and Schuster, 1979], p. 11). That this is not always a happy condition, but the product of "shock," even for a writer, Didion suggests in her treatment of Doris Lessing in the same book (pp. 124-25).

29. Keppler, *Literature of the Second Self*, p. 164.

30. Brown's era was of course not without a powerful consciousness of doubling at many levels, as Michael Kammen attests in *People of Paradox: An Inquiry Concerning the Origins of American Civilization* (New York: Alfred A. Knopf, 1972; reprinted, New York: Random House, 1973). For Kammen, what we have been calling identity becomes political and cultural legitimacy, issuing in a paradoxical social form called "collective individualism" (p. 75). Instead of psychoanalysis, Kammen turns to biology for a controlling concept: "I might invoke here an ugly word of classical origin—syzygy—meaning the conjunction of two organisms without loss of identity, a pair of correlative things, a paradoxical coupling of opposites. An easier word-concept, but one almost as ugly, is biformity," which he maintains to be inescapable in the American character and its institutions (p. 89). My point is merely that against Kammen's backdrop it might be odder if biformity were not reflected in Brown's stories. Sacvan Bercovitch traces another tradition of early American doubling in his *Puritan Origins of the American Self* (New Haven: Yale University Press, 1975). Bercovitch's point is precisely that Cotton Mather's treatment of John Winthrop asserts an individual identity joined "through an act of submission to a transcendent absolute" (p. 13), and that this is a stubbornly American habit. Bercovitch's sources are remarkably parallel to Fletcher's and Keppler's, although "allegory" is supplanted in his critical vocabulary by "figura" and "typology." How an aesthetic in which allegory looms large and significantly might become the property of a Puritan culture is described at length in Barbara Kiefer Lewalski, *Protestant Poetics and the Seventeenth-Century Religious Lyric* (Princeton: Princeton University Press, 1979). Ursula Brumm's *American Thought & Religious Typology* (New Brunswick, N.J.: Rutgers University Press, 1970) would have benefited in its treatment of Brown from a more conventional literary application of Bercovitch's exciting speculations, had they been available to her.

31. Joel Porte spells out the Brown-Shelley relationship in "In the Hands of an Angry God: Religious Terror in Gothic Fiction," in *The Gothic Imagination: Essays in Dark Romanticism*, ed. G. R. Thompson (Pullman: Washington State University Press, 1974), pp. 42-64.

Index